Diverging the Popular, Gender and Trauma

UNIVERSITY OF CALGARY
Press

Diverging the Popular, Gender and Trauma AKA
THE JESSICA JONES ANTHOLOGY

EDITED BY
Mary Grace Lao, Pree Rehal, and Jessica Bay

University of Calgary Press
2500 University Drive NW
Calgary, Alberta
Canada T2N 1N4
press.ucalgary.ca

LIBRARY AND ARCHIVES CANADA CATALOGUING IN PUBLICATION

Title: Diverging the popular, gender and trauma : AKA the Jessica Jones anthology / edited
   by Mary Grace Lao, Pree Rehal, and Jessica Bay.
Other titles: AKA the Jessica Jones anthology
Names: Lao, Mary Grace, editor. | Rehal, Pree, editor. | Bay, Jessica, editor.
Description: Includes bibliographical references and index.
Identifiers: Canadiana (print) 20240372212 | Canadiana (ebook) 20240372239 | ISBN
   9781773855738 (hardcover) | ISBN 9781773855745 (softcover) | ISBN 9781773855769
   (PDF) | ISBN 9781773855776 (EPUB) | ISBN 9781773855752 (Open Access PDF)
Subjects: LCSH: Jessica Jones (Television program) | LCSH: Jones, Jessica (Fictitious
   character) | LCSH: Women superheroes on television. | LCSH: Superhero television
   programs—United States—History and criticism.
Classification: LCC PN1992.77.J3635 D58 2024 | DDC 791.45/72—dc23

The University of Calgary Press acknowledges the support of the Government of Alberta
through the Alberta Media Fund for our publications. We acknowledge the financial support
of the Government of Canada. We acknowledge the financial support of the Canada Council
for the Arts for our publishing program.

Alberta Government   Canada   Canada Council for the Arts   Conseil des Arts du Canada

Printed and bound in Canada by Imprimerie Gauvin
♻ This book is printed on Enviro paper

Copyediting by Ryan Perks
Cover image: Colourbox 30578872, 24079048, 18935865, 12197741, 5702168
Cover design, page design, and typesetting by Melina Cusano

Contents

List of Figures

Introduction

Mary Grace Lao, Pree Rehal, and Jessica Bay

The idea of an edited collection began when we realized that there was collective interest within our department in a critical engagement with the highly acclaimed Netflix series *Marvel's Jessica Jones* (henceforth referred to as *Jessica Jones*). What started out as a discussion about co-authoring papers moved to co-organizing a panel for the meeting of the Film and Media Studies Association of Canada (formerly the Film Studies Association of Canada) at the 2016 Congress of the Humanities and Social Sciences, held at the University of Calgary. We were pleasantly surprised at how full the room was, despite ours being an early morning panel. We received both productive and positive feedback from the engaged and diverse attendees. It indicated to us that there was a need for this anthology.

But why did this television series speak to us so strongly? After bringing a solo woman-led show to the Marvel Cinematic Universe (MCU) with *Marvel's Agent Carter* (2015–16), the company had to show that it was willing to do something different to fit in with the Netflix aesthetic set by *Marvel's Daredevil* (2015–18). *Jessica Jones* immediately set itself apart from the rest of the MCU and helped to cement the Netflix branch as grittier and more anchored in the real world of New York than the fantasy world of the MCU as seen in *The Avengers* Infinity Saga (2012–19). As Netflix continued to build up the hype in advance of the release of *Jessica Jones* in late 2015, we had questions: How would the company represent her? How would her story be told? How different is this story from the rest of the MCU? How would she be positioned in relation to her character in the comic series? Would she be the gritty noir character, or the wife and mother?

Jessica Jones is unique in that she is a comics character without a long history in comic-book form, and she completely rejected her superpowers to first live a life as a private investigator in the *Alias* (2001) run, and then as a wife and mother in various other series. Jones's lack of extensive history as a comics character affords the show's creators the opportunity to expand her story beyond the brief glimpses we have been given in the comics to explore her identity as a survivor of trauma and to focus on her time as a private investigator. These are both smart business and content decisions—they allow for more seasons while, as our contributors point out later in the book, exploring the experiences of women in abusive relationships. But choosing Jessica Jones as the second Defender in the Netflix expansion of the MCU also says something about how these shows hope to be different from the films and even the broadcast series, such as *Marvel's Agents of S.H.I.E.L.D.* (2013–20). The Netflix shows have set themselves apart by focusing on lesser-known anti-heroes working mostly independently in the gritty streets of New York.

Netflix started as a mail-in DVD subscription service in 1999, added streaming in 2007, and has become a powerhouse in terms of global film and television streaming providers (Keating 2012). Part of this success is due to its use of effective and sophisticated algorithms, good business decisions and lucrative deals with rights holders, and the quality of its "original" content. The deal that allowed Netflix to produce *Jessica Jones*, a Marvel product, began in 2012 when the company gained exclusive rights to new-release Disney products starting in 2016 (Graser 2012). From there, Marvel worked with Netflix to develop a television deal that included, in addition to *Jessica Jones*, *Daredevil* (2015–18), *Luke Cage* (2016–18), *Iron Fist* (2017–18), and the ensemble piece *The Defenders* (2017) (Lewis 2013). Netflix's model of releasing original series as complete seasons, rather than releasing one episode a week, not only encourages binge-watching among its viewers, but also allows for more seamless storytelling and fan investment. With *Jessica Jones*, this translates to a more complex superhero who can truly engage in the real world of New York's underground and with the trauma she is experiencing.

Jessica Jones actively leans in to its role as "different," even oppositional, through its main character's blatant refusal to smile; her eschewal of acceptable standards of femininity, or even acceptable standards of social interaction; the show's focus on trauma and refusal to shy away from calling Kilgrave's invasion anything but rape; its marketing—including a Twitter account attributed to Jessica herself, who regularly claps back at haters; and by actively recruiting women behind the camera and in the writer's room (Prudom 2016). By approaching a character and topics that are normally ignored, *Jessica Jones* introduces tough topics to the MCU and chooses to grapple with them rather than superficially "solving" them. The general, and presumably superhero-loving audience is introduced to the concept of gaslighting and, through Jessica, is allowed to follow a woman as she works through the lasting trauma of domestic abuse and rape while also finding her place within the world—both the world of New York, as shown in the show, and the larger world of the MCU itself.

Jessica is a compelling character and a unique choice for the MCU. The show started a conversation that has gone beyond comic book or superhero fans, offering many people a way to discuss their own trauma with others, and it serves as a political statement on the ways that narratives focused on gender-based violence, militarization, and toxic masculinity continue to persist in North American popular culture, as well as the role of the hero. Through this anthology we want to explore this character, who is, in many ways, exactly the kind of hero that feminist detective fiction author Mary Wings said she wanted; Jessica unapologetically "fucked and drank and detected [her] way through exciting stories" (quoted in Tasker 2006, 236) in the show's first season, and that allows her to push back against the norms that too often govern superhero stories.

We chose *Jessica Jones* as our focus for this collection for the popularity it won for engaging headlong with concepts of heroism, gender, female relationships, and trauma. At the time of season 1's release, it was revolutionary in its depiction of a woman (super)hero who did not care to be liked. Jessica Jones was being compared to the likes of Agent Carter or the members of S.H.I.E.L.D., and the audience found her to be very different from these depictions of femininity and heroism. *Jessica Jones* spoke to the wider sociological and political commentary of its time. The overwhelming audience response to the innovative content in the first season set it apart from the middling response to the more traditional superhero narratives of subsequent seasons, with season 2 focusing more on Jessica's past and origin story as she came to terms with the consequences of killing Kilgrave, and season 3 showing Trish Walker's descent into evil and Jessica's own reckoning with being a more permanent superhero in New York. In addition, the other series in the Netflix branch of the MCU (e.g., *Luke Cage*, *Iron Fist*) suffered a decrease in ratings (Clark 2018), likely due to the introduction of Disney+, which owns the MCU. It has been suggested that Netflix accounted for this drop, and, rather than investing in substantial plot development for season 3, as it had for the first season, it was more concerned with bringing the series to an end (Clark 2019).

This collection places considerable focus on season 1, originally released in November 2015, as its themes continue to be relevant to contemporary discussions of gender and race, not just in popular culture but also in the news. For example, season 1 came to resonate with audiences again in October 2017 with the advent of the viral #MeToo social media campaign[1] (Green 2019; MacDonald 2019) and subsequent discussions surrounding male entitlement and toxic white masculinity.

This Collection

Our vision for this anthology was to gather as academics, artists, and fans to critically engage with the political and gendered themes surrounding the representations of trauma for which the series was known. What we ended up with was far beyond our initial vision: there were a number of similarities as well as differences in the issues and themes on which our contributors chose to focus—the way the show deals with trauma, abuse, gaslighting, and masculinity, among other topics, and the way it fits into larger conversations surrounding its place in both the MCU and the world at large. As academics familiar with the barriers of institutional access and accessibility issues themselves, we intended for this collection to have a space in television and media studies as well as fan studies, while being accessible to both the general public and the academic community. Joli Jenson (1992), Henry Jenkins (1992), and, more recently, Paul Booth (2010) have problematized the divide between scholar and fan, with Booth in particular suggesting that fans can be seen as media scholars due to their critical engagement and consumption of the content they enjoy. As an example of an academic journal that successfully incorporates the academic and general voice, the Organization for Transformative Works and Cultures publishes *Transformative Works and Cultures*, which regularly features critical works written by both academics and non-academics. This blending of engagement with popular content allows for a diversity of critical voices and an expansion of our understanding of the material. Likewise, we wish for this collection to be read beyond the "ivory tower," as it were, so that we can engage in a more interesting and expansive dialogue on popular culture in the spaces where it is consumed.

The authors gathered here use different theoretical frameworks and methodologies in order to provide nuanced analyses of *Jessica Jones*, ranging from film, media, surveillance, urban, psychoanalysis, and affect studies. While acknowledging that much of our work is located within these theories, we also recognize that theories are subject to critique and interrogation. For example, some chapters (Ross; Moll) have used Michel Foucault's foundational theories (panopticon and sexuality). In light of recently published allegations of Foucault's sexual exploitation of young boys during his time in Tunisia (Sorman 2021), we must be cognizant of how his personal indiscretions have an overall impact on our scholarship, especially since many of the themes from *Jessica Jones* are rooted in sexual violence and trauma. We are not calling for Foucault to be "cancelled"; instead, we wish to reflect on his actions and how they serve as an example of the ways that the academy has historically viewed (and in many cases still does) marginalized groups as mere objects to be studied. This perspective reinforces the colonial structures that our institutions are built upon. Our intention is to challenge these colonial structures by engaging rather than theorizing these lived experiences.

Keeping with the tradition of fandom scholarship and previous feminist collections like *This Is What a Feminist Slut Looks Like: Perspectives on the SlutWalk Movement* (Friedman et al. 2015), which considers the historical, contemporary, and future directions of the SlutWalk movement, our approach to this collection reflects Donna Haraway's (1998) notion of situated knowledges, according to which feminists neither want nor need a "doctrine of objectivity" or some other single transcending theory. Instead, feminists want modern critical theories to understand "how meanings and bodies get made, not in order to deny meanings and bodies, but in order to build meanings and bodies that have a chance for life" (580). This feminist analytical perspective considers the "class, race, culture, and gender assumptions, beliefs, and behaviors of the researcher," arguing that the researcher "must be placed within the frame of the picture that [they] attempt to paint" (Harding 2004, 461).

Acknowledging this feminist analytical perspective, the authors in this collection have made use of a number of methodologies, including auto-ethnography, close reading, content analysis, Laban movement analysis, discourse analysis, and semiotic analysis. This interdisciplinary analytical approach provides nuanced insight into the impact of the series and its main characters' portrayal and trauma narratives, which in turn allows us to reflect on the issues of stigmatization, trauma, mental illness and addiction, as well as rape culture and race in an era of #MeToo, and racialization and police brutality in an era of Black Lives Matter.

This book begins with an episode guide and is divided into three parts, each focusing on a different aspect of the series and accompanied by brief editorial introductions. The episode guide provides a synopsis of the first season episodes. We encourage you to flip through it, and to refer to it with each proceeding chapter. That way, you do not have to rewatch the entire series—though we are not trying to stop you from doing so!

The first part of the book focuses on Jessica Jones, the hero and protagonist. What is interesting to note here are the various themes that overlap in our contributors' chapters having to do with the gendered ways in which women are portrayed. Jessica is a flawed woman. She may not have a heart of gold, but she is doing what she can to survive. Despite her rough demeanour, she cares deeply for her best friend, Trish Walker. The character of Jessica allows us to consider what it means to be a woman through her positions as super, troubled, and hero.

When considering Jessica as "woman," our text looks to feminist theories. Beginning particularly with Simone de Beauvoir and Judith Butler, we understand that there is nothing naturally feminine about being a woman. While de Beauvoir (1974) suggests that we "become" women, Butler ([1990] 2006) says that we "perform" our femininity. The work of these two scholars influenced future feminist scholars in their ability to break the essentialist conception of "girl" and "girlhood." While de Beauvoir has fallen out of favour with some, the ideas presented by Butler continue to be reimagined by scholars in North America and remain relevant to our understandings of gender and its representation. Jenny Bavidge (2004) suggests that "the notion of the Girl—her identity, her body and sexuality, as well as her moral, physical and intellectual education—has been recognised as a site around which many of culture's concerns and anxieties cohere" (44). *Jessica Jones* offers a space to examine those anxieties through an extraordinary "girl." Meanwhile, feminist theory offers an opportunity to approach Jessica's gendered position through class and gender structures, power and its imbalances, while also offering space to consider how this show can act as a call to arms for political action and social justice.

We show how Jessica Jones challenges our preconceived notions of what a superhero is, through her gender, her adherence to a moral compass, and her behaviour (Chestopalova; Jenkins; Stang). Shana MacDonald (2019) describes Jessica as a feminist killjoy and a foil to the neoliberal, post-feminist sensibilities of girl power. Unlike other female superheroes, Jessica's other job is less than meritorious, as she makes a living as a private investigator spying on cheating spouses. Her career and personal choices, along with her trauma, are justified rather than vilified (MacDonald 2019). The series focuses on the violation of personal space, not just at the hands of Kilgrave, but also Jessica's own actions as a private investigator (Ross). As a character in the larger MCU, Jessica offers a connection between the sleek fantasy world of the movies and the gritty noir world of the other MCU series on Netflix while challenging the superhero genre itself (Fitzgerald).

The second part of the book focuses on the male characters in the series. While *Jessica Jones* has been critically acclaimed for its representation of female characters, it is equally important to look at the many ways masculinities are portrayed in the show, as these reflect the highly gendered society within which it situates itself. Part 2 looks at constructions of masculinities through bodily performance, and it does so to illustrate gendered relations among the characters in the series. The focus here on masculinities, as opposed to masculinity, recognizes the concept's fluidity. As R. W. Connell (2005) argues, masculinity is not described by a concrete set of definitions, but instead changes such that a dominant masculinity emerges and re-emerges, so long as it maintains the patriarchal system. It is this relationality that, according to Connell, naturalizes or marginalizes men who do not fit this dominant form of masculinity. More recently, critiques of masculinities studies have highlighted this relationality, as it is said to create a dichotomy between masculine and feminine (Connell and Messerschmidt 2005), as well as between Western (white) and non-Western (non-white) masculinities (Beasley 2008).

In part 2, we begin with Jessica Seymour's chapter. Seymour argues that the presentation of these different masculinities across a gender spectrum is a way to portray feminine gender performance positively while also recognizing that there is a need to portray Black masculinities positively in popular culture. Next, we explore Western notions of hegemonic masculinity through the idea of toxic masculinity. Brett Pardy, for example, connects toxic masculinity to the militarization of law enforcement, focusing on Will Simpson's character development. Anastasia Salter and Bridget Blodgett's chapter on Kilgrave's representation of toxic masculinity draws on the increasing presence of geek masculinity, a masculinity that at one point was considered something like the opposite of mainstream masculinity. These nuanced portrayals of the villain give way to a different kind of relationship with the audience, one that is deeply rooted in gender, power, and violence (both physical and emotional) in order to uphold a Eurocentric (white) patriarchy (Lao).

Indeed, the gendered performances analyzed in parts 1 and 2 feed into a greater scholarly debate surrounding popular representations of sex and gender. Both Jessica's and Kilgrave's representations as the epitomes of the feminist killjoy and toxic masculinity, respectively, flourish under neoliberalism (MacDonald 2019). However, it remains that these performances are cis-normative and rooted in Western (and white) definitions of gender. While the show has been criticized for these depictions, as we discuss in our conclusion (Bay), our contributors have made use of these normative representations of gender to problematize and further our understandings of intersectional gender representations in media more generally.

The third and final part of the book brings our attention back to the series characters and the ways in which trauma is portrayed. The series makes clear that anyone, regardless of their past circumstances, is affected by Kilgrave, and it leaves them in a state of trying to reconcile the aftermath of the trauma. But at the same time, the series also reflects how women have historically been seen as hysterical and irrational (Moll). Kiera Obbard interrogates the different ways trauma narratives are presented in the series. In this section of the book, some of our authors address trauma as it applies to the character of Jessica Jones through other theoretical concepts and, in some cases, personal reflection on the experience of past traumas. Trauma theory's basis in psychoanalysis certainly has a place in film and media studies, as it helps us understand our affective relationships with media artifacts and events. This is especially the case when we think about the ways in which Jessica represents different types of traumas, such as post-traumatic stress disorder, alcoholism, and gender-based violence (see Rayborn and Keyes 2018). Other scholars, such as Rakes (2019) and their work on feminist crip trauma theory, have successfully started from the position of trauma theory to critically engage with *Jessica Jones* and its narrative of gendered violence and the resulting trauma.

However, as Susannah Radstone (2007) asks, "To what extent . . . are the insights offered by trauma theory generalizable to the whole field of representation?" (12). The dangers of depending too much on trauma theory can result in an unnecessary pathologization of popular culture's representation of trauma. To pathologize could be to do damage to those members of the general population who experience trauma themselves. We are concerned here with media representations of trauma. Thus, our focus is on how trauma is *represented* (and managed)—not, for the most part, the trauma itself. In this book, we have attempted to approach Jessica's trauma through other forms of analysis in order to remain true to our goal of presenting an interdisciplinary media perspective on *Jessica Jones*.

Despite this desire to maintain an interdisciplinary media perspective, there are hints of trauma theory laced throughout this book, though these aren't explicitly stated. For example, in the process of examining Jessica's physical movements and how they convey her internalized trauma, Michelle Johnson discusses the roots of that trauma and its psychological effect on Jessica. While this work is not grounded in trauma theory per se, it does draw from that important work.

While it is clear that trauma and surviving trauma is a significant theme in the first season, the chapters all contribute unique perspectives that reach beyond the individualization of trauma theory to access a more global understanding of how trauma can be presented on screen, including its effects on bodies in space (Johnson; Jacob and DiEmanuele) and sisterhood (Thomas). On the other hand, we also dive into how the (white) feminist narratives in the series are shaped by trauma and anti-Blackness (Rehal and Fairbarns).

This collection is aimed at academics and fans alike, with the intention of amplifying diverse critical voices in an accessible way. We hope the individuality of the authors' perspectives and arguments not only expand upon but also challenge what readers know about Jessica Jones. While we recognize that the series is fictional, its impact on the realm of superhero media has been tangible. Whether or not you love the show, or our critiques of it, we invite you to carry this discussion forward.

NOTE

1   In this collection, we make a distinction between #MeToo, the viral social media campaign started by Alyssa Milano, and Me Too, the movement started by Tarana Burke in 2006.

References

Bavidge, Jenny. 2004. "Chosen Ones: Reading the Contemporary Teen Heroine," In *Teen TV: Genre, Consumption and Identity*, edited by Glyn Davis and Kay Dickinson, 41–53. London: British Film Institute.

Beasley, Christine. 2008. "Rethinking Hegemonic Masculinity in a Globalizing World." *Men and Masculinities*, 11 (1): 86–103.

Booth, Paul. 2010. *Digital Fandom: New Media Studies*. New York: Peter Lang.

Butler, Judith. (1990) 2006. *Gender Trouble: Feminism and the Subversion of Identity*. New York: Routledge.

Connell, R. W. 2005. *Masculinities*, 2nd ed. Los Angeles: University of California Press.

Connell, R. W., and James W. Messerschmidt. 2005. "Hegemonic Masculinity: Rethinking the Concept." *Gender and Society*, 19(6): 829–59.

Clark, Travis. 2018. "Interest in Netflix's 'Luke Cage' and 'Iron Fist' Dropped Dramatically Over Time, and Its Other Marvel Shows Could Also Be in Trouble." *Business Insider*, October 27, 2018. https://www.businessinsider.com/interest-in-netflixs-luke-cage-iron-fist-had-huge-drop-over-time-2018-10.

———. 2019. "The final 'Jessica Jones' Season Marks the End of Netflix's Marvel TV shows—Here Are the Likely Reasons They Were All Canceled." *Business Insider*, June 14, 2019. https://www.businessinsider.com/jessica-jones-final-season-why-netflixs-marvel-shows-were-canceled-2019-6.

De Beauvoir, Simone. 1974. *The Second Sex*. Translated by Constance Borde and Sheila Malovany-Chevallier. New York: Random House.

Friedman, May, Andrea O'Reilly, Alyssa Teekah, and Erika Jane Scholz. 2015. "Introduction." In *This Is What a Feminist Slut Looks Like: Perspectives on the SlutWalk Movement*, edited by Alyssa Teekah, Erika Jane Scholtz, May Friedman, and Andrea O'Reilly, 1–16. Bradford, ON: Demeter Press.

Graser, Marc. 2012. "Disney Inks Exclusive Deal with Netflix." *Variety*, December 4, 2012. https://variety.com/2012/digital/news/disney-inks-exclusive-deal-with-netflix-1118063070/.

Green, Stephanie. 2019. "Fantasy, Gender and Power in *Jessica Jones*." *Continuum: Journal of Media & Cultural Studies* 33 (2): 173–84.

Haraway, Donna. 1988. "Situated Knowledges: The Science Question in Feminism and the Privilege of Partial Perspective." *Feminist Studies* 14 (3): 575–99.

Harding, Sandra, 2004. "Is There a Feminist Method?" In *Social Research Methods: A Reader*, edited by Clive Seale, 456–64. London: Routledge.

Jenkins, Henry. 1992. *Textual Poachers: Television Fans and Participatory Culture*. New York: Routledge.

Jenson, Joli. 1992. "Fandom as Pathology: The Consequences of Characterization." In *The Adoring Audience: Fan Culture and Popular Media*, edited by Lisa A. Lewis, 9–29. New York: Routledge.

Keating, Gina. 2012. *Netflixed: The Epic Battle for America's Eyeballs*. New York: Penguin.

Lewis, Hilary. 2013. "Netflix Orders Four Original Marvel Series." *Hollywood Reporter*, November 7, 2013. https://www.hollywoodreporter.com/heat-vision/marvel-netflix-agree-create-original-654171.

MacDonald, Shana. 2019. "Refusing to Smile for the Patriarchy: Jessica Jones as Feminist Killjoy." *Journal of the Fantastic in the Arts* 30 (1): 68–84.

Prudom, Laura. 2016. " 'Jessica Jones' Boss on Increasing Diversity On-Screen and Off: 'It's Still Not Enough.' " *Variety*, May 5, 2016. https://variety.com/2016/tv/news/jessica-jones-female-directors-diversity-1201767692/.

Radstone, Susannah. 2007. "Trauma Theory: Contexts, Politics, Ethics." *Paragraph* 30 (1): 9–29.

Rakes, H. 2019. "Crip Feminist Trauma Studies in Jessica Jones and Beyond." *Journal of Literary and Cultural Disability Studies* 13 (1): 75–91.

Rayborn, Tim, and Abigail Keyes, eds. 2018. *Jessica Jones, Scarred Superhero: Essays on Gender, Trauma and Addiction in the Netflix Series*. Jefferson, NC: McFarland.

Sorman, Guy. 2021. "Talent Is No Longer an Excuse for Crime." *France-Amérique*, January 9, 2021. https://france-amerique.com/en/talent-is-no-longer-an-excuse-for-crime/.

Tasker, Yvonne. 2006. "Feminist Crime Writing: The Politics of Genre" [1991]. In *Cultural Theory and Popular Culture: A Reader*, edited by John Storey, 3rd ed., 232–6. New York: Pearson Education.

Episode Guide

Season 1

1.01: "AKA LADIES' NIGHT"

We are introduced to many of the main characters in this first episode. Jessica Jones is a private detective, Jeri Hogarth is a tough lawyer, Trish is a former child star and Jessica's long-suffering best friend. We also learn that Jessica has PTSD from her time with Kilgrave, and that she is a functional alcoholic who hates the world. Jessica takes a case to find a missing woman named Hope, whom she finds in a hotel after being left by Kilgrave.

1.02: "AKA CRUSH SYNDROME"

The aftermath of Hope's compelled murder of her parents includes Jessica being questioned, Luke Cage being questioned because Jessica was surveilling him, and Hope in jail. We learn that Luke also has powers.

1.03: "AKA IT'S CALLED WHISKEY"

Luke and Jessica discuss their place in the superhero universe and how they got their powers. Jessica begins to put her plan for capturing and destroying Kilgrave into place by looking for the drug to incapacitate Kilgrave. Jessica saves Malcolm, and Trish confronts Kilgrave over the radio, leading him to send Officer Simpson to kill her.

1.04: "99 FRIENDS"

Jessica is tracking her stalker to find Kilgrave. While looking for other Kilgrave victims, Hogarth and Jessica inadvertently set up a support group for the survivors. Jessica is catfished and attacked for having superpowers. Trish and Simpson connect over their trauma.

1.05: "AKA THE SANDWICH SAVED ME"

Despite conflict over who should be in charge and how they should proceed, Jessica, Simpson, and Trish capture Kilgrave. Jessica gives Malcolm a choice about his future, and he chooses a drug-free life. Kilgrave has escaped and has found a way to continue controlling Jessica by forcing her to send daily photographs of her smiling.

1.06: "AKA YOU'RE A WINNER!"

Luke needs Jessica to help him find someone so he can get information on his deceased wife. Hope tries to kill herself when she realizes she is pregnant with Kilgrave's baby. Hogarth and her secretary, Pam, are moving forward in their relationship. Jessica finally reveals her role in Luke's wife's death to stop him from killing another person.

1.07: "AKA TOP SHELF PERVERTS"

Kilgrave kills a neighbour in Jessica's apartment and Malcolm and Trish clean up for her. Jessica's new plan to capture Kilgrave and save Hope involves getting arrested and placed in a supermax prison so that Kilgrave will have to expose himself to get to her. Kilgrave issues an ultimatum to Jessica, threatening the lives of an entire police precinct if she doesn't meet him at her childhood home to give him a chance to show her that they are, in his words, "inevitable."

1.08: "AKA WWJD?"

Kilgrave is attempting to win Jessica over with nostalgia and by promising not to use his powers on her while they live together in her childhood home, but he is still controlling the people around them to keep Jessica in line. Jessica discovers that Kilgrave was never taught how to be good, so she takes him out to show him how to help people with his powers. He feels empowered, but she is conflicted and ultimately decides to follow through with her original plan to drug him rather than try to reform him. Meanwhile, Officer Simpson has tried to help Jessica by blowing Kilgrave up, but he ends up on the receiving end of his own bomb.

1.09: "AKA SIN BIN"

Kilgrave has been captured and is enclosed in the chamber, where he can't control anyone, while Jessica tries to organize a way to prove he controlled Hope for her defence. She enlists Hogarth, Trish, and Detective Clemons as help and/or witnesses to Kilgrave's powers. To better understand Kilgrave and get under his skin, Jessica finds his parents, but their introduction to the situation allows him to escape. Everyone but Jessica is controlled during Kilgrave's escape.

1.10: "AKA 1,000 CUTS"

Hogarth helps Kilgrave escape, and in the process destroys her relationships with both of the women in her life. Kilgrave makes promises to have Hope released in exchange for the return of his father. The survivor's group searches for Jessica for revenge, and Kilgrave uses them against her; Hope gets caught in the middle and makes the ultimate sacrifice for the promise that Jessica will kill Kilgrave.

1.11: "AKA I'VE GOT THE BLUES"

Simpson has gone off the program the military prescribed for him and has turned his anger toward Jessica for not letting him control the situation or kill Kilgrave from the very beginning. He attacks Jessica while on experimental drugs, and Trish takes the same drugs to protect Jessica and fight him off. The military takes him away. Meanwhile, Kilgrave is jealous and blows up Luke's bar with him in it just as Jessica arrives to watch it happen.

1.12: "AKA TAKE A BLOODY NUMBER"

Jessica and Luke get closer during this episode and Jessica seems almost ready to accept his forgiveness as they search for Kilgrave and his father, Albert. Albert has been helping Kilgrave improve the range of his powers. Meanwhile, Trish's mother reaches out with some information about the organization that makes the drug Simpson was taking, as well as their connection to Jessica. She promises more if Trish will agree to rekindle their business relationship. In the end, Jessica must fight Luke when she realizes he has been under Kilgrave's control this whole time.

1.13: "AKA SMILE"

Claire Temple from *Daredevil* makes her first crossover appearance as she recognizes Luke as a man with powers and agrees to help Jessica get him out of the hospital and watch over him as he recovers from a gunshot wound. Kilgrave is no longer trying to convince Jessica they are destined to be together as he now just wants her dead. Jessica and Kilgrave have their final showdown: Jessica finally kills Kilgrave, with multiple witnesses to the murder and the mind control, including police officers. The season ends with Jessica and Malcolm cleaning up and people calling them for help.

PART 1

A New Kind of Superhero:
Film Noir and the Anti-hero

A New Kind of Superhero: Film Noir and the Anti-hero

Jessica Bay

We open this collection with five chapters that critique the concept and genre of the superhero through Jessica Jones's unique position, in terms of her character, the genre in which the show and comic book exist, and the show's specific production elements. Jessica Jones the character serves an interesting role in the pop-culture landscape of the late 2010s; she is, as the authors in this section show, both heroic and not a hero, while also being a woman and misanthrope who inspires others to support and help her on her journey. This show and these chapters allow for an interrogation of what it means to be a hero.

In many ways Jessica embodies the traditional hero's journey as defined by Joseph Campbell ([1949] 2008) or Northrop Frye (1957), however, she is a woman on a personal journey as well. Films of the 1990s, as Jeffrey A. Brown recounts, began showing women heroes "who are more than capable of defending themselves and vanquishing the bad guys" (1996, 52). Brown goes on to suggest that "the development of the hardbody, hardware, hard-as-nails heroine who can take it, and give it, with the biggest and the baddest men of the action cinema indicates a growing acceptance of nontraditional roles for women and an awareness of the arbitrariness of gender traits" (52). While Jessica herself very clearly presents as this type of character, her superhuman strength means that she has personally moved beyond that definition. At the same time, the show's creators have recognized that women heroes no longer need to simply be men in drag performing that "hard-as-nails" role: they can be action heroes while also exploring personal journeys that are specific and recognizable to many women. Jessica has nothing to prove to others, but she does have to prove something to herself—her own worth. The audience sees her working through her trauma and PTSD, discovering herself as she tries to save the figure of [H]ope.

In this way Jessica is a different kind of hero, and the authors in this first section consider both her role as a hero and the show's role in the hero genre. We have a number of chapters that consider Jessica across media. As an adaptation of a character from a comic book, these examinations of Jessica Jones allow for our authors to incorporate analyses that pull from comic book studies, media studies, genre theory, and media industry studies. In the first chapter, Catherine Jenkins makes use of Michel Foucault's theories to build a habitus of the superhero class, analyzing Jessica's position as a superhero by holding her character and actions up to this habitus. She considers Jessica in relation to ideas of the post-human as discussed by Sheryl Vint and Katherine Hayles, while placing Jessica within a history of comics superheroes, particularly from the two major publishers (Marvel and DC). Ultimately, Jenkins uses this discussion to construct a superhero habitus for the Modern Age of comics (1985–present).

After this strong introduction to Jessica as a multimedia superhero identity, we move to a consideration of the hero narrative within genre. Natalja Chestopalova carves out a new (sub)genre through her analysis of Jessica Jones, that of the rebel femme noir. This genre critiques the traditional superhero character, while also pushing back against heteronormativity and patriarchal control in popular culture. Jessica is not fully a noir detective; rather, she is enacting the role of superhero rebel who is fighting for femme empowerment. Sarah Stang then shows how Jessica Jones questions the (super)hero as a concept through the ideas of duty, responsibility, and morality. Stang demonstrates that Jessica fits neither the traditional superhero nor the anti-hero role, suggesting that she is instead a sort of neo-noir "hero." This conception works to further critique the superhero character and genre.

Finally, we have two chapters that consider how the show works within its larger production context. Eric Ross examines Jessica Jones with reference to Foucault's concept of the panopticon to discuss the role of the camera within the show, the camera recording the show, and the various actors controlling or viewing those cameras, including Jessica, us as viewers, and Netflix, which surveils us as we watch Jessica watch others. Ross's chapter takes us from the story world to our own experience of both viewing the show and being viewed in the new era of digital production. We close this section with a chapter by Ian Fitzgerald, who argues that the production and distribution context of *Jessica Jones* and the other Netflix Marvel adaptations offer the opportunity for a change in genre. This change allows for *Jessica Jones*, in particular, to critique the superhero genre—including Marvel's other major film adaptations—by showing a character and a world that has to deal with the consequences of the actions of those larger-than-life heroes.

The chapters in this section take *Jessica Jones* as a new perspective on the (super)hero—both as a character and a genre. Through these discussions we can better understand the changing roles of women, and gender in general, in traditionally male-centred stories and production contexts.

References

Brown, Jeffrey A. 1996. "Gender and the Action Heroine: Hardbodies and the *Point of No Return*." *Cinema Journal* 35 (3): 52–71.

Campbell, Joseph. (1949) 2008. *The Hero with a Thousand Faces*, 3rd ed. Novato, CA: New World Library.

Frye, Northrop. 1957. *Anatomy of Criticism: Four Essays*. Princeton, NJ: Princeton University Press.

When Is a Superhero Not a Superhero?

Catherine Jenkins

Long before the Netflix series, Jessica Jones came to life in 2001 in the *Alias* comic book series written by Brian Michael Bendis, with art by Michael Gaydos, for Marvel's Max imprint. *Jessica Jones* is a gritty comic book for grown-ups, full of hardship and social isolation. The title character is aggressive, sexually active, and foul-mouthed (the comic's opening word is "fuck," which is repeated several times in the opening pages). Her comics carry "Explicit Content" warnings. She has a strong, if sometimes confused, moral compass. She has superpowers: with super strength, she can throw a two-ton car; her body has beyond-human durability; and she can fly (sort of). She also has problems with alcohol, and post-traumatic stress disorder. So is Jessica Jones, the woman behind Alias Investigations, a superhero, some kind of twisted anti-superhero, a post-human enterprise, a troubled young woman, or something else?

Marvel comics legend Stan Lee suggests that "a superhero is *a person who does heroic deeds and has the ability to do them in a way that a normal person couldn't*" (2013, 115; italics in original). Comic scholar Peter Coogan suggests that the defining conventions of the superhero genre are "*mission, powers,* and *identity*" (Rosenberg and Coogan 2013, 3; italics in original). In this context, "identity" might refer to both the superhero's identifiable costuming, and their "secret identity" or civilian persona, which they use when not in their superhero role. In his essay "The Myth of Superman," semiotician Umberto Eco observes that "Often the hero's virtue is humanized, and his powers, rather than being supernatural, are the extreme realization of natural endowments" (1979, 107). He also suggests that in a post-industrial society, in which humanity's personal power has been usurped by machines, the hero becomes representative of "the power demands that the average citizen nurtures but cannot satisfy" (107).

Jessica Jones certainly accomplishes things in ways that regular people cannot, having powers beyond regular human capacities, although it is questionable whether these are consistently used for heroic deeds. She takes on missions and has a sometimes-confused identity that is more often affiliated with her civilian role rather than that of a costumed superhero, and for eight months she was possessed by the Purple Man (a.k.a. Zebediah Killgrave[1]), who manipulated her to act against her will (Bendis and Gaydos 2003b, n.p.). In the cynical Bronze and Modern Ages of comics (ca. 1973–present), in which superheroes are humanized and forced to cope with common problems like money, substance abuse, and death, Jessica Jones still represents capacities beyond those of regular people; however, her powers seem only slightly beyond us, and having discarded her superhero garb, she even looks like one of us. Earlier generations of superheroes were virtually indestructible and infallible, aligned with a naive American ethos. Jessica Jones does represent the superhero mythos, but in an unconventional way. By exploring Golden Age comic book superheroes against the background of Pierre Bourdieu's notion of habitus, as well as contemporary conceptions of post-humanism, this chapter explores Jessica Jones as a superhero who diverts from the classic model, thereby evolving the superhero habitus.

Although a narrow view of Pierre Bourdieu's construction of habitus focuses on cultural capital and socio-economics—"class habitus, the internalized form of class condition and of the conditionings it entails" (1984, 101)—the concept has a much broader cultural reach. Bourdieu refers to three types of social capital that tend to locate who we are in terms of class: embodied cultural capital, such as linguistic dialect; objectified cultural capital, such as a house; and institutionalized cultural capital, such as professional credentials (437–8). Although these may be shared by certain social classes, creating part of that group's identity and a foundation for social inequality, they can also be acquired by other classes (471).

Bourdieu, however, also discusses cultural capital in terms of lifestyles, as "systematic products of habitus, which, perceived in their mutual relations through the schemes of the habitus ... transform the distribution of capital ... into a system of perceived differences" (172). For Bourdieu, lifestyle includes aesthetic tastes, skills, fashion, mannerisms, etc. Habitus is the unconscious and acquired embodiment of all forms of cultural capital: "The schemes of the habitus, the primary forms of classification, owe their specific efficacy to the fact that they function below the level of consciousness and language, beyond the reach of introspective scrutiny or control by the will" (466). These are the habits, aesthetic sensibilities, characteristics, and skills that are our second nature, and that seem obvious or intuitive ("Profile: Pierre Bourdieu" n.d.); in this way habitus "becomes internalised in the form of dispositions to act, think, and feel in certain ways" (Fleming n.d.). Habitus can be defined as "the way society becomes deposited in persons in the form of lasting dispositions, or trained capacities and structured propensities to think, feel and act in determinant ways" (Wacquant 2005, 316). Our habitus enables us to move readily within certain environments and social contexts. Habitus is, however, culturally and socially developed, rather than naturally ingrained ("Profile: Pierre Bourdieu" n.d.); we are enculturated to our habitus through family, peers, gender, and other forms of identity (Fleming n.d.). Because habitus is learned, it is also flexible, and therefore adaptable to different situations or over time (Navarro 2006, 16). One's habitus can change by way of the flexibility between its intrinsic and relational properties; in other words, through the interplay between its socially entrenched structures and free will (Bourdieu 1984, 170).

Based on this very brief overview of Bourdieu's notion of habitus, one can construct a habitus of the superhero class by observing the lifestyles and practices of its members. Drawing on the previous definitions, the superhero habitus indicates one who (a) accomplishes heroic deeds or missions, (b) embodies powers beyond those of regular humans, and (c) has both an identifiable superhero identity and a secret civilian identity. Comic book superheroes, including popular, long-running series such as *Superman* (1938), *Batman* (1939), and *Wonder Woman* (1941), began publishing during the Golden Age of comics (1938–50). During the Second World War, such superheroes took on Hitler and single-handedly defeated hordes of spies and other Nazis; during the Silver Age, (ca. 1956–73), they defeated a variety of super villains who often had their own superpowers. These superheroes accomplished their heroic missions by exercising extraordinary powers. As a native of Krypton, Superman has super strength, speed and durability, the ability to fly, X-ray vision, super breath, and high intelligence. Batman is a different type of superhero: the vigilante. Although he is intelligent, he embodies no special physical abilities, other than being well trained and in peak physical condition. He is aided by high-tech devices, afforded largely by inherited wealth. As a demigod,

Wonder Woman is yet another type of superhero. Similar to Superman, she has superhuman strength, speed and durability, as well as longevity, training in hand-to-hand combat, and access to magical devices, such as the Lasso of Truth, her indestructible bracelets, sword, and shield. As a female superhero, she is also a rarity. All three have distinctive costumed superhero identities, as well as secret civilian identities: Superman is also reporter Clark Kent; Batman is also billionaire Bruce Wayne; and Wonder Woman is also Diana Prince, first an army nurse, and later part of military intelligence, a civilian employee, and a United Nations staffer. Typical of Golden Age superheroes, all three have a strong moral grounding; as an audience, we know that they represent the power of good over evil.

Does Jessica Jones fit this classic superhero habitus? In the original comic book, Jessica begins life as Jessica Campbell, attending Midtown High School, where she has a crush on Peter Parker (a.k.a. Spider-Man). She is an ordinary teenager whose superpowers only manifest after her family car collides with a military convoy carrying radioactive "Hazardous Experimental Material." The accident kills her parents and younger brother and leaves her in a coma for six months. She awakens after the hospital is plunged into darkness as a result of the Fantastic Four's battle with Galactus, which releases additional radiation. From the Moore House for Wayward Children, she is adopted by the kindly and supportive Mr. and Mrs. Jones (quite different from the Netflix conception), becoming Jessica Jones (Bendis and Gaydos 2003a, n.p.). Her return to Midtown High is difficult, with school bullies teasing her about being a freak for waking from a coma. Peter Parker, having also experienced family loss, tries to talk to Jessica, but misinterpreting his advances as pity, she runs away. For two pages, Jessica is seen running and experiencing traumatic flashbacks, when she suddenly discovers that she has left the ground and is floating, beyond her control, above the Hudson River. Suddenly conscious of her flying, she falls into the river, and is rescued by Thor. Her second attempt at flight is equally uncontrolled, ending when she lands on the villainous Scorpion trying to rob a laundromat. Jessica discovers her increased strength by pushing over a very solid-looking tree. During the awakening of her powers, she and her adoptive father discuss the varied public perceptions of superheroes. When asked whether she is a superhero by stunned witnesses at the laundromat, she answers with a hesitant yes (Bendis and Gaydos 2003a, n.p.).

Jessica's subsequent experience as a costumed superhero is, however, short-lived. The story is told in flashbacks to her on-again, off-again partner, Luke Cage. Almost unrecognizable in a form-fitting silver costume with aqua trim, Jessica flits overhead as Jewel, wondering about getting a job and a decent boyfriend. Swooping down to break up a fight, she encounters the Purple Man (a.k.a. Zebediah Kilgrave). Exposure to experimental nerve gas left Kilgrave the colour purple, but also gave him mind control over others through psychoactive pheromones, paving the way for his criminal career. Kilgrave overcomes Jessica's will and orders her to delay the police so he can finish his steak. Jessica remains under Kilgrave's control for eight months. In the original comic book, when Cage asks whether Kilgrave raped Jessica during this incarceration, she responds, "He didn't. What he did was—He fucking made me stand there and watch him fuck other girls. Telling me to **wish** it was me. . . . But when there **weren't** any girls around, on a rainy night with nothing to do . . . he would make me **beg** him for it" (Bendis and Gaydos 2003b, n.p.; bold in original).

While Jessica's second trauma in the Netflix series is her repeated rape and her stronger connection with Kilgrave's other rape victims, in the original comic book, the second trauma is Kilgrave's mind control. When Kilgrave orders Jewel (a.k.a. Jessica Jones) to destroy Daredevil, she finally escapes the vicinity of his pheromone-based mind control. Unfortunately, she attacks the Scarlet Witch, having mistaken her for Daredevil, before fully returning to her senses. The unprovoked attack on one of their own causes the amassed Avengers to beat Jessica into another coma. While recovering, she is offered a position as a S.H.I.E.L.D. liaison for the Avengers, which she declines (Bendis and Gaydos 2003b, 2003c). Although the X-Men's Jean Grey builds Jessica a mental block to prevent Kilgrave from ever gaining control of her mind again, subsequent mentions of Kilgrave cause Jessica extreme anxiety. After the Kilgrave incident, Jessica retires her Jewel identity. Comic scholar Terrence Wandtke suggests that differences between the original comic book and the Netflix series denote "two different understandings of the character" (personal communication, April 13, 2017). Although Jessica's eight-month encounter with Kilgrave is a pivotal part of the comic book, it forms only a brief chapter in her story. The Netflix series gives Kilgrave a much more prominent role.

Jessica's second attempt as a costumed superhero is as Knightress, another story told in flashbacks to her newborn, Danielle. Upon reflection, Jessica considers the Knightress chapter a brief, but dark and cynical, period of her life. As the Knightress, Jessica is a vigilante, attempting to defeat a kingpin called the Owl. The Owl and his henchmen are defeated by a joint effort of the Knightress, Luke Cage (Danielle's eventual father), and Iron Fist (a.k.a. Danny Rand). When asked her superhero identity, Jessica declines to answer. As the police arrive, Jessica discovers that one of the thugs has brought his children, and that they are in the back seat of the villain's car. When an officer indicates that the children will be taken to the police station before going to child services in the morning, Jessica responds, "You can't have kids in a police station in the middle of the night." Seeing the children's distress, Jessica removes her mask—thus retiring her Knightress identity—and gives her full name and a S.H.I.E.L.D. reference so she can gain custody of the children overnight (Bendis and Gaydos 2006, n.p.). Subsequent to this second failure as a costumed superhero, Jessica establishes Alias Investigations and begins working as a private investigator, often looking into mutant- or superhero-related crimes.

Returning to the Golden Age notion of the superhero habitus, through her attempts as a costumed superhero, Jessica Jones can be seen to accomplish heroic deeds, but on a small scale. She brings down low-level thugs, using powers of flight and strength beyond those of regular people; however, both of her attempts at creating a costumed superhero identity are short-lived, ending in failure. As Bourdieu suggests, habitus can change over time owing to a flexibility between its socially entrenched structures and free will (1984, 170). Certainly the superhero habitus has changed since the Golden Age. One of the starkest changes was the 1954 introduction, and subsequent abandonment by Marvel in 2001, of the Comics Code Authority, briefly discussed by Sarah Stang in this volume. *Jessica Jones: Alias* began publication in 2001, so how does Jessica Jones fit the superhero habitus of either the Bronze Age (1973–ca. 1985) or Modern Age (ca. 1985–present) of comics?

Watchmen (1987) is often cited variously as the end of the Bronze Age or the beginning of the Modern Age, although these periods share many common traits. Superheroes of this latter period are more often troubled anti-heroes. *Watchmen* offered an alternative reality in which superheroes were publicly recognized after the Second World War. In this reconstructed history, superheroes are outlawed by the Keene Act in 1977, and most subsequently retire. A few, like Doctor Manhattan, remain as government-sanctioned agents, giving the United States an edge as a world power. Others, like the story's featured anti-hero, Rorschach (a.k.a. Walter Kovacs), operate as vigilante outlaws. According to comic book scholar Bradford Wright, unlike previous generations of superheroes, those of *Watchmen* "talked and behaved like real people" (2003, 271). Wright adds, "Rorschach, was perhaps the most disturbing superhero ever created for comic books. His brutal perception of black-and-white morality reflected writer Alan Moore's critical deconstruction of the whole notion of heroes" (275). Moore's superheroes are positioned against the backdrop of the Reagan and Thatcher era, when politicians were often seen as harming their country's populations. Comics scholar Geoff Klock suggests that *Watchmen*'s revisionism "sends waves of disruption back through superhero history . . . devalu[ing] one of the basic superhero conventions by placing his masked crime fighters in a realistic world" (2002, 63).

The dark urban world of *Watchmen* is perhaps best described by Rorschach himself: "The streets are extended gutters and the gutters are full of blood and when the drains finally scab over, all the vermin will drown. The accumulated filth of all their sex and murder will foam up about their waists and all the whores and politicians will look up and shout 'save us!' . . . and I'll look down and whisper 'no' " (Moore and Gibbons 1987, 1). The bullied child of a prostitute and absentee father, Kovacs lashes out in violent self-defence and is subsequently placed in the Lillian Charlton Home for Problem Children. The real-life murder of Kitty Genovese (Gansberg 1964) prompts Kovacs to become a vigilante, and his work in the garment trade provides access to the revolutionary fabric for his chameleon-like black-and-white mask. The mask's changing ink-blot nature provides the name Rorschach. While siding with a helpless underclass, Rorschach exhibits a rarely seen level of violence toward criminals. Rorschach's most obvious power is his ability to intimidate; however, he is also a genius investigator and strong-arm interrogator, trained in espionage and hand-to-hand combat. He is often perceived as a sociopath, and after an incident in which a kidnapped child is fed to a dog, he completely loses his original Kovacs identity: "It was Kovacs who closed his eyes. It was Rorschach who opened them again" (Moore and Gibbons 1987, no. 6, p. 21). He confides to his psychologist that this was the point after which the mask became his face and he became "Rorschach, who sometimes pretends to be Kovacs," rather than "Kovacs pretending to be Rorschach" (Moore and Gibbons 1987, no. 6, p. 14).

As with earlier eras of comics, female superheroes exist in the Bronze Age, but they are still fewer in number. One of the most enigmatic of this period is Elektra, first appearing in *Daredevil* no. 168 (Miller 1981). Elektra's mother dies while giving birth to her, so she is raised by her father, as well as various martial arts experts. She is plagued by dark childhood memories, has a psychotherapist, and occasionally self-harms. Her work as a freelance assassin and bounty hunter sometimes puts her on the side of good working for S.H.I.E.L.D., but other times on the side of evil working for mobsters. Lacking a strong moral compass of her own, she is targeted by both sides, finally killed by mobsters, but is then resurrected (Miller and Janson 1983). Mercenary and assassin, Elektra is a master martial artist, with ninja stealth and acrobatic training. She has learned to control her nervous system in order to deaden pain, harness her emotions, and prevent blood loss, and she gains telepathic and telekinetic abilities, heightened vigilance and awareness, a fatal silent Chi scream, and strong weapons skills, especially with her trademark twin Okinawan Sai blades. Her skills are the result of years of disciplined training, rather than being inbred or the result of an accident. Her alter ego, Elektra Natchios, is essentially non-existent, as she always appears in her red costume (Miller and Sienkiewicz 1986a, 1986b).

Based on these examples, superheroes or anti-heroes of the Bronze or Modern Ages of comics still retain the following characteristics: (a) they accomplish heroic deeds or missions, although with an ambivalent sense of good; (b) they embody powers beyond those of regular humans, but often through their own labour, rather than from birth or by accident; and (c) they have both a superhero identity and a "secret identity," but their superhero identity often dominates their civilian identity, to the degree that their civilian identity may be entirely lost. The pure habitus of the Golden Age has eroded, leaving characters who are less obviously good and who face real-world problems and psychological issues.

While acknowledging that both Rorschach and Elektra are much darker characters than Jessica Jones, some commonalities are apparent. Rorschach and Jessica both lose their parents during their teens and are consigned to institutions, although the version of Jessica in the comics is adopted by a kind and loving family, while Rorschach is not. Jessica lives briefly at the Moore House for Wayward Children, perhaps an acknowledgement of Alan Moore's *Watchmen* as Jessica's antecedent. Elektra never knows her mother, and although she is close to her father, he is killed during an anti-terrorist police action when she is at university. Although Elektra is an assassin for hire, both Rorschach and Jessica strive to aid the helpless against larger and uglier forces. Both Rorschach and Jessica have super strength and are intelligent investigators. All three—Rorschach, Elektra, and Jessica—have varying degrees of psychological issues.

Jessica Jones can readily be seen as one of these more contemporary superheroes, engaged in the dialectical process of an evolving habitus through conflicting notions of staid Golden Age structure and her own agency. Her independence and volatility are more akin to contemporary superhero models, as are her substance abuse and psychological issues. Unlike her contemporaries, Jessica has twice abandoned a superhero identity and costume, becoming instead a private detective in street clothes. She has more in common with the hard-boiled detectives of the 1930s and '40s, than she does with Superman. *Jessica Jones*, like the work of Moore, Miller, and others, comes even closer to rendering the superhero a regular person. Her powers of strength and flight are all that separate her from the rest of us. In Jessica, the superhero becomes us, and the superhero habitus undergoes a radical revision without the costume or absurdly high moral standards.

In *Jessica Jones*, the superhero is redefined not as a superhero, or even an anti-superhero, but as a form of post-human. Through accident, Jessica takes on superhuman powers, combining her natural biology with science. Theologian Elaine Graham defines post-humanism as "denoting a world in which humans are mixtures of machines and organism, where nature has been modified (encultured) by technologies, which in turn have become assimilated into 'nature' as a functioning component of organic bodies" (2002, 10). This definition resembles Donna Haraway's earlier conception of the cyborg as "the offspring of implosions of subjects and objects and of the natural and the artificial" (1997, 12). As is apparent from these definitions, post-humanism requires a substantial ontological shift from the biological human being, but the cyborg is not the only theoretical post-human construction.

Rejecting the technologically driven model, cultural theorist Sherryl Vint calls for an "embodied notion of posthumanism" (2007, 16). Similarly, postmodern literary critic Katherine N. Hayles (1999) suggests that the post human is a new conception of human, an emergent being, rather than the end of humanity. Instead of incorporating the sometimes clumsy prostheses of cyberpunk science fiction, Vint, Hayles, and sociologist Nikolas Rose perceive that advances in the biological sciences, such as the Human Genome Project, actually render us *more* biological, *more* embodied, by manipulating human beings at the organic level. Rose suggests that "we are inhabiting an 'emergent form of life,' " (2007, 80) one in which genetic augmentation and transformation will allow us to produce better children, improve our physical performance, and acquire ageless bodies. We are, in short, becoming post-human, and in so doing we are striving to meet the superhero habitus. Characters like Jessica Jones allow us to recognize our everyday selves in the post-human superhero who is only slightly augmented.

Regardless of how post-humanism is conceived, whether as a cyborg hybrid or a biological enhancement, Haraway (1997) and others suggest that its conception opens the door for humanity to take on a multiplicity of acceptable human forms, and Jessica's is just one of these. This concept is liberating, especially in light of genetics research that tends to focus on homogeneity and perfectibility, thwarting natural evolutionary trends. In evolving the superhero habitus, Jessica Jones supersedes the superhero and moves toward the post-human. Bourdieu supports this flexible evolution of habitus:

> To reconstruct the social conditions of production of the habitus as fully as possible, one also has to consider the social trajectory of the class or class fraction the agent belongs to, which, through the probable slope of the collective future, engenders progressive or regressive dispositions towards the future; and the evolution, over several generations, of the asset structure of each lineage, which is perpetuated in the habitus. (1984, 123)

Taking her place in the Modern Age of comics, several generations into superhero evolution, Jessica Jones may be perceived as both progressive and regressive. Although her character abandons key elements of Golden Age superheroes, she embodies a post-human superhero habitus, making her more readily identifiable and closer in status to her readers.

NOTE

1   The name for the character of the Purple Man is spelled differently in both the Netflix series and the comics on which it was based (i.e., "Kilgrave" and Killgrave," respectively). Henceforth, I employ the "Kilgrave" spelling to avoid switching between different versions of the name and to maintain consistency with other chapters in the collection.

References

Bendis, Brian Michael, and Michael Gaydos. 2003a. *Jessica Jones: Alias* 1, no. 22. New York: Marvel, 2003.

———. 2003b. *Jessica Jones: Alias* 1, no. 25. New York: Marvel, 2003.

———. 2003c. *Jessica Jones: Alias* 1, no. 26. New York: Marvel, 2003.

———. 2006. *Jessica Jones: Pulse* 1, no. 14. New York: Marvel, 2006.

Bourdieu, Pierre. 1984. *Distinction: A Social Critique of the Judgement of Taste*. Translated by Richard Nice. Cambridge, MA: Harvard University Press.

Coogan, Peter. 2013. "The Hero Defines the Genre, the Genre Defines the Hero." In *What Is a Superhero?*, edited by Robin S. Rosenberg and Peter Coogan, 3–10. New York: Oxford University Press.

Eco, Umberto. 1979. "The Myth of Superman." In *The Role of the Reader: Explorations in the Semiotics of Text*, 107–24. Bloomington: Indiana University Press.

Fleming, Diana. n.d. "Pierre Bourdieu: Habitus." Center for Neural Science, New York University, accessed March 26, 2024. www.cns.nyu.edu/~pillow/gradforum/content/habitus_Diana_Fleming.doc

Gansberg, Martin. 1964. "37 Who Saw Murder Didn't Call the Police; Apathy at Stabbing of Queens Woman Shocks Inspector." *New York Times*, March 27, 1964. https://www.nytimes.com/1964/03/27/archives/37-who-saw-murder-didnt-call-the-police-apathy-at-stabbing-of.html.

Graham, Elaine L. 2002. *Representations of the Post/Human: Monsters, Aliens and Others in Popular Culture*. New Brunswick, NJ: Rutgers University Press.

Haraway, Donna. 1997. *Modest_Witness@Second_Millennium: FemaleMan_Meets_ OncoMouse*. New York: Routledge.

Hayles, Katherine N. 1999. *How We Became Posthuman: Virtual Bodies in Cybernetics, Literature, and Informatics*. Chicago: University of Chicago Press.

Klock, Geoff. 2002. *How to Read Superhero Comics and Why*. London: A. & C. Black.

Lee, Stan. 2013. "More Than Normal, but Believable." In *What Is a Superhero?*, edited by Robin S. Rosenberg and Peter Coogan, 115–24. New York: Oxford University Press.

Miller, Frank. 1981. *Daredevil*, no. 168. New York: Marvel, 1981.

Miller, Frank, and Klaus Janson. 1983. *Daredevil*, no. 190. New York: Marvel, 1983.

Miller, Frank, and Bill Sienkiewicz. 1986a. *Elektra Assassin*, no. 1. New York: Epic, 1986.

———. 1986b. *Elektra Assassin*, no. 2. New York: Epic, 1986.

Moore, Alan, and Dave Gibbons. 1987. *Watchmen*. New York: Warner Books.

Navarro, Zander. 2006. "In Search of Cultural Interpretation of Power: The Contribution of Pierre Bourdieu." *IDS Bulletin* 37 (6): 11–22. https://opendocs.ids.ac.uk/opendocs/bitstream/handle/123456789/8355/IDSB_37_6_10.1111-j.1759-5436.2006.tb00319.x.pdf?sequence=1&isAllowed=y.

"Profile: Pierre Bourdieu." n.d. Social Theory Re-wired, accessed March 26, 2024. https://www.routledgesoc.com/profile/pierre-bourdieu#:~:text=Habitus%20is%20one%20of%20Bourdieu.

Rose, Nikolas S. 2007. *The Politics of Life Itself: Biomedicine, Power, and Subjectivity in the Twenty-first Century.* Princeton, NJ: Princeton University Press.

Wacquant, Loic. 2005. "Habitus." In *International Encyclopedia of Economic Sociology*, edited by Jens Beckert and Milan Zafirovski, 315–19. London: Routledge.

Wright, Bradford. 2003. *Comic Book Nation: The Transformation of Youth Culture in America.* Baltimore, MD: Johns Hopkins University Press.

Defining "Rebel Femme Noir" through Genre Hybridization in Cinematic and Comics Narratives of *Jessica Jones*

Natalja Chestopalova

The hybridization of the superhero genre in print, film, and comics has allowed for the creation and expansion of superhero sub-genres that shift the attention toward the femme experience and the spaces of difference that non-heteronormative protagonists can occupy. Within these multi-modal comics and cinematic spaces of difference, new heroines are helping rebuild and even heal fictional universes that have been oriented toward portrayals of predominantly male superheroes. This is especially applicable to genre hybridization in film and comics as types of media that have over time developed a symbiotic relationship with audiences of mass and popular culture phenomena. New comics aligned with critical feminist frameworks, graphic novels written as well as drawn by women, and television series with narratives that break with traditional genre staples—all of these contribute to the emergence of exciting literary and media hybridization. In fact, the growing demand for non-heteronormative superheroines has helped to diversify comics and film, while directing superhero sub-genres toward the exploration of the empowered *rebel femme* as a superhero in her own right.

The definition of the rebel femme superhero cannot be obtained through limiting conventional methods that have been used as cornerstones in traditional superhero narratives. Peter Coogan, who has written extensively on the nature of the superhero genre, suggests that these key defining characteristics are bound by embodied conventions in the form of the superhero's mission as the champion for the oppressed, explicit power, and superhero identity through specific costumes and code names or aliases (Coogan 2009,

77–82). Although all of these have become essential signifiers of the super-hero genre, they have received criticism for generating a dynamic driven by the regurgitation of abstract traits that come dangerously close to homogenizing the genre. The new approaches to genre hybridization can act as a welcome narrative destabilizer and a way of making cinematic and multi-modal superhero narratives a source of storytelling rebellion.

One such empowered narrative comes in the form of the *rebel femme noir* sub-genre, which merges the crime thriller aesthetic with the psychological intensity of a superhero gone rogue. This chapter looks at *Jessica Jones* as a manifestation of this sub-genre, tracing the variety of implicit as well as explicit ways in which Jones's characterization generates liberating tensions and new types of social agency. Jones is an unusual, and in some ways uncanny, superhero with a distinct sense of unease verging on suspicion about the superhero scene, institutional justice, and intimacy. Jones's identity and life decisions complicate her femme superhero identification and status because they shatter the linear conception of what a woman superhero is capable of and is expected to embody. This narrow spectrum of characteristics tends to insist on binaries between heroes and villains by locating characters like Wonder Woman, Storm, and Batwoman toward one end, and Catwoman, Harlequin, and *Red Lantern*'s Bleez toward the other. The subtle aim of Jessica Jones's narrative is precisely to question such binaries by exposing them as part of the homogenizing agenda that caters to a phallogocentric superhero universe.

She made her first appearance in Marvel's "Max" adult reader titles as the protagonist of a twenty-eight-issue series titled *Jessica Jones: Alias* (2001–4), written by Brian Bendis and illustrated by visual artist Michael Gaydos. Jones's narrative gained a much wider popular audience through the cinematic reimagining of her story in the Netflix original television series *Jessica Jones* (2015–19). Rather than function as versions of the same story, the television series and *Alias* comics occupy a complementary narrative space where Jessica Jones sets a precedent for a highly engaging rebel femme superhero. In the introduction to the first volume of *Alias*, producer and comics writer Jeph Loeb affectionately calls Jessica Jones "a blessing and a curse" (Loeb 2015, 4). He goes on to suggest that this dichotomy is attributed to her being a not-so-hard-boiled detective living and working in the gritty underbelly of the Marvel Universe. However, there is much more to this separation. Although she shares the fictional New York realm with the militarized Avengers and the heteronormative Marvel "superstars" such as Spider-Man, Ant-Man, and Daredevil, Jones exhibits an unconscious desire to distance herself from organized superhero communities. In fact, both the comics and the television series ensure that Jones's character remains relatable precisely because of her non-superhero qualities and her capacity to experience and learn from failures, flaws, and weaknesses.

Jones's identification as a superhero is superseded by her role as an independent private investigator and a deeply traumatized woman with PTSD and a severe addiction to alcohol. What this order of identification priorities implies is a proud acceptance of complexity and psychological trauma in progress. This chapter approaches Jones's narrative as complementary comics and television series that dissect the notion of regenerative counter-normativity and rebel femme empowerment. It further suggests that the *Jessica Jones* comics and television series try to reinvent the concepts of domesticity, agency, and consent through the figure of a femme superhero who confronts the stigmatization of mental illness, the victimization of women, and rape culture, among other issues.

To properly talk about the narratives of *Jessica Jones* it is necessary to accept her as a tumultuous and rebellious woman who is in many ways a counterintuitive embodiment of a superhero. She is further positioned outside of the habitual discourse on graphic novels and comics because of the connotations that the rebel femme noir sub-genre introduces into her storyline. Examining the domestic/suburban/chick noir genre hybridization, A. J. Waines writes that the crime thriller category featuring female protagonists has been rapidly growing through sub-genres that are concerned with the figure of the empowered femme and the uncanny dimension of her subjectivity. In Waines's sub-genre classification, suburban noir is, to use her phrasing, "the dark side of suburban living" as it is very "close to home. It is on our doorstep, [in] the neighbourhood—and [it] breeds threat with themes of secrets, being trapped, being watched/stalked and things not being what they seem—all seen from behind those twitching net curtains" (Waines 2014). Compare that to the opening sequence for the Netflix original series, saturated with an uncanny noir quality and offering a series of city close-ups reminiscent of Hitchcock's *Rear Window* (1954). Instead of the phallogocentric gaze of Hitchcock's L. B. "Jeff" Jefferies tracing the deceptively intimate tranquility of the neighborhood, the series opens with sinister rows of high-rise windows, as if each one is being tracked by Jones's contemplative stare. Behind every window the viewer seems to recognize a micro-stage that illuminates rather than hides the darker dimensions of relationships, privacy, domesticity, and homeliness. Jason Bainbridge summarizes fictional New York as a largely archetypal city (Bainbridge 2010, 163–4), a quality that makes it in many ways an ideal setting for hybridized genre narratives.

New York as a site of the darker side of modernity and of its urbanization and industrialization is a type of space that is implicitly about survival against odds and obstacles (Bainbridge 2010, 167). The first episode of the television series reinforces its noir aesthetic by situating Jones as someone who spends her nights on dirty staircases watching, drinking, and photographing people for her hired and personal cases, while at the same time being watched and photographed herself. The honesty with which the noir city acknowledges its flaws makes it an emotional sanctuary of sorts. For instance, in *Alias* vol. 3, no. 16, the collaborative tensions introduced through Bendis's narrative rhythm and Gaydos's visual comics introduces a sequence that includes a full-page bleeding panel, situating Jessica as someone who is in many ways in sync with this noir city (Bendis and Gaydos 2015b, 54).

In particular, no. 16 narrates the middle part of a case Jones chooses to investigate as it resonates with her own experience of abuse and physical as well as emotional torture resulting from her abduction by the Purple Man, known as Kilgrave in the television series. This investigation revolves around the retrieval of the third version of Spider-Woman, Mattie Franklin, who has been abducted, drugged, and then mutilated. The particulars of Franklin's bodily harm are especially telling as she is violated sexually, and parts of her shoulder flesh are removed in a cannibalistic and abject manner to be ingested and sold as a drug. In fact, the job of locating and retrieving Franklin sets up a lot of the trauma-conscious tension and affective dynamics relevant to the final confrontation between Jones and the Purple Man at the end of *Alias* vol 4, no. 28. As a fellow superhero, Franklin's victimization and rape force Jones to recognize the problematic nature of her own relationships and accept that she will need to address some of her ongoing anxieties. It is in the middle of this case that Bendis and Gaydos insert a full-page bleeding panel of New York City in all its noir glory. When talking about New York, Bainbridge notes that the city effectively functions as a "grid for the Marvel Universe," since it makes the events and characters "*legible*" by offering the audience a sense of connectivity through an urban space functioning as a community and a dimension of realism (Bainbridge 2010, 168; emphasis in the original).

It is within this noir city grime, rain, pollution, and alienation that Jones is situated, her greyish, slouching body melting into the lower-right corner as if part of the landscape. This is Jones's narrative at its darkest, but also at its most infectiously regenerative in terms of counter-normative superheroism. The figure of Jones as the rebel femme persists against the odds and against a fictional universe that is so adept at replicating the reality of stigmatization faced by women suffering from mental illness, anxiety, addiction, and PTSD.

In Jones's noir world, to be a rebel femme is to accept that personal demons can take on a variety of physical and emotional forms. Jennifer K. Stuller, writing about rebellious female comics characters like Lois Lane and their connection to second-wave feminism, insists that it is not enough to critique the pop-culture representation of women; rather, it is necessary to diversify the kinds of questions being asked about femme superheroines (Stuller 2012, 235–51). For the *Jessica Jones* comics and television series this entails asking questions about the representations of addiction, domestic violence, and the wide range of subtle and not-so-subtle ways in which gendered discrimination and violence can occur. The use of genre hybridization in both comics and television series, as well as how this hybridity is manifested through the series' rebel femme noir sub-genre, is highly effective since it creates the necessary visual and psychological climate for the dissection of alternative types of femme social agency.

One of the reasons why the *Alias* comics and the *Jessica Jones* series work so well as examples of counter-normative narratives about a rebel femme superhero is because of their meticulous commitment to allocating space for Jones's habits, weaknesses, flaws, and emotional boundaries. Complemented by carefully chosen investigative cases, these habits and boundaries become nothing short of a collection of psychological symptoms. In fact, within six minutes of the series's first episode, Krysten Ritter as Jones can be observed in the carnivalesque glory of empowerment through failure and rebellion that she embodies. After throwing her disgruntled male client through the front door, Jones heads over to her occasional lawyer/employer to beg—or as she put it, to "ask very strongly"—for a job (ep. 1.01, "AKA Ladies' Night"). Meanwhile, in the background, Jones's voiceover casually comments, "People do bad shit. I just avoid getting involved with them in the first place. That works for me. Most of the time" (ep. 1.01 "AKA Ladies' Night"). She goes on to use drinking as a personally valid reason to excuse her inability to function in a punctual and reliable manner, and yet she still manages to secure a new work contract. The case she is offered involves serving a court summons to the owner of a gentlemen's club where an exotic dancer fell off a stage and as a result suffered permanent brain damage. Jones's first question, directed at the woman the lawyer intends to represent, reflects a deep and immediate concern for women's rights and the institutionalized victimization of women in corporate and mainstream culture. As the interests of the exotic dancer are being represented, Jones takes the assignment, and we immediately find her working the case from the comfort of her toilet seat. Nonchalant and effective, Jones proceeds to falsify her identity to obtain sensitive case information; she then reaches for the empty toilet roll: "Shit," she says, slapping it.

The inclusion of the working-on-the-toilet scene is incredibly revealing, not only in terms of counter-normative portrayals of women superheroes, but also in terms of mainstream portrayals of women's bodies and their perfect as well as imperfect boundaries. In the *Alias* comics, a similar washroom scene occurs in vol. 1, no. 7, where Jones is depicted sitting comfortably on a toilet in a contemplative manner while staring at something in front of her (Bendis and Gaydos 2015a, 150). The bleeding-style panel takes over the entire page and forces the reader to trace a total of eighteen separate speech bubbles. The scene's layout, style, and narrative pace successfully work together to compel readers to maintain their focus on Jones's body at its most vulnerable and intimate. In classic noir narratives, blood and flesh is generally affiliated with the actions and behaviours of men, while the women remain at a distance, untainted by bodily harm or bodily functions. A notable example of a classic noir woman is Goldie, who appears in "The Hard Goodbye" from the *Sin City* series by Frank Miller. On the one hand, Goldie is a distressed and haunted woman incapable of taking care of herself, while on the other, she is portrayed as possessing such incredible beauty that even her dead body does not show any signs of imperfection, broken surfaces, or decomposition. *Alias* and *Jessica Jones* can be easily distinguished from this type of noir precisely because they turn toward rather than away from imperfection, flaws, and various physical and emotional boundaries. Jones's narrative is about seeking new types of femme agency and empowerment in places that a normative or homogenizing gaze might dismiss as unnerving and even abject. Graphic novel researcher Frederik Byrn Køhlert, writing on the work of Julie Doucet, notes that comics narratives have been quite effective in raising new questions about women's bodies, their functions, and their boundaries by relying on "unconventionally drawn stories" (Køhlert 2012, 19). Specifically, Køhlert suggests that the representation of bodily transgression and its celebratory violence can be accomplished through the introduction of Mikhail Bakhtin's notion of the carnivalesque.

What the carnivalesque entails for the *Alias* comics, and by extension the television series, is that it injects elements of grotesque "parodic excess" in the form of the visible and functioning body. Such a body is, by definition, a rebellious and empowered body, capable of shattering the gaze of visual objectification and unravelling its scopophilic pleasure potential (Køhlert 2012, 20–1). It is in moments like the toilet scene, where Jones is in a position of imaginary vulnerability, that she is at her most characteristic as a rebel femme noir.

Jones's empowerment does find its counterpart in her difficulty expressing thoughts and feelings about sexual violence, the experience of rape, the fear of domesticity, repressive behaviours, and addiction. In both the television series and *Alias* comics narratives, the process of interviewing each new client is structured in a distinctly artificial manner. In the cinematic narrative, the Alias Investigations office doubles as an apartment and channels Dashiell Hammett's classic noir aesthetic. In fact, during the client interviews the arrangement conveys a sense of uncanny familiarity and, at the same time, dislocation. In the comics form, the interview process is stylistically designed to take over a two-page spread in which Jones's character occupies six identical panels aligned horizontally in the upper space of the page. Below each of these smaller panels are six elongated panels devoted to the frenetic client and his or her immediate investigative emergency. In each of the six arranged upper panels, Jones is drawn as lacking in physical movement, narrative progression, and visible emotional reaction. She remains utterly still throughout the client's narration of the case monologue, leaving the reader with only one temporal progression marker in the form of smoke escaping her lit cigarette. The choice to dedicate this particular storytelling dynamic to the client interviews is both intentional and symbolic insofar as it acts as a commentary on Jones's role as investigator and on her own much more personal relationship with the cases at hand.

What this duality of visual narration suggests is not a lack of response or emotionality, but rather a habit of restraint or boundary setting when it comes to traumatic content that either overlaps with or sits at a tangent with Jones's own affective trigger areas. For instance, in *Alias* vol. 1, no. 1, Jones is approached by a potential client who wants to locate her missing younger sister, Miranda. While the case turns out to be a hoax, the description of the missing sister divulges several critical triggers for Jones's character: "she was always kind of a lost one, kind of always drifting with the wrong crowd and getting into trouble. Uch—so stupid. She had an abortion," and "the family really didn't support her very well on that and it kind of led her to some trouble with drugs" (Bendis and Gaydos 2015a, 20). This description does satisfy some of the traditional noir narrative investigation parameters as it features a woman in distress who has been exposed to familial as well as social hostility, judgment, alienation, and stigmatization. Jones, however, is not a traditional noir detective but a complex superhero rebel seeking social justice, emotional resolution, and femme empowerment. This makes her a uniquely qualified professional capable of thinking beyond the schemes of heteronormativity and victimization.

Another instance of client interviews where Jones exhibits the same type of boundary formation and affective restraint is narrated in *Alias* vol. 1, no. 7. In this case, a heartbroken Jane Jones is desperate to find her missing husband, Rick, who eventually turns out to be a superhero impersonator, consistent philanderer, and an occasional pseudo–rock star musician (Bendis and Gaydos 2015a, 146–7). The emotional boundary that Jones sets up during the original client interview remains a constant source of support throughout the case, especially since many of the prolific lies developed and sustained by Rick facilitate dangerous misogynistic stereotypes about women and women's mental health. Instead of admitting that he is suffering from *pseudologia fantastica*, or pathological and compulsive lying syndrome, Rick chooses to evoke the mythical mad-woman-in-the-attic trope by claiming that Jane is "so wacked out of her mind sometimes" that "she concocts these theories" and then "she decides they're **true**. All of a sudden they're fact," "she's **nuts**, okay! I married a **lunatic**! So excuse **fucking** me for not wanting to come out and tell a complete **stranger** that I married a complete **lunatic**" (Bendis and Gaydos 2015a, 175–6; emphasis in original). Jones's capacity to navigate this case and her own emotions is bound by the tense negotiation between her responsibility as a superhero rebel and an empowered femme in the process of accepting her own history of trauma and PTSD.

Comics researchers, including Ruth J. Beerman, have made a connection between how women's bodies and affect experiences are narrated in comics and their connection to the development and control of superpowers (Beerman 2012, 2010). Beerman's writing on representations of heroism in popular culture suggests that there is a delicate threshold between empowerment and disempowerment, and this threshold is defined through the heroine's ability to regain a positive understanding of her body and sexual desires. The work of Sara Ahmed on emotion and affectivity can also help elucidate Jones's process of boundary creation and distancing. For Ahmed, the contact between individuals and/or objects resembles a type of *sticky point of contact* and that allows active engagement with the spaces of trauma as defined by contact, rather than caused by an affect that always remains at a distance and outside of one's role as a conscious subject (2004, 6–11). In Ahmed's affective approach, emotions come to life and are shaped by *contact*, instead of being caused by the subjects and objects themselves. It is these sticky points of contact that make Jones stand out as a femme superhero who uses counter-normativity and vulnerability as a source of strength. This type of superheroism also makes her character feel right at home in the rebel femme noir sub-genre and its fascination with the points of contact that define the domestic, homely, and private as intrinsically uncanny.

In Jones's noir environment, her role as a rebel femme is contingent on remaining transparent and vocal about these sticky points of contact, especially if they elicit strong physical and affective responses. In the television series, as well as certain *Alias* issues, Jones's apartment functions as a point of such sticky connectivity, since her contact with it becomes an instant trigger of anxiety, obsessive behaviours, and an overpowering sense of dread. Unlike the processes of empowered emotional restraint and boundary formation generated during difficult case interviews, Jones's relationship with the Alias Investigations office-apartment amounts a narrative about the loss of legitimacy when it comes to heteronormative domesticity, homeliness, privacy, and the types of relationships that help sustain them. Both the television series and comics embrace Jones's paranoiac relationship with her domestic space. *Alias* vol. 1, no. 2 begins with an internal monologue dedicated to addressing Jones's apprehensive attitudes toward the apartment and what it signifies as a manifestation of indefinitely violated physical and psychological space. Panels with barely visible outlines of Jones's face are accompanied by a self-assessment or confession-style phrasing: "My name is Jessica Jones. This is my apartment. In a spectacularly paranoid move I have been standing here staring at it for—let's see—forty two minutes," and "I can tell you—reason or no reason—the act of staring at my own curtains for the last twenty minutes, trying to decide if they moved because of a breeze or because someone might be in there waiting for me—is an altogether surreal experience" (Bendis and Gaydos 2015a, 32–3). This uncanny combination of urban alienation and lucid-dream awareness is at the core of Jones's character and the rebel femme noir storyline built around her. Furthermore, both the cinematic and comics narratives are always structured in a way that makes the audience hyper-conscious of the narrative's connotation when it comes to the systemic stigmatization of mental illness and victimization of women, especially women who identify as survivors of rape and domestic abuse.

The paranoiac symptoms and self-destructive habits exhibited by Jones over the course of her storylines are carefully contextualized within the experience of psychological and physical torture inflicted by the Purple Man, or Kilgrave. During her abduction, Jones was violated and controlled in a sadistic manner that took away her sense of agency over her emotional and physical experiences. On the one hand, she was denied key boundaries that help an individual ground themselves, including but not limited to access to her familiar clothing, safe domestic space, and supportive relationships. On the other, Kilgrave's mind control also deprived her of the basic infrastructure that legitimizes sensory and psychological reality as a lived experience. As Jones phrases it in *Alias* vol. 4, no. 25, "in your head—it doesn't *feel* any different than when you think it *yourself*," and "Not only does it *feel* the same, it actually feels *better* because the thought, the *command*— is pure" (Bendis and Gaydos 2015c, 88; emphasis in the original). Although both types of Kilgrave's mind control function as instances of violation and rape, the latter is more so responsible for Jones's prolonged state of severe depression, anxiety, and PTSD. In the television series, for instance, one of Kilgrave's abuses entails forcing Jones to smile for painfully prolonged periods of time while simultaneously experiencing the emotions associated with such a facial expression. Not only does this perverse affect-based exercise in abusive control amount to torture, but it also undermines Jones's capacity to distinguish between the real and the imaginary emotional states.

Such an utter lack of affective and cognitive clarity and awareness plays a critical role when it comes to forming questions about the nature of consent and its portrayal in popular mass media. In fact, Jones reflects on a similar type of abuse in *Alias* when she confides about her extreme paranoia and anxiety to friend and lover Luke Cage. Prompted by the need to address the Purple Man's escape from prison, Jones recounts how for eight months, "He fucking made me stand there and watch him fuck other girls. Telling me to *wish* it was me. Telling me to *cry* while I watched," and "when there **weren't** any girls around, on a rainy night with nothing to do . . . he would make me *beg* for it" (Bendis and Gaydos 2015c, 85; emphasis in the original). To complicate this abuse even further, the Purple Man introduces sinister intimacy and domesticity into these acts of torture by forcing Jones to lie at his feet, sleep on the floor, and bathe him. The confession-like nature of these traumatic recollections emphasizes Jones's renewed capacity to voice and share memories of past suffering and her ongoing regeneration and self-empowerment. This is an essential shift in noir comics storytelling, since the majority of traditional superhero comics employ sexual and physical assault as narrative triggers for the hero to seek revenge or justice. As part of their research on the introduction of new comics content into libraries, Anna Jorgensen and Arianna Lechan indicate that there is a distinct absence of comics and graphic novels that commit to looking at what happens to the female victim of assault in the long term (2013, 281). Specifically, they call for the inclusion of more content that seeks to understand the consequences of violence against women for the victims as well as the perpetrators. Jorgensen and Lechan argue for an almost paradigmatic genre shift, where rape and domestic violence cease to be a recurrent plot device that obscures what happens to women characters and whether they overcome trauma through rehabilitation.

The rebel femme noir tropes shaping both comics and television series are very useful for narrating how Jones develops in response to the intensity of incurred trauma. The counter-hegemonic rebel femme noir sub-genre of the series benefits from a consistent commitment to concentrating on Jones and her journey toward integrating various psychological resistance mechanisms into her daily life and work. Many of these resistance mechanisms and boundary-forming techniques are manifested through Jones's appeal to helpful transitional objects and experiences, quite similar to the method defined by psychoanalyst D. W. Winnicott. Transitional objects in Winnicott's sense act as a type of special possession that allows the subject to learn and then process the fact that they are separate from a particular object or person (Winnicott 2009). Winnicott's concept of transitional objects can be extremely helpful to survivors of domestic abuse and rape since they might feel overwhelmed by the conscious as well as unconscious triggers surrounding them. In addition to the already mentioned triggers, such as emotionally framed client interviews and uncanny domestic spaces, Jones has to address the fact that Kilgrave's presence as her abuser continues to haunt her. In response to this presence, Jones integrates a number of transitional objects, some of them physically embodied and some symbolic.

To illustrate, in the television series, Jones uses variations of the street names from around her childhood neighbourhood, and we often observe her chanting, "Birch Street, Main Street, Higgins Drive, Cobalt Lane" in moments of intense and overwhelming anxiety, fear, or paranoia (ep. 1.02, "AKA Crush Syndrome"). Her friend and fellow empowered femme with some superhero abilities, Trish Walker, encourages this practice by suggesting that "reciting street names from back home" is a "proven method for managing PTSD" (ep. 1.01, "AKA Ladies' Night"). Comments such as these help ensure that the audience can witness the importance of preventing the stigmatization of mental illness and victimization of women suffering from PTSD. In fact, as an example of an empowered femme, Walker herself functions as a type of transitional object for Jones, who has difficulties dealing with the accidental death of her parents. Jones's use of resistance techniques and transitional objects creates the type of narrative and psychological complexity that can satisfy even the requirements of the test based on the ideas of Alison Bechdel and Liz Wallace, who argue that the film, and by extension the comics storyline, "has to have at least two women in it" who "talk to each other about" something "besides a man" (Bechdel and Wallace 2005). Not only do the television and comics series succeed in this, but they also manage to expand the rebel femme noir sub-genre to include female characters of extreme emotional and psychological intensity.

Looking at the empowered superhero noir narrative elements of Jones's storyline, the *New Yorker*'s Emily Nussbaum awards Jessica Jones with an even more apt description: "superhero survivor" (Nussbaum 2015). There is something intrinsically counter-hegemonic about a broken woman surviving against the odds while coming face to face with the horror of violence against women. By embracing her counter-normativity and regenerative otherness, she becomes a superhero-survivor in the cinematic and graphic noir genre where women can be held captive and raped for months, and where a woman in a superhero costume becomes a fetish or a trophy. As an empowered rebel femme, Jessica Jones is not afraid to ask critical questions about agency, domesticity, consent, boundaries, and mental rehabilitation. Her narrative takes the counter-normativity discourse outside of the theoretical realm and into noir urban, domestic, and sacred spaces. Jones's commitment to finding new types of femme agency embody the incredible difficulty of living through violence, surviving its effects, and even thriving as an empowered rebel femme. She may say, "I was never the hero you wanted me to be" (ep. 1.01, "AKA Ladies' Night"), but she is the rebel femme superheroine audiences, libraries, and bookstores desperately need.

References

Ahmed, Sarah. 2004. *The Cultural Politics of Emotion*. New York: Routledge.

Bainbridge, Jason. 2010. " 'I am New York'—Spider-Man, New York City and the Marvel Universe." In *Comics and the City: Urban Space in Print, Picture and Sequence*, edited by Jörn Ahrens and Arno Meteling, 163–82. New York: Continuum.

Bechdel, Alison, and Liz Wallace. 2005. "The Rule." In *Dykes to Watch Out For: The Blog*, August 16, 2005. http://alisonbechdel.blogspot.ca/2005/08/rule.html.

Beerman, Ruth J. 2012. "The Body Unbound: *Empowered*, Heroism and Body Image." *Journal of Graphic Novels and Comics* 3 (2): 201–13.

Bendis, Brian Michael, and Michael Gaydos. 2015a. *Jessica Jones: Alias* 1, nos. 1–9. Edited by Stuart Moore, Kelly Lamy, and Nanci Dakesian. New York: Marvel Worldwide.

———. 2015b. *Jessica Jones: Alias* 3, nos. 10, 16–21. Edited by Stuart Moore, Joe Quesada, C. B. Cebulski, Kelly Lamy, and Nanci Dakesian. New York: Marvel Worldwide.

———. 2015c. *Jessica Jones: Alias* 4, nos. 22–8. Edited by C. B. Cebulski, Tom Brevoort, Andy Schmidt, Marc Sumerak, and Stephanie Moore. New York: Marvel Worldwide.

Coogan, Peter. 2009. "The Definition of the Superhero." In *A Comics Studies Reader*, edited by Jeet Heer and Kent Worchester, 77–93. Jackson: University Press of Mississippi.

Jorgensen, Anna, and Arianna Lechan. 2013. "Not Your Mom's Graphic Novels: Giving Girls a Choice beyond Wonder Woman." In *Technical Services Quarterly* 30:266–84.

Køhlert, Frederik Byrn. 2012. "Female Grotesques: Carnivalesque Subversion in the Comics of Julie Doucet." *Journal of Graphic Novels and Comics* 3 (1): 19–38.

Nussbaum, Emily. "Graphic, Novel: 'Marvel's Jessica Jones' and the Superhero Survivor." *New Yorker*, December 13, 2015. https://www.newyorker.com/magazine/2015/12/21/graphic-novel-on-television-emily-nussbaum.

Stuller, Jennifer K. 2012. "Feminism: Second-Wave Feminism in the Pages of *Lois Lane*." In *Critical Approaches to Comics: Theories and Methods*, edited by Matthew J. Smith and Randy Duncan, 235–51. New York: Routledge.

Waines, A. J. 2014. "Suburban, Domestic and Chick-Noir—New Genres in Psychological Thrillers." *A. J. Waines* (blog), August 19, 2014. https://awaines.blogspot.com/2014/08/suburban-domestic-and-chick noir-new.html.

Winnicott, D. W. 2009. "Playing: A Theoretical Statement." In *Playing and Reality*, 51–70. New York: Routledge Classics.

"My Greatest Weakness? Occasionally I Give a Damn": (Super)Heroic Duty, Responsibility, and Morality

Sarah Stang

Jessica Jones is unquestionably an unusual hero: a bitingly sarcastic, unapologetically cynical alcoholic who refuses to consider herself a superhero, preferring to use her powers of super strength and incredible jumping solely in the service of her shady work as a private investigator. While Netflix's series encourages audience identification with Jessica as the protagonist, it quickly becomes clear that she is a person of questionable moral integrity. Her own self-doubts and skewed sense of self-worth are directly related to the abuse she suffered at the hands of the first season's mind-controlling villain, Kilgrave. *Jessica Jones* fits well within the film noir genre, presenting a heavy-drinking, cynical, self-pitying private eye who has a "heart of gold" buried under layers of anguish and rage. In many ways, *Jessica Jones* is similar to DC's *Watchmen*, a groundbreaking comic written in 1986 by Alan Moore. *Watchmen* was an attempt to subvert the superhero genre by presenting heroes who are not really "super," but who are instead deeply flawed, psychologically damaged individuals who happen to wear costumes and fight crime. Writing about *Watchmen*, Iain Thomson asks an important question: "What does it mean when we seek not just to destroy our heroes—gleefully expose their feet of clay, their human, all-too-human failings—but to *deconstruct* the very idea of the hero?" (2005, 100–1; emphasis in original). That same desire to deconstruct superheroism can be found in other series like *The Boys* and *Umbrella Academy*, suggesting that perhaps this is a cultural moment in which audiences want to see "bad"—that is, petty, egotistical, and emotionally damaged—superheroes, at least on the small screen. Certainly, several films have attempted to do the same thing, such as *Hancock*, *The Dark Knight* trilogy, *Man of Steel*, and several of the Marvel superhero films, especially *Captain America: Civil War* and *The Avengers* franchise, but television series allow for a slower, deeper look at all the flaws and failings of their characters, and seem to especially focus on the cynical aspects of genre deconstruction. This chapter offers an exploration of how the first season of *Jessica Jones* embraces that cynicism and attempts to deconstruct the idea of the (super)hero, particularly in its complicated exploration of duty, responsibility, and morality. As I demonstrate, while the season engages with the themes of superpowered anti-heroism, instead of simply dwelling in cynicism and presenting a protagonist whose trauma prevents her from being a "proper" superhero, it instead presents a cautiously hopeful exploration of how one could be heroic despite one's traumatic experiences. In this way, *Jessica Jones* presents an alternative and perhaps more nuanced vision of who and what a superhero can be, and what it means to be one.

This chapter begins with a discussion of the superhero genre, which has historically been dedicated to the triumph of good over evil, with the superhero primarily defined by their goodness and sense of righteousness. Much of the "goodness" attributed to superheroes is tied to their unwillingness to kill, even when it would be the most logical and efficient choice. As Jessica discovers throughout the show, holding to such principles can cause more harm than good. Although Jessica is certainly not the first reluctant or self-doubting superhero, she embodies a very different articulation of duty, responsibility, and morality than any other superhero in the Marvel Universe, to the extent that she could be considered a kind of anti-superhero, superpowered, but not heroic in the traditional sense. As this chapter demonstrates, *Jessica Jones*'s unique approach to these questions is directly related to its thematic and stylistic design as a neo-noir series and Jessica's characterization as a noir "hero." In order to underscore Jessica's uniqueness as a superhero, this chapter compares her sense of, approach to, and articulation of duty, responsibility, and morality to those expressed by the superheroes in two of Netflix's other Marvel series, *Daredevil* and *Luke Cage*. While Jessica shares similarities with the other characters, particularly the reluctant Luke Cage, she remains a uniquely ambivalent superhero.

"With Great Power There Must Also Come—Great Responsibility!"[1]

Although this chapter focuses on the Netflix adaptation of the *Jessica Jones* comics, a brief detour into the history of comic book superheroes is useful. Comic book superheroes have almost always been bastions of truth and justice (and the American way),[2] particularly since the Comics Code Authority (CCA) was formed in 1954 by the Comics Magazine Association of America (Daniels 1971; Nyberg 1998). Established in response to public concern over violent comic book content, the CCA was a self-regulating organization headed by New York magistrate Charles Murphy. Murphy specialized in juvenile delinquency, a rising problem that had recently been associated with violent comic books by the Senate Subcommittee on Juvenile Delinquency. The subcommittee held public hearings in 1954 to investigate graphic violence in crime and horror comic books, and these hearings led to unfavourable press coverage, including a front-page story in the *New York Times* on September 17, 1954. In response, comic book publishers opted to form a self-regulatory body, rather than risk being submitted to government regulation. The code was revised and loosened in 1971 and again in 1989 to allow for more sympathetic criminal activity, corruption of public officials, seduction, and violence. Marvel Comics abandoned the code altogether in 2001, and DC Comics followed suit in 2010, both adopting their own private in-house rating system instead (Nyberg n.d.; Wolk 2011).

Similar to the Hollywood Production Code, which established the moral guidelines for cinematic content from 1934 to 1968, the Comics Code developed by the CCA banned graphic depictions of violence, sexuality or sexual innuendo, and, most importantly for our purposes, declared that "in every instance good shall triumph over evil and the criminal [shall be] punished for his misdeeds."[3] As Jeff Brenzel (2005, 149–50) points out, this provision explains why the notion of "goodness" is central to the superhero genre, though it evidently did not detract from the form's immense popularity. Clearly, the narrative set-up of good versus evil, with good winning every time, resonated with American society's desires and values both in terms of what content moderators felt was appropriate and what mainstream audiences were looking for. This was certainly shaped by a very specific definition of "goodness" as that which adhered to American cultural norms and values, as well as a narrow vision of the ideal hero; in the United States that hero was (and still is) likely to be heterosexual, white, male, and able-bodied. This is important because, as Iain Thomson (2005) states, referencing Heidegger, "the heroes we choose focus our common sense of what is most important in life, shaping our feel for which battles we should fight as well as how we should go about fighting them" (100). Superheroes, then, embody idealized heroics—how our heroes would act if they had the power or technology to do nearly anything they wanted—and communicate ideologically laden messages regarding ideal (i.e., normative) behaviour.

Many superheroes have an origin story to explain why they chose to fight crime. Sometimes it is simply because they were raised by good people who instilled in them a strong sense of morality, like Superman or Spider-Man (Finger 1948; Lee 1962). Other times it is due to some horrible trauma they experienced, like Batman helplessly witnessing the deaths of his parents as a child (Finger and Fox 1939). For both the comic book and Netflix versions of *Jessica Jones*, the same accident that killed her family gave her preternatural abilities, though Netflix's Jessica never feels any internal drive to use those abilities for the greater good (Bendis 2003; ep. 1.11, "AKA I've Got the Blues"). After months of psychological torture at the hands of the villainous Kilgrave, who used her as his personal companion, dress-up doll, sex slave, bodyguard, and henchwoman, Jessica finally managed to break free of his control. The catalyst for her liberation appeared to be the horror at her own actions, as Kilgrave had ordered her to "take care of" a woman named Reva, an order that Jessica carried out by murdering her (ep. 1.03, "AKA It's Called Whiskey"). This event is gradually revealed to the audience through a series of flashbacks that clearly suggest that Jessica suffers from overwhelming feelings of guilt and self-loathing. This self-loathing, combined with the survivor's guilt she feels from the accident that killed her family, has left Jessica psychologically damaged. She suffers from PTSD, anxiety, paranoia, and moral injury,[4] causing her to self-medicate with excessive alcohol consumption and push away everyone who tries to help her.

Marvel's comic book auteur Stan Lee (1975) has written that, "in writing the typical Marvel type of tale, it's almost impossible not to become involved in some extraneous philosophical or moralistic side issue" (188). These "side issues" often reveal a superhero's stance regarding duty, responsibility, and morality, particularly in the case of Spider-Man, a reluctant hero who has often questioned the ethics of his own actions. Just as Jessica uses her powers to solve cases for money, Peter Parker uses his powers for his own financial gain since his job is to photograph Spider-Man in action. Although Spider-Man occasionally waffles and gives up being a superhero, he always returns to it, reassuring audiences that he is still the hero they know and love. Jessica, on the other hand, continually fails and disappoints the people around her. While the main struggle in *Jessica Jones* is between Kilgrave and Jessica, there are many "side issues" that intertwine with the central narrative and serve to reveal Jessica's own dubious sense of moral responsibility.

Luke Cage, the man with unbreakable skin, was first introduced in *Jessica Jones* as Jessica's love interest, though their relationship quickly sours when Jessica reveals that Kilgrave had forced her to murder Luke's wife, Reva. Jessica's impact on Luke's life was entirely negative: lying to him, emotionally manipulating him, causing him to lose his beloved bar, and nearly killing him with a shotgun blast to the head. By seducing the husband of the woman she murdered—an act that haunts her—Jessica reveals her weak sense of moral responsibility. While she clearly feels guilt and distress at her actions, particularly when she sees the picture Luke keeps of his late wife, she only feels compelled to tell him the truth to prevent him from murdering someone else he mistakenly blames for Reva's death. While this intervention does indicate that Jessica feels some moral responsibility, it seems to only emerge in extreme life-or-death situations. When Luke calls Jessica "a piece of shit" for lying to him, spying on him, and seducing him, both Jessica and the audience cannot help but agree (ep. 1.06, "AKA You're a Winner").

A second side story that reminds audiences of Jessica's anti-hero tendencies sees Jessica nearly kill an innocent woman in order to frighten her into signing divorce papers (ep. 1.07, "AKA Top Shelf Perverts"). As a favour to the high-powered lawyer who feeds her cases, Jeri Hogarth, Jessica agrees to help expedite Jeri's painful divorce by making her wife sign the divorce papers by any means necessary. Jessica dangles Jeri's wife over subway tracks, threatening to drop her if she does not sign the papers. Unfortunately, Jessica accidentally drops her, though she manages to toss her out of harm's way at the last moment. As media critic Alyssa Rasmus (2016) has observed of this scene, "this show[s] us what kind of person Jessica is without Kilgrave: how far she'll go and how much she'll hurt someone." This is an extremely dark moment for Jessica, in which her sense of self-loathing has undoubtedly reached its peak. For a second or two, Jessica stares at the oncoming subway train, contemplating whether she should bother jumping out of the way at all.

These moments of moral weakness certainly indicate that Jessica is no superhero, though she is not exactly an anti-hero, either. The archetypical Marvel anti-hero is Frank Castle, also known as the Punisher. One of the main antagonists in the second season of *Daredevil*, and also the protagonist of his own series, Frank is burdened with guilt for failing to protect his wife and daughter, who both apparently died as innocent bystanders of a gang war, but who were actually killed during an attempt to assassinate him. This kind of survivor's guilt is a common motivation for superheroes to dedicate their lives to fighting crime, but for Frank, the guilt drives him to swear vengeance on those responsible. He embarks on a killing spree, mercilessly murdering everyone who he feels deserves to die. Although both superheroes and anti-heroes fight evil, the key differences are that anti-heroes generally fight for selfish reasons, believe that the end justifies the means, and are willing to kill for their cause. While anti-heroes and superheroes share a sense of duty and responsibility, their moral compasses are calibrated very differently (DeScioli and Kurzban 2008). These questions are addressed in many superhero comics, films, and television series, but the willingness or unwillingness to kill is the most commonly articulated tension within the genre.

Refusing to kill is part of a sacred ethical code that many superheroes adopt, perhaps to convince themselves that they really are the "good guys." Instead, they insist on turning the criminals and supervillains over to the authorities, even when those authorities have proven to be ineffectual at detaining and convicting them. As Peter DeScioli and Robert Kurzban (2008) observe,

> [Superheroes] fail to kill evildoers even when they know the villains will escape prison and that innocent lives will be lost in the next round of capture. . . . Superheroes don't kill even when their restraint risks others' lives. Yet somehow we all admire superhero restraint, despite the reckless endangerment to humanity entailed by leaving villains like Lex Luthor or Kingpin alive. (256)

For most of the season, Jessica attempts to abide by this code, though not in order to hold herself to any higher standard of moral responsibility. Jessica wants to capture Kilgrave alive to prove to the world that he and his powers are real, thereby proving the innocence of Hope, who murdered her own parents while under Kilgrave's control. Proving Hope's innocence and revealing

Kilgrave to the world will also allow Jessica to vindicate her own actions and, possibly, even begin to forgive herself. Proving that Kilgrave's powers are real becomes an obsession for Jessica, partially because even those who know about him—Trish, Luke, and Jeri—do not fully believe her until they experience his mind control for themselves. Early on, the only person who fully understands the threat Kilgrave poses is Officer Will Simpson, another victim of Kilgrave's powers. Under Kilgrave's control, Will attempted to murder Trish and then commit suicide. Jessica thwarted both attempts, but the experience left Will traumatized, haunted by his own powerlessness. Instead of using alcohol to drown his sorrows, he turns to experimental combat-enhancement drugs to increase his own power. Will is (correctly) convinced that killing Kilgrave is the only way to stop him, though his obsession with doing so leads him to abuse the drugs and turn against Trish and Jessica, who both get in the way of his plans. In his ruthlessness, pragmatism, and willingness to kill, Will is undoubtedly an anti-hero, and while Jessica refuses to kill Kilgrave for most of the season, in the end their approaches align.

Episode 10, "AKA 1,000 Cuts," is a turning point for Jessica. Kilgrave takes Hope hostage to trade her for his father, the scientist responsible for giving him his powers and who may have a way to increase their potency. Although Jessica is immune to Kilgrave's powers, she is willing to risk making him more powerful in order to save Hope. Realizing the other woman's folly, Hope kills herself in order to "free" Jessica to finally murder Kilgrave. Hope's self-sacrifice is the catalyst that finally spurs Jessica's willingness to get her already dirtied hands even dirtier. In the following episode, "AKA I've Got the Blues," Jessica's sense of moral responsibility has changed: she declares her intention to "rip Kilgrave's throat out" and her antagonistic neighbour Robyn, whose brother was forced to slit his own throat at Kilgrave's command simply for being in love with Jessica, challenges her, asking, "No matter who gets dead along the way?" Jessica retorts that "it's less people than he'd kill," though this response comes rather late, as Jessica's unwillingness to kill the villain up until that point had already caused the death and suffering of countless people. Becoming an anti-hero (or, at least, a hero who is willing to kill) right away, rather than at the very end of the season, would have been the more ethically pragmatic course. As Will remarks later in the same episode, "You could have killed him a dozen times. Now I'm just doing what has to be done. Someone has to." Although Simpson is by no means a bastion of moral integrity, he is right—Jessica could have killed Kilgrave many times but chose not to. Again, this is not because she holds herself to some higher ideal of morality like Superman or Batman; rather, it was to prove the innocence of one person, and, vicariously, to vindicate herself.

In the final episode, "AKA Smile," Jessica finally succeeds in killing Kilgrave, snapping his neck after tricking him into thinking she was back under his control. The scene, although perhaps not as spectacular as the deaths of other villains, is appropriately intimate. Although "gifted," Kilgrave was not a supervillain—he did not have any grand scheme for world domination—rather, he was a delusional, narcissistic sexual predator who had convinced himself that Jessica was his soulmate. He was consumed with the desire to make her love him, and, failing that, to destroy her. This final confrontation between hero and villain, so central to superhero narratives, was, like the rest of *Jessica Jones*, very atypical of the genre. However, a scene from *Wonder Woman* vol. 2, no. 219, from September 2005, provides such a blatant parallel that it likely served as inspiration for this violent yet unsettlingly emotionless murder. Maxwell Lord, a supervillain with mind-control abilities, takes over Superman's mind, forcing him to carry out his criminal schemes. He tricks Superman into believing that Wonder Woman is a villain threatening his beloved Lois Lane, causing him to attack her. Wonder Woman manages to fight Superman off and catch Lord in her Lasso of Truth, with which she learns that his mind control is irreversible, and the only way of freeing Superman is to kill Lord. Not wanting to leave Superman as an omnipotent weapon in the hands of a villain, Wonder Woman makes the only choice she can: she murders Lord by snapping his neck. Like Jessica, Wonder Woman's face remains cold and impassive as she kills the villain, yet unlike Jessica, she has broken a moral code that she and her cohort had always lived by. While those who understood the extent of Kilgrave's threat supported Jessica's choice, Wonder Woman's actions were met with disgust and scorn from her allies, Superman and Batman, who felt that she should have found another way to defeat Lord. The weight of her sin is so heavy that Wonder Woman gives up her superheroics for a year to meditate on her actions and redeem herself. As Marco Arnaudo (2013) observes, this segment "clearly demonstrates the high price superheroes must pay for defying their most sacred rule" (89–90).

It is important to remember, however, that Jessica Jones is *not a superhero*; at least she does not consider herself one, nor does she aspire to be one. In her chapter in this collection, Catherine Jenkins discusses the comic book version of Jessica as a modern, post-human superhero who allows us to recognize ourselves in her habitus. Jessica's many flaws are vital components of this relatable disposition, especially when she recognizes herself as a complex individual: a survivor, a murderer, and, to others, a hero. Jessica's journey is one of self-recognition, and the process is undoubtedly painful. Her final voice-over monologue of season 1 reveals that killing Kilgrave did not alleviate her sense of guilt and self-loathing:

> They say everyone's born a hero, but if you let it, life will push you over the line until you're the villain. The problem is, you don't always know that you've crossed that line. Maybe it's enough that the world thinks I'm a hero. Maybe if I work long, and hard, maybe I could fool myself. (ep. 1.13, "AKA Smile")

Indeed, if refusing to kill is a sacred rule of the superhero, it is obvious that committing murder would not make Jessica feel more like a hero. She is still "a piece of shit"—even Luke's apparent tender forgiveness of Jessica was sadistically orchestrated by Kilgrave. No one forgave Jessica for her sins, so how could she ever forgive herself?

Jessica Jones as a Neo-noir "Hero"

Jessica's inability to heal psychologically is at least partially due to her refusal to ask for help. Although she is indirectly responsible for starting a support group for Kilgrave survivors, she refuses to join them, acting as though such weakness is below her. Her self-imposed isolation is heavily critiqued by those who care about her, particularly Trish and her neighbour Malcolm. Whereas Jessica sees her isolation as a mark of strength and independence, it is actually a sign of weakness—she is too afraid to let others get close to her. Many superheroes keep their distance from others in order to protect them from becoming targets, and while this protective impulse does motivate Jessica to an extent, she also struggles with emotional detachment and an inability to express her affection to others. This emotional distance is used as a plot device in the final episode: Jessica uses "I love you" as a code to prove to Trish that she is not under Kilgrave's control, since it is a phrase she would never normally say. After losing her entire family, being raised by a cruel foster mother, and suffering psychological and sexual abuse for months, it is not surprising that Jessica is emotionally withdrawn. It is also a characterization that connects *Jessica Jones* to the film noir genre. As Paul Arthur (2001) observes, in film noir "a cynical and soured individualism, however disoriented or distorted by underworld affiliations, takes precedence over communal goals" (162). Indeed, film noir protagonists are often anti-heroes, unpleasant and blatantly self-destructive detectives or private eyes who walk a tenuous line between hero and criminal. Noir protagonists are often described as "hard-boiled" detectives, though, as media critic Laura Durkay (2016) correctly observes, "[Jessica] is not so much hardboiled as she is broken."

Like many noir protagonists, "hard-boiled" or not, Jessica's darkest, most insecure moments are almost always also violent moments, such as when she almost beats Kilgrave to death while trying to force him to use his powers (ep. 1.09, "AKA Sin Bin"). Jessica loses control, like a true noir "hero," and Trish must electrocute her to make her stop. As Arthur (2001) points out, the film noir universe is blanketed in a "shroud of personal insecurity" that reinforces "the treatment of physical brutality as a pervasive, endlessly refractive existential crisis" (168). The tonally ambivalent ending of *Jessica Jones* fits perfectly into the noir genre: the villain is killed in a final confrontation that occurs beyond the control of the incompetent authorities, bypassing the justice system, yet the narrative tension is not fully resolved. Jessica is still traumatized and bitter, and she may even face murder charges. While other film genres, such as the Western, often involve a final, fatal confrontation between hero and villain that takes place outside of any legal process, in film noir this ending is never really presented as heroic. To illustrate this point, Arthur (2001) contrasts film noir endings with Richard Slotkin's description of endings in the Western genre:

> What is crucially absent from most noir endings is any sense of a "regeneration through violence," the consummatory act as "*necessary* and *sufficient* resolution of all the issues the tale has raised." While concluding violence in Westerns contributes to the reassertion of stable personal identity, in noir it often adds to the burden of self-abnegating loss, the final stage in a process of assuming the mantle of criminal "other." (160; emphasis in original)

Noir endings often fail to resolve the narrative tensions and restore social equilibrium. Like Jessica, the noir protagonist is not always cleared of all criminal charges once the villain has been exposed and killed. Instead, noir endings are marked with a "sense of ambiguous or inadequate finality," or unsettled closure, which "has been widely recognized and debated in noir literature" (Arthur 2001, 160). Some examples of this type of ambiguous or tragic film noir ending are *Scarlet Street* (Lang 1945), in which the protagonist is left homeless and mentally unstable, tormented by the voice of the woman he killed; *Kiss Me Deadly* (Aldrich 1955), which ends with an explosion and countless deaths; *Vertigo* (Hitchcock 1958), ending with the heartbroken protagonist standing on a ledge, looking down; *In Cold Blood* (Brooks 1967), which closes with the protagonist's hanging; *Chinatown* (Polanski 1974), in which a lead character is killed, leaving her daughter in peril; and *Night Moves* (Penn 1975), in which nearly everyone is dead at the end. The ending of *Jessica Jones* is similarly dark and ambiguous, though perhaps not quite so tragic. These noir elements, combined with the centralization of a protagonist who is far more anti-hero than superhero, sets *Jessica Jones* apart from Netflix's other Marvel productions. *Daredevil* and *Luke Cage* do, however, incorporate moral ambivalence, reluctance, and self-doubt, albeit to a far lesser extent than *Jessica Jones*.

Jones, Cage, and the Devil

The Netflix adaptations of Marvel properties were very successful while they lasted, with three seasons of *Jessica Jones*, three seasons of *Daredevil*, two seasons of *Luke Cage*, two seasons of *Iron Fist*, and two seasons of *The Punisher* released before Netflix cancelled all its Marvel Cinematic Universe series. Netflix also aired one season of *The Defenders*, which featured Jessica Jones, Luke Cage, Daredevil, and Iron Fist working together to fight crime in New York City. *Daredevil*, *Jessica Jones*, and *Luke Cage* all ask important questions about what it means to be a hero and how to know whether or not you are one, though each series has its own particular answers. As I have discussed, *Jessica Jones* focuses on morality, whereas *Daredevil* focuses more on duty and suffering, and *Luke Cage* focuses on stoic responsibility. Because these three shows spend considerable time ruminating on what it means to be a hero, it is worthwhile to tease out some comparisons between them. I will not discuss Danny Rand, the protagonist of *Iron Fist*, or Frank Castle, the protagonist of *The Punisher*, in any depth here because neither character has the same level of overt concern for notions of superheroic duty, responsibility, or morality as Jessica, Luke, and Matt Murdock, a.k.a. Daredevil. Danny lacks the inner turmoil and self-reflexivity of the other Netflix Marvel heroes, while Frank is an anti-hero, and so *The Punisher*'s approach to morality is considerably different, as I discuss below regarding his relationship to Daredevil. In addition, Luke and Matt share several similarities with Jessica that Danny does not, and while the extreme personality differences between Jessica and Danny make for amusing conversations and situations in *The Defenders*, it does little for my discussion here.

Out of the four series, *Daredevil* presents perhaps the most standard Marvel "superhero" type. Matt Murdock is a lawyer by day, and at night he dons a costume and fights crime as "the Devil of Hell's Kitchen." However, unlike many superheroes, he gained his powers as a child, after an accident that also left him blind. Although he learned to use his powers to compensate for his disability, his blindness provides another layer of protection to prevent others from uncovering his secret superhero identity. In the first season of *Daredevil*, Matt's primary antagonist is Wilson Fisk, known in the comics as Kingpin, who believes he is saving Hell's Kitchen by ruthlessly removing anything and anyone that he sees as tainting it. Like many of the most interesting villains, Fisk believes he is the hero, working tirelessly to save his city. Unlike *Jessica Jones*, which presents its villain as an unquestionably terrible person, *Daredevil* embraces a moral ambiguity that is rare for Marvel productions. Before the first season aired, showrunner Steven DeKnight boasted that audiences will not always be sure who to root for, claiming that "there are no heroes or villains . . . just people making different choices" (quoted in Dornbush 2014).

This ambiguity continues in the second season, particularly when Matt confronts the anti-hero Frank Castle, also known as *The Punisher*. Many of the tense conversations between the two centre issues of duty, responsibility, and morality. Frank calls Matt's own sense of self and purpose into question many times, berating him for taking half measures by refusing to kill (his accusations are reminiscent of those levied by Will against Jessica) and for refusing to see that he and Frank are not that different. While Matt consistently denies these accusations and insists on his own righteousness, there is truth to Frank's words. Regardless of his verbal convictions, Matt's adoption of the devil for his alter ego, complete with red armour and horns, reveals his own complicated sense of morality. Unlike Jessica and Luke, who try to avoid violence when they can, Matt not only embraces violence, but actually enjoys beating his enemies senseless. As he confesses in the final episode of season 2, he needs to fight in order to feel alive (ep. 2.13, "A Cold Day in Hell's

Kitchen"). Although he struggles with this guilty pleasure, Matt sees himself as an instrument of justice, both as a lawyer and a hero.

When Matt's best friend and partner, Foggy Nelson, discovers the truth about Matt's secret superhero identity, he is not so easily convinced. Foggy is presented as a moral voice in the series, a kind-hearted everyman who only wants what is best for the people he cares about. He is, understandably, concerned about his friend's night-time behaviour because not only is it highly illegal (which is particularly worrisome, given that they are *lawyers*), Matt has also almost died several times. The psychological implications are also frightening, as not only is Matt secretly an incredibly violent person—he *enjoys* that violence immensely. Although Matt abides by the superhero code of not killing, his behaviour also betrays anti-heroic tendencies: he has decided that protecting Hell's Kitchen is his duty, yet Wilson Fisk felt the exact same way; he sees himself as delivering justice, yet Frank Castle saw himself the same way. *Daredevil* demonstrates that simply having a strong sense of duty and responsibility does not necessarily make someone a hero, and while he might not make as many bad choices as Jessica, Matt is certainly not without his flaws.

Luke Cage, on the other hand, actually is a "good" person, although he, like Jessica, is reluctant to call himself a hero (as late as episode 11, he still insists that he's "not the hero type"). Although Luke Cage actor Mike Colter claimed that his character is morally ambiguous, compared to Matt and Jessica, Luke is consistently calm, kind, and stoic (White 2016). He also chooses not to kill, though the choice is never centralized as a moral dilemma as it is in *Daredevil* and *Jessica Jones*. Like Jessica, Luke would rather keep his head down and live as close to a normal life as possible than use his powers for good. However, in *Luke Cage* he gradually decides to take responsibility for protecting Harlem from criminals who would abuse its residents for their own gain. The entire first season of *Luke Cage* sees Luke being encouraged to "take responsibility" in various ways: using his powers for good, becoming Harlem's resident superhero, defeating his villainous half-brother who wants him dead, and, finally, by giving himself up to the authorities. Luke also has the most personal reason for deciding to become Harlem's hero: the death of his father figure, Pop, who was gunned down by criminals working for Cottonmouth, one of the first season's main villains. The death of a family member, especially a father figure, is a traditional catalyst for a hero's decision to fight crime—the pain of the traumatic loss feeds into their sense of duty, morality, and responsibility. Pop always encouraged Luke to use his powers to help people, and so his subsequent actions are fulfilling his father figure's last wish.

While each of the heroes are unique, there are overlapping elements in their stories that are worth teasing out. Jessica and Luke are both reluctant heroes, though Luke's sense of morality is much clearer and more unambiguous than Jessica's. Luke is also the most selfless of the group, embracing his responsibility as a hero without ulterior motives. While Matt also insists on his duty to protect others, unlike Luke, he does so because he is addicted to violence. Matt and Jessica both have a selfish reason for fighting, even if it might not be their primary motivation: for Matt, to feel alive through hurting people, and for Jessica, to free herself from the pursuit of her nemesis. Luke is willing to work with and rely on others for help, but both Matt and Jessica push their friends away from them. Although this is ostensibly done to protect them, both heroes clearly feel that relying on others is a weakness and a liability. Whereas Matt quickly embraces what he views as his duty and chooses the life of a superhero for himself, Jessica and Luke both initially reject the duty and responsibility that others try to force upon them. Once he has made the decision to become the hero of Harlem, however, Luke fully accepts his responsibility. Jessica, on the other hand, takes nearly the entire first season to learn that she must try her best to live up to the expectations of those who see her as a hero, even if she might never consider herself one. Each of these characters has unique powers and motivations, but their diverse approaches to duty, responsibility, and morality provide the most interesting and tense interactions between them when they come together to form the Defenders.

Not "Super," but Certainly Human

Although Jessica is not as selfless in her approach to responsibility as Luke, in her own way she tries to fix the problems she causes. Jessica's heroism lies not in her decision to finally kill Kilgrave, but in her much earlier decision to stay in the city even after finding out Kilgrave was alive and hunting for her. She articulates this decision at the end of the first episode in a voice-over: "Knowing it's real means you gotta make a decision. One, keep denying it, or two, do something about it" (ep. 1.01, "AKA Ladies' Night"). This is a remarkable moment for Jessica, especially in hindsight, after the audience comes to learn the extent of her trauma, her selfishness, and her isolation.

By comparison, while Matt and Luke certainly have traumatic pasts, neither of them experienced trauma that made them feel worthless and tainted. Both men briefly struggle with feelings of guilt for the deaths of their father figures, but they are able to attribute their past traumas to external factors beyond their control, and so they are not paralyzed by this self-blame. Jessica, on the other hand, internalized her trauma, allowing it to warp her sense of self-worth. This distinction is important because Jessica experienced long-term gender-based abuse and sexualized trauma, which affected her in specific ways. Rape trauma syndrome is a unique kind of complex PTSD that can be exacerbated by social and cultural aspects—such as rape culture and victim blaming—and symptoms can differ even based on whether the sexual assault resulted from force, incapacitation, or verbal coercion (Brown, Testa, and Messman-Moore 2009). For Jessica, it might have felt like a combination of all three, given Kilgrave's ability to make his victims *want* to follow his orders. While it is not necessarily useful to compare trauma and to make claims about who suffered more, it is clear that Jessica's trauma is very different from Matt's or Luke's. Origin stories are central to the motivations and morality of the superhero, and so Jessica's unique past trauma both explains and emphasizes the fundamental differences between her and the other two heroes. As media critic Roz Kaveney (2008) has observed of the comic book version of Jessica Jones, "Jessica thinks of herself as someone who is deeply unlovable and unworthy of love, even though she has friends and lovers who care deeply about her" (70). Jessica's embittered self-loathing, as well as her repugnant and violent mistakes, are what make her feel more human than any other superhero; though Jessica is not really a superhero, at least not yet. While she is not an anti-hero like the Punisher, she might be what Rasmus (2016) refers to as a postmodern anti-hero: "not someone who's evil, but someone who's conflicted about how to do good, be good, and the point of being good at all."

These questions are certainly brought up in *Daredevil* and *Luke Cage*, but *Jessica Jones* really digs into them and tears them apart. Although *Jessica Jones* was not as culturally impactful as *Watchmen*—which has, after all, been hailed as indicating "the moment comic books grew up" and ushering in the ongoing cultural obsession with graphic novels (Barber 2016)—it certainly endeavours to deconstruct the very idea of the hero by presenting viewers with a woman who is almost entirely the opposite of what a hero is supposed to be. If heroes are meant to inspire us to change and to be better than we are, however, Jessica is the perfect woman for the job. As show creator and writer

Melissa Rosenberg stated in an interview with *Variety*, "at her core, [Jessica is] someone who ultimately wants to do something good in the world, though that is buried under many layers of damage" (quoted in Ryan 2015). The fact that Jessica was eventually able to work with others, face her deepest fears, risk her life and mental integrity, and defeat an almost undefeatable enemy *despite* those layers of damage and self-loathing is far more impressive, meaningful, and nuanced than most superhero narratives. Presenting audiences with a "piece of shit" neo-noir hero who tries her best and keeps trying even when her best is not good enough is a bold, subversive, and inspirational move. Her moral compass might be somewhat broken, but then again, so is she.

NOTES

1   Lee (1962, 11).

2   This is practically Superman's catchphrase, as he fights "a never-ending battle for truth, justice and the American way." He always fought for truth and justice, and "the American way" was added in 1942 in the *Adventures of Superman* radio series. The series ran from 1940 to 1951 and introduced and popularized many key elements in the Superman mythos. The "American way" part was dropped in 1944 (replaced with "tolerance"), then added again during the Cold War in the *Adventures of Superman* TV series, which ran from 1952 to 1958 (Lundegaard 2006).

3   As of this writing, the full text of the Comics Code can be found online at http://www.mit.edu/activities/safe/labeling/comics-code-1954.

4   Moral injury refers to damage done to one's own conscience, which usually results in intense feelings of guilt and shame. For more on *Jessica Jones* and moral injury, see Glaser (2016).

References

Aldrich, Robert, dir. 1955. *Kiss Me Deadly*. Los Angeles: Parklane Pictures.

Arnaudo, Marco. 2013. *The Myth of the Superhero*. Translated by Jamie Richards. Baltimore, MD: Johns Hopkins University Press.

Arthur, Paul. 2001. "Murder's Tongue: Identity, Death, and the City in Film Noir." In *Violence in American Cinema*, edited by J. David Slocum, 153–75. New York: Routledge.

Barber, Nicholas. 2016. "Watchmen: The Moment Comic Books Grew Up." *BBC*, August 9, 2016. https://www.bbc.com/culture/article/20160809-watchmen-the-moment-comic-books-grew-up.

Bendis, Brian Michael. 2003. *Alias* 1, no. 22. New York: Marvel Comics.

Brenzel, Jeff. 2005. "Why Are Superheroes Good? Comics and the Ring of Gyges." In *Superheroes and Philosophy: Truth, Justice, and the Socratic Way*, edited by Tom Morris and Matt Morris, 147–60. Chicago: Open Court Publishing.

Brooks, Richard, dir. 1967. *In Cold Blood*. Los Angeles: Pax Enterprises.

Brown, Amy L., Maria Testa, and Terri L. Messman-Moore. 2009. "Psychological Consequences of Sexual Victimization Resulting from Force, Incapacitation, or Verbal Coercion." *Violence against Women* 15 (8): 898–919. https://dx.doi.org/10.1177%2F1077801209335491.

Daniels, Les. 1971. *Comix, a History of Comic Books in America*. New York: Outerbridge & Dienstfrey.

DeScioli, Peter, and Robert Kurzban. 2008. "Cracking the Superhero's Moral Code." In *The Psychology of Superheroes*, edited by Robin S. Rosenberg, 245–59. Dallas, TX: Benbella Books.

Dornbush, Jonathon. 2014. "7 Things We Learned about Netflix's New 'Daredevil' Series." *Entertainment Weekly*, October 11, 2014. http://ew.com/article/2014/10/11/daredevil-new-york-comic-con-footage-details-netflix-marvel/

Durkay, Laura. 2016. "Surviving Is Her Superpower." *Socialist Worker*, January 14, 2016. http://socialistworker.org/2016/01/14/surviving-is-her-superpower.

Finger, Bill. 1948. *Superman* 1, no. 53. New York: DC Comics.

Finger, Bill, and Gardner Fox. 1939. *Detective Comics* 1, no. 33. New York: DC Comics.

Glaser, Jessica. 2016. "Beyond Surviving: On Sexual Violence, Moral Injury, and Jessica Jones." *The Toast*, January 6, 2016. http://the-toast.net/2016/01/06/on-sexual-violence-moral-injury-and-jessica-jones/.

Hitchcock, Alfred, dir. 1958. *Vertigo*. Encino, CA: Alfred J. Hitchcock Productions.

Kaveney, Roz. 2008. *Superheroes! Capes and Crusaders in Comics and Films*. New York: I. B. Tauris.

Lang, Fritz, dir. 1945. *Scarlet Street*. Los Angeles: Walter Wanger Productions, Fritz Lang Productions, and Diana Production Company.

Lee, Stan. 1962. *Amazing Fantasy* 1, no. 15. New York: Marvel Comics.

———. 1975. *Son of Origins of Marvel Comics*. New York: Simon and Schuster.

Lundegaard, Erik. 2006. "Truth, Justice and (Fill in the Blank)." *New York Times*, June 30, 2006. http://www.nytimes.com/2006/06/30/opinion/30iht-ederik.2093103.html.

Nyberg, Amy Kiste. 1998. *Seal of Approval: The Origins and History of the Comics Code*. Jackson: University Press of Mississippi.

———. n.d. "Comics Code History: The Seal of Approval." Comic Book Legal Defense Fund, accessed March 24, 2024. http://cbldf.org/comics-code-history-the-seal-of-approval/

Penn, Arthur, dir. 1975. *Night Moves*. Los Angeles: Hiller Productions.

Polanski, Roman, dir. 1974. *Chinatown*. Los Angeles: Penthouse, Long Road Productions, and Robert Evans Company.

Rasmus, Alyssa. 2016. "Keeping Up with Jessica Jones, the Postmodern Anti-hero Next Door." *Popmatters*, February 9, 2016. http://www.popmatters.com/feature/keeping-up-with-jessica-jones-the-postmodern-anti-hero-next-door/.

Ryan, Maureen. 2015. " 'Jessica Jones' Showrunner Melissa Rosenberg Talks about Her Tough Heroine." *Variety*, November 20, 2015. http://variety.com/2015/tv/features/jessica-jones-marvel-melissa-rosenberg-1201644912/.

Thomson, Iain. 2005. "Deconstructing the Hero." In *Comics as Philosophy*, edited by Jeff McLaughlin, 100–29. Jackson: University Press of Mississippi.

White, Brett. 2016. "Luke Cage's Colter Praises Moral Ambiguity of His Characters." *CBR*, April 13, 2016. http://www.cbr.com/luke-cages-colter-praises-moral-ambiguity-of-his-characters/.

Wolk, Douglas. 2011. "R.I.P.: The Comics Code Authority." *Time*, January 24, 2011. http://techland.time.com/2011/01/24/r-i-p-the-comics-code-authority/.

Watch Party: Watching Jessica Jones Watch Others

Eric Ross

The first season of *Jessica Jones* asks viewers to see it as a story about rape, patriarchal control, and female agency, but the formal elements of the show's construction reveal that tensions between public and private spaces, and the subsequent violation of those spaces, are integral to its representation of justice, vengeance, and agency in an increasingly murky universe. This tension calls into question how far one should be willing to go for justice. Violation of personal space is manifested most explicitly by the villainous Kilgrave and his ability to control people. However, Jessica herself routinely violates the personal space of others in her capacity as a private investigator, and as the series progresses, the line between hero and villain begin to blur. This is a particularly important point for twenty-first-century audiences as the power and ubiquity of digital surveillance technology grows and laws and law enforcement are slow to catch up. As such, ordinary citizens are more and more at the mercy of this technology as they cling to whatever shred of privacy there is left. As Michel Foucault wrote in 1975, "Our society is one . . . of surveillance" ([1975] 1995, 217).

Jessica Jones illustrates for its audience what Michel Foucault in *Discipline and Punish* called "panopticism." A panopticon is a kind of building originally designed by Jeremy Bentham in the late eighteenth century. It consists of a central tower surrounded by a circular building. This outlying building would contain a number of cells with each one having a window facing toward the tower and an opposite window facing away. As Foucault describes it, "By the effect of backlighting, one can observe from the tower, standing out precisely against the light, the small captive shadows in the cells of the periphery" ([1975] 1995, 200). The whole structure is designed to allow one guard to be able to observe all of the inmates simultaneously, consolidating power into the central structure. This state of "permanent visibility . . . assures the automatic functioning of power" (201).

The title credits of *Jessica Jones* immediately establish this theme by using a highly stylized animation that shows a montage of scenes around New York City, culminating in a close-up of an eye before the start of every episode. The first three shots in this sequence establish the voyeurism that will become a mainstay of the show's cinematography. At first the viewer sees mostly dark colours as the camera moves slowly to the right before emerging behind a building to peer into an alley as a dark figure walks away from the viewer. This is immediately followed by a shot of another shadowy-looking woman in profile walking down the street, but this time we as viewers are positioned as though we are riding in a car and slowly driving alongside the woman: watching out the window while she remains seemingly oblivious. Finally, we transition to a view of a window with the shadowy outline of a figure standing in it. Here, we are positioned outside the building and at least two storeys below the window, looking up.

The rest of the title sequence is accompanied by a montage of similar windows with similar figures and other people in alleyways as the music crescendos and a human face is finally revealed, presumably Jessica's, in profile with the focus on her eye. The image fills the left half of the screen before fading again to reveal the series title. And then the episode begins. The giant eye appearing at the end of this montage of urban scenes implies that each of the images was taken from the point of view of the eye, or in this case from Jessica. So right away, the show establishes Jessica's role as the voyeur surveilling the city, peering into the private lives of others through windows or stalking individuals outside without their noticing.

Surveillance has long been a trope of literature, especially in the superhero, detective, and noir genres, genres that *Jessica Jones* borrows heavily from. In detective fiction, in particular the works of Raymond Chandler or Agatha Christie, surveillance is often employed in a transgressive way by detectives and private investigators as a means to uncover the crimes and abuses of the rich and powerful. However, the role of surveillance in fiction has been complicated in the post-9/11 era. The war on terror has led to a number of different breakthroughs in visual surveillance technologies, and the resulting images have filtered into popular culture through mass and popular media, whether it is drone footage of the Middle East (Parks 2013), home surveillance technologies like doorbell cameras, or, to use another superhero-related example, the climactic scene in 2008's *The Dark Knight* in which Batman uses surveillance data in cell phones to locate the Joker. In many of these instances, surveillance is seen, at worst, as a technology of the powerful rather than a tool to be used against them, and, at best, as an ambivalent put powerful tool available to anyone. This is the terrain that *Jessica Jones* is operating in, at once appealing to the traditional use of surveillance in detective fiction while also engaging with some of the wariness surrounding post-9/11 surveillance technology.

Foucault's panopticon is, again, instructive. He goes to great lengths to demonstrate how the functioning of power is so automatic that the panopticon no longer requires a guard at all, the goal being

> to arrange things [so] that the surveillance is permanent in its effects even if it is discontinuous in its action; that the perfection of power should tend to render its actual exercise unnecessary; that this architectural apparatus should be a machine for creating and sustaining a power relation independent of the person who exercises it; in short, that the inmates should be caught up in a power situation of which they are themselves the bearers. ([1975] 1995, 201)

Essentially, the functioning of the panopticon ensures that anyone can operate its mechanisms, even the prisoners themselves. Indeed, it even comes to rely on the assumption of the constraints of power: "He who is subjected to a field of visibility, and who knows it, assumes responsibility for the constraints of power . . . ; he inscribes in himself the power relation in which he simultaneously plays both roles; he becomes the principle of his own subjection" (202). Thus, in this state where the threat of surveillance is constant, people take it upon themselves to enforce discipline on themselves and on the others around them in order to avoid punishment. This resembles what Deleuze calls a society of continuous control. Under continuous control, the state cares only that the individuals under its control are in the correct zone or in the right place, that one fits the algorithm (1992, 7).

Jessica Jones demonstrates several things about surveillance in our twenty-first-century world. It demonstrates the power of surveillance to objectify individuals as specimens to be observed, and questions how we, the viewers, should feel about it. It demonstrates how the mechanisms of surveillance can be used by just about anyone for a variety of purposes. Michalis Lianos points out that by the early twenty-first century, what had seemed like a coherent project of control, as described by Foucault, has been fractured by privatization, the easy access to technology, and the diffusion of control (2003, 426). This situation has created a reality in which the many are able to see and monitor the few, or even in which the many can monitor the many, using digital technology. This is what Thomas Mathiesen refers to as the "synopticon" (1997, 215), where individuals use peer-to-peer surveillance or "lateral surveillance" (Andrejevic 2005) for security purposes. Crucially for Mathiesen, we live in what he calls a "viewer society" (1997, 219), a society that normalizes the experience for everyone of being both constantly watched by others and constantly watching others. This is especially relevant for both Jessica Jones the character and *Jessica Jones* the show.

The first scene of the show continues with all of these themes. The camera follows a couple as they walk back to their car at night and proceed to have sex in the back seat. As the viewer follows them, they are always seen from a distance: from behind a fence, through a car window, or from odd angles—above them as they walk, or very low to the ground once they reach the car. As they move, the camera occasionally stops in a freeze-frame, accompanied by the sound of a shutter, to imply that Jessica is taking pictures of them. All this happens while we hear Jessica in a voice-over saying,

> New York may be the city that never sleeps, but it sure does sleep around. Not that I'm complaining, cheaters are good for business. A big part of the job is looking for the worst in people. Turns out, I excel at that. Clients hire me to find dirt, and I find it; which shouldn't surprise them, but it does. Knowing it's real means they've got to make a decision. One: do something about it, or two: keep denying it, shoot the messenger, tell me I'm getting off on ruining their already shitty lives. Option two rarely pans out. (ep. 1.01, "AKA Ladies' Night")

As her monologue continues the scene shifts to a view of the door to her apartment with a frosted glass window that reads "Alias Investigations." Behind the window we can see silhouettes and hear a muffled argument. As the monologue ends, a man crashes through the glass window; Jessica then emerges to say, "and then there's the matter of your bill" as the scene ends. Besides establishing that Jessica spends her time watching others, especially "at their worst," with its implications of privacy violation, Jessica's introductory monologue sets up a shallow defence of her violations by first appealing to morals. Her first line seems to chastise New York City and its residents for their loose morals as "cheaters," before she ultimately pivots to appealing to business and talent.

Jessica seems to be trying to persuade the viewer that what she is doing is not wrong, because she is being paid. She is a small business owner who is hired to watch people. This is what her clients ask her to do, and she is very good at her job. For Jessica, her role is to find the truth and to report that truth to her clients in the form of photographic and eyewitness evidence. Here she has positioned herself pre-emptively opposite Kilgrave, whose violations of personal space and privacy aim simply to serve himself and his own agenda, while Jessica is serving others and "the truth." Despite Jessica's defence of her own actions, the work of the camera during this scene, as well as several others, seems to suggest that her actions are less than noble.

The most salient point of this conception of the surveillance state is that it completely democratizes power. Technology "subtly arranged so that an observer may observe, at a glance, so many different individuals, also enables everyone to come and observe any of the observers" (Foucault [1975] 1995, 207). For Foucault, the panopticon functions because the inmates allow it to function by doing most of the work themselves. Mark Andrejevic extrapolates from this idea in his analysis of the modern surveillance state, where the constant threat of surveillance encourages individuals to police themselves and others, or, as he writes, where everyone is "simultaneously urged to become spies" (2005, 479). Anyone can exercise such power as long as the threat exists, and while that power is primarily exercised by states and other kinds of institutional authority, "it would be wrong to believe that the disciplinary functions were confiscated and absorbed once and for all by a state apparatus" (49). Rather, some of the work of surveillance and discipline is left to ordinary individuals within a society (Foucault [1975] 1995, 215). Indeed, modern video and electronic surveillance functions in the same way by surrounding us with digital recording devices, such that we never know who or if anyone is watching (Koskela 2000, 243).

The distribution of surveillance technology was supposed to occasion a sense of security and safety, but instead it mostly just makes a society where people are always afraid. In *Jessica Jones*, nearly all of the main characters—Jessica, Kilgrave, Trish, Simpson, Luke Cage, and Malcolm—engage in some form of surveillance of others, whether by stalking them, or breaking into their homes, or watching them on camera. As the show progresses toward its final confrontation with Kilgrave, it takes on a more traditional superhero-action format with a series of smaller confrontations leading to the final battle, but for the first half of the show's first season Jessica engages in a significant amount of stalking, snooping, and sleuthing around the city as she attempts to find Kilgrave and solve a number of mysteries around his return and their mutual past together.

During these scenes, as Jessica sneaks around looking in windows and breaking into buildings in search of clues, the camera's positioning reflects the scenes of stalking that we see in the show's opening title credits. These sequences serve to heighten the self-awareness on our part as viewers that implicates us in Jessica's actions. We are stalking her as she stalks other characters in the show. Christian Metz (1982) calls this phenomenon primary cinematic identification. Scott Richmond applies this idea specifically to superhero films, writing that the viewer is encouraged to think of themselves as an observer within the world of the film, unraveling the boundary between diegetic and non-diegetic space: "such unraveling follows directly from the perceptual arrangement of the cinema, which gives us a world from which we are constitutively absent and therefore in which I am 'all-perceiving' " (2012, 131). So we are encouraged not only to identify and sympathize with Jessica, but our identification with the camera itself encourages us to be critical of her as well.

Kilgrave is first seen in the season's second episode. Without ever directly showing his face, the camera follows him as he enters an apartment and informs the residents that he will be their guest, and he uses his powers to command the family several more times in the scene. All of this is in full view of the viewer. We see Kilgrave's actions fully and we understand him to be the villain of the show because of it. Over the season's first two hours we learn more and more about Kilgrave's terrible powers and his obsession with Jessica, but in his first appearance we see the true nature of his powers. Not only is Kilgrave violating the physical space of this family by forcibly entering their home and taking up residence, but he continues to rob them of their free will and agency by forcing the children to stay in the closet while forcing the adults to serve him dinner with a smile on their faces.

Whenever Kilgrave is violating the space of others the camera makes no attempt to hide or distort him. He is rarely shown through another object or in reflection. Knowing they are witnessing the show's villain, the viewer has no illusions about his wrongdoing. Whether it his casually telling someone to stab themselves, or to cut their own heart out, or to jump off a ledge, the show wants the viewers to see Kilgrave's evil head-on: to hear him issue the commands, and for the victims to follow orders while Kilgrave goes about his business. It is important for the series to establish Kilgrave as the villain, and to do so it is important that he be observed fully.

Setting herself apart from the sociopathic Kilgrave, Jessica declares that "My greatest weakness is that occasionally I give a damn" (ep. 1.02, "AKA Crush Syndrome"). It's this distinction that grows more important as the series progresses and the line between the two characters blurs even more. At the end of the third episode, it is revealed that someone has been taking photographs of Jessica all over the city for Kilgrave. This unsettling revelation is made more interesting because of the similarities between these pictures of Jessica and the pictures that she herself has taken of others, including her now lover, Luke Cage.

Jessica has invested a great deal of effort into creating a distinction between herself and Kilgrave, frequently justifying her actions in her voice-over monologues or in conversation with other characters. Despite often operating outside of the law, she frequently refers to herself as a small business owner, and later, as the series sees her pivot to hunting down Kilgrave full-time, she speaks of her sense that her mission is for the "good" of everyone. In an early scene, after it has been revealed that Jessica has been stalking Luke and taking pictures of him and his lover, Jessica lies to protect herself by claiming that the woman's husband had hired her to see if she was cheating. It is, however, later revealed that this is not the case, and that the woman's husband had no idea. When the woman comes to Jessica's office to confront her, Jessica dodges the accusation that she is a stalker by telling the woman that she "ruined her own marriage" (ep. 1.02, "AKA Crush Syndrome"). Later still, when Jessica is attempting to steal an anesthetic called Sufentanil to use on Kilgrave, she says in her monologue, "Knocking out one clerk to catch Kilgrave? Worth it. Knocking out two people? Still the right call" (ep. 1.03, "AKA It's Called

Whiskey"). Jessica ultimately reconsiders, but only after the arrival of a pregnant doctor and a security guard.

Perhaps Kilgrave would have gone ahead with the heist and knocked everyone out, but this scene illustrates what Jessica meant by "occasionally giv[ing] a damn." Jessica's initial desire to commit assault in order to commit theft in order to track down and apprehend Kilgrave represents an appeal to a broader sense of social good. In her mind, the elimination of Kilgrave is worth breaking the law. This sense of vigilante justice is common in superhero stories. In these incidents, superheroes often justify their unlawful actions as eventually benefitting the community that they hope to protect and serve.

Setting aside the legality of Jessica's actions, this devotion to the community and to her ideas about justice embodies the disciplinary ideals of Foucault. Despite the fact that Jessica breaks the law a number of times during the show's first season, her desire to protect her community shows her allegiance to the institutional authorities already in place. The main driver of the show is Jessica's desire to capture Kilgrave and prove the innocence of Hope Shlottman, the young NYU student whom Kilgrave compelled to murder her own parents. Rather than simply break Hope out of prison using her own superpowers, Jessica seeks, at first, to preserve the integrity of the justice system by working within its limits to put Kilgrave behind bars. Jessica is constantly reminded by Hogarth of the need to complete her investigation by the book, or rather to give Hogarth a real story that will be usable in a court of law. Thus, much of the first part of the season focuses on Jessica's attempts to either elicit a confession out of Kilgrave or collect usable evidence of him wielding his powers—evidence that she attempts to collect through digital video surveillance.

During the season's fourth episode, Jessica begins the hunt for the person who has been taking photographs of her around the city. As she combs through hours of police footage, she says in voice-over, "Now I know how it feels. Someone watching your every move, seeing you in private moments" (ep. 1.04, "AKA 99 Friends"). The pain she feels at having been watched grants her a degree of empathy for the people that she watches. However, just as this feeling begins to set in, Jessica goes out to complete another job, and what follows is the season's most extensive use of the stalking camera effect.

Earlier, Jessica had been hired by a woman named Audrey Eastman to find out whether or not her husband had been cheating on her. Jessica initially suspects that Audrey is being used by Kilgrave to set a trap for her, but after observing her for thirteen hours, she is convinced that she is not under his influence. For a full two minutes the camera alternates between shots of Audrey's husband and Jessica as she follows him around a dark and mostly abandoned neighbourhood. During this time, the two figures are partially obscured behind fence posts, walls, and glass windows as Jessica watches the husband enter a building and then a room to meet with his "mistress." When Jessica enters the room, it is revealed that the "mistress" in question is actually Audrey. Only then do we learn that the whole situation was contrived so that Audrey could try to kill Jessica as revenge for her mother's death during the events depicted in the first *Avengers* film.

This scene does little to alter the arc of the story, but it does present the stalking camera effect in a way that had not been seen before in season 1. The extended use of the stalking camera in this scene serves two purposes. First, it serves to heighten the sense of pain that Jessica felt at being watched earlier in the episode and to transfer some of that unease to the viewer. By partially obscuring the figures around corners or behind objects, the viewer's position in relation to Jessica and the husband is foregrounded, as are the camera's attempts at observing without being seen. This is especially apparent when we consider the previous scene, in which Jessica feels the pain of having her space violated by her as yet unknown stalker.

Second, the technique itself illustrates the democratization of power through surveillance. It forces viewers to be aware of the fact that they are watching Jessica just as she watches the husband. As we have seen, the whole situation is merely a trap set for Jessica, and so the use of the lurking camera serves as a warning for Jessica that she is in fact being watched, and not just by her stalker or by the viewers, but by the Eastmans, who are trying to kill her.

Jessica is the titular character of the series, the hero and the protector of the streets of Hell's Kitchen; it is her duty to observe and to watch. She is the guard in the guard tower. But, as in any fully realized surveillance state described by Foucault or Lianos, power functions here so as to "enable everyone to come and observe any of the observers" (Foucault [1975] 1995, 207). And indeed, anyone with access to a Netflix account can observe Jessica Jones as she observes others, and the camera's positioning and movement draws attention to that. But Netflix viewers must also be aware of the ways in which they are themselves watched, not by Jessica or Kilgrave, but by Netflix itself. Users are constantly reminded of this when the streaming service asks if they would like to continue watching their chosen show or movie, or whether they would like to watch something else. Netflix's algorithms watch us so well, and are so sophisticated, that they recommend additional content based on the aggregate viewing data of users ("Privacy Statement" 2022).

By the season's second half, however, Jessica has devoted her energy full-time to tracking down Kilgrave, her PTSD driving her more and more to focus solely on her mission of justice. But the closer she gets to Kilgrave, the more her quest for justice seems like a quest for revenge. By this point in the series, having seen the full and gruesome extent of his powers with each new and shockingly evil punishment that he inflicts on people across the city, the audience has no illusions about Kilgrave. The show has now completely abandoned the lurking camera aesthetic, and there is no longer any question that what Jessica's doing is the "right" thing to do. Kilgrave is evil and must be stopped by any means necessary. By abandoning the lurking camera effect, the series is no longer questioning the potentially sinister nature of modern surveillance, and is instead falling back on the typical vigilante notion that to act in the face of evil is not only morally justified, but necessary.

As the hunt for Kilgrave grows more desperate, Jessica's and Kilgrave's methods begin to take on ever closer resemblances. The audience witnesses the decentralization of power and surveillance as Jessica and Kilgrave simultaneously stalk each other using video and digital technologies, tracking each other's movements throughout the city. About halfway through the first season, Kilgrave kidnaps Jessica and holds her prisoner in her childhood home, threatening the lives of a chef and maid that he has hired to make their lives more comfortable together should she attempt to escape. Jessica manages to escape after knocking Kilgrave unconscious with drugs. She then kidnaps him and holds him prisoner in a sealed, soundproof room that has been flooded with water and contains an exposed wire.

Jessica's kidnapping of Kilgrave is constantly normalized by her motivation to prove Hope Shlottman's innocence by catching Kilgrave's powers on camera, as well as by Kilgrave's manipulations of Jessica's friends to later secure his own escape. However, in addition to Kilgrave's illegal abduction, both he and Jessica put innocent lives at risk: Kilgrave with the chef and maid at Jessica's home, Jessica when she sends Kilgrave's biological parents into the sealed room to goad him into using his powers. Up until the point where Kilgrave escapes, one could even reasonably claim that Jessica's actions are worse. Kilgrave did not coerce Jessica to return to her childhood home, and while there he did not force her to do anything; he threatened the lives of the staff, to be sure, but that claim would be difficult to defend in a court of law. Jessica, by contrast, abducted Kilgrave and held him in a sealed room, and videotaped the entire incident. These scenes also feature a kind of literal acting out of the panopticon as Jessica, Trish, and Hogarth each take turns monitoring the video equipment while Kilgrave remains locked in his cell.

Despite her determination to see justice done within the confines of the American criminal justice system, Jessica is reminded by her adopted sister, Trish Walker, and her employer, the lawyer Jeri Hogarth, that any evidence she might collect while holding Kilgrave prisoner would be obtained under duress and therefore deemed inadmissible. In response, Jessica lures a police detective to the room, holds him prisoner by handcuffing him to a pipe, and forces him to witness Kilgrave using his powers on his biological parents. The police detective, forced as he is to observe the proceedings, serves as a stand-in for the institutional authority to which Hogarth and Jessica need to appeal. All of this is done so that Jessica can "bring down" Kilgrave and prove Hope's innocence. During the demonstration, Kilgrave eventually drops the innocent exterior and reveals himself to be as evil as he is accused of being. In the room with his parents, Kilgrave forces his mother to kill herself; when Jessica's electrical trap then fails to go off, she must enter the room to save Kilgrave's father, allowing Kilgrave to escape with the help of the detective and Hogarth.

Kilgrave's actions further solidify his status as an evil character and emphasize the need for Jessica to stop him by any means necessary. His actions cannot and should not be tolerated, but by failing to call into question Jessica's actions in pursuit of him, the series chooses not to challenge Jessica's own illegal and often dangerous methods. Her past experiences with Kilgrave—the rape, assault, and other violations—have caused her significant trauma that she has not truly begun to adequately deal with beyond her own self-medicating. This PTSD resulting from her being forced to confront her rapist have turned this mission of justice into a dangerous quest for revenge. The moment before the lurking camera effect is abandoned, Jessica realizes how damaging it is to be the object of surveillance and illegal stalking, and she seemingly has a realization that she must begin to question her own methods. In the end, however, she does not change her methods even as the series loses the self-reflexivity of the lurking camera. This seems to suggest that, no matter Jessica's own actions, because her hunt for Kilgrave is based in a desire to see justice done, for the good of all, she must be free to defeat Kilgrave even if this means compromising her own desire for justice. Her clarity of purpose demands it. But what does it demand of us, and are we willing to accept those terms?

References

Andrejevic, Mark. 2005. "The Work of Watching One Another: Lateral Surveillance, Risk, and Governance." *Surveillance & Society* 2 (4): 479–97.

Deleuze, Gilles. 1992. "Postscript on the Societies of Control." *October* 59 (Winter): 3–7.

Foucault, Michel. (1975) 1995. *Discipline and Punish*. Translated by Alan Sheridan. 2nd ed. New York: Vintage Books.

Koskela, Hille. 2000. " 'The Gaze without Eyes': Video Surveillance and the Changing Nature of Urban Space." *Progress in Human Geography* 24 (2): 243–65.

Lianos, Michalis. 2003. "Social Control after Foucault." *Surveillance & Society* 1 (3): 412–30.

Mathiesen, Thomas. 1997. "The Viewer Society: Michel Foucault's 'Panopticon' Revisited." *Theoretical Criminology* 1 (2): 215–34.

Metz, Christian. 1982. *The Imaginary Signifier: Psychoanalysis and the Cinema*. Translated by Celia Britton. Bloomington: Indiana University Press.

Parks, Lisa. 2013. "Zeroing In: Overheard Imagery, Infrastructure Ruins, and Datalands in Afghanistan and Iraq." In *The Visual Culture Reader*, edited by Nicholas Mirzoeff, 196–206. London: Routledge.

"Privacy Statement." 2022. Netflix, last modified November 1, 2022. https://help.netflix.com/legal/privacy.

Richmond, Scott C. 2012. "The Exorbitant Lightness of Bodies, or How to Look at Superheroes: Ilinx, Identification, and Spider-Man." *Discourse* 34 (1): 113–44.

5

"So Go After the Big Green Guy or the Flag Waver.": The MCU Reality Bridge

Ian Fitzgerald

The Netflix series *Marvel's Jessica Jones* situates itself in a curious place within the Marvel Cinematic Universe (MCU). Like the series preceding *Jessica Jones* (*Marvel's Daredevil* [2015–18]), and those that follow (*Marvel's Luke Cage* [2016–18], *Marvel's Iron Fist* [2017–18], and *Marvel's The Defenders* [2017]), *Jessica Jones* relies heavily upon adult storylines and portrayals of sex and violence. This also separates the various Netflix series from those produced in conjunction with ABC (*Marvel's Agents of S.H.I.E.L.D.* [2013–20] and *Marvel's Agent Carter* [2015–16]). *Jessica Jones* airs on a streaming service, rather than on a broadcast network, rendering Netflix closer to a cable or satellite channel in this regard. Yet within the Netflix section of the MCU, *Jessica Jones* is a series that differs by virtue of its position as a story centred around a female protagonist in a real-world situation that is both gritty and supernatural. Jessica as a character is a victim of violence and the driving force of her story is that of recovery, not heroic ambition. In fact, the source of her powers is unknown, and the investigation into them—which in many other origin stories would serve as the main plot—here constitutes a subplot that remains unresolved at the end of season 1. She is a shameless anti-hero, one that spends far less time than Daredevil being apologetic or contrite about it. In *Jessica Jones*, both the series and its main character are set apart from the rest of the MCU on both the big and small screens. The series is positioned as a bridge between the glossy, colourful fantasy world in which most of the MCU takes place and the dark but realistic world of Netflix's *Defenders*. It is a series and a character of difference, and in that sense *Jessica Jones* links the two realms of the MCU.

How and Why Do Netflix's Defenders Series Differ from the Rest of the MCU?

The primary reason the various Defenders series work as a place of difference within the MCU is because their home is on Netflix. This privilege allows the Defenders to narratively tell and visually show stories that would not be seen in the MCU, either on network television (ABC) or on film (Disney). Compared to the high-flying antics of the agents of S.H.I.E.L.D., the Defenders acknowledge that in the MCU there are still actions that occur in the real world. While S.H.I.E.L.D. agents are chasing after demons and monsters, the Defenders deal with cops, private investigators, lawyers, and vigilantes as they fight day-to-day crime on the street.

Much like the subscription channel HBO and the cable channel Showtime, Netflix's platform allows the network to produce television programs that heighten the violence and sexuality portrayed onscreen. Much of that comes from Netflix's switch from a mail-order DVD library to a streaming service (Cronin 2014). The decision by the company to offer cinema-level aesthetics for a monthly eight-dollar subscription fee was an expensive one, yet Netflix has succeeded by producing high-quality shows, beginning with the American adaptation of *House of Cards* (2013–18) (Keyes 2013).

Netflix's deal with Disney and Marvel was made in 2013, with the first delivery of product occurring in 2015 with *Marvel's Daredevil*, a property that had just returned to the Marvel fold after being licensed to 20th Century Fox for years (Keyes 2013).[1] The Defenders universe is the brainchild of Marvel Television head Jeph Loeb, who envisioned an ensemble similar to *The Avengers* (2012) (Li 2017, 29). Loeb approached Netflix soon after *House of Cards* first aired, seeing the bingeable appeal of multiple intersecting series (Li 2017, 29). Daredevil was the natural starting place as the character had already been exposed to a larger population by way of the critically panned (Rotten Tomatoes n.d.) 2003 film.

Much of the criticism of the *Daredevil* film revolves around the perceived watering down of the property's central characters, narrative, and aesthetics (Otto and Patrizio 2004). The problem with this criticism is twofold. First, genre cinema, for the most part, tends to cater to young, white, middle-class males (Grant 2007). In 2003, the superhero film was still establishing itself as a genre unto itself, rather than as an offshoot of action films, noir/crime films, or adaptations of comic books. Since the genre was still new and still inherently bound to the comic book—an object itself tied to childhood or "deviant adulthood" (Legman 1948)—the film had to be marketed to a younger audience of mostly teens and young men. The film could be violent, but not so violent as to alienate the parents of the under-eighteen audience or jeopardize film's ability to garner a PG-13 rating (14A in English Canada) from the Motion Picture Association of America. The director's cut, which earned an R rating, did not receive a theatrical release. That said, in the book *Marvel Encyclopedia: Marvel Knights, Daredevil* is named one of the most authentic comic book movies ever made, but only from the standpoint of fans of the comic from which it came (Kiefer 2004, 26).

The second problem with the criticism of the 2003 film is that the genre was still trying to figure out its own rules, both aesthetically and narratively. In the mid- to late 2010s, superhero films played around with the workings of genre much easier because superhero films came out so rapidly, such that the workings and aesthetics easily evolved from piece to piece. Each installment in the *Captain America* trilogy differs slightly in style and story: *Captain America: The First Avenger* (2011) is a historical piece telling Cap's origin story during the Second World War; *Captain America: The Winter Soldier* (2014) is reminiscent of a 1970s conspiracy film wherein alliances and institutions are questioned; and *Captain America: Civil War* (2016) is more of a third Avengers film than a third Captain America film, featuring both old and new members of the MCU in a fun but epic showdown. Regardless of these differences, the three films still function as related parts in Captain America's cinematic arc. Opposing this is something like 2016's *Deadpool*, which criticizes and parodies an entire genre in a single piece. This self-awareness is not always present in superhero films. However, the number of superhero films being released in any given year requires a degree of experimentation on the part of creators to keep the films fresh and innovative in a genre that can easily become static.

The emerging superhero genre had to find its footing by creating expectations for its audience back in 2003. *Daredevil* stands as something different within a world of more straightforward narrative films that follow characters like Superman, Batman, the X-Men, and Spider-Man, especially with regards to their origin stories. Apart from Tim Burton's take on Batman (1989, 1992), the genre was still quite light, so even the aesthetics of the 2003 *Daredevil* seem dark by comparison. Peter Coogan explains that, prior to the early 2000s, superhero films were silly and pure fantasy (2014, 9–10). The advent of the *Spider-Man* films and their preference for computer-generated imagery over prosthetics, costumes, and makeup allow for "realism or believability" (Coogan 2014, 10). *Daredevil* as a narrative was odd in 2003; by 2015, the Netflix series, while still dark, could fit within the superhero genre, regardless of its quirks. In Hollywood cinema, the genre wouldn't fully accept dark superhero films until 2005's *Batman Begins*, even if there were occasionally silly films with lighter themes (e.g., the *Fantastic Four* films from the 2000s).

Throughout this evolution, the superhero genre tended to cater to the "average" audience of young, white, middle-class males: the MCU is in this regard no different. Both MCU films and TV series look like ones that could be viewed by youth and adult audiences alike. The ABC series that are part of the MCU continue these aesthetic and narrative choices by way of more traditional, serialized storytelling. The violence and dark narrative set the Netflix series apart, and this is again tied to Netflix being the producer rather than ABC.

Using HBO as an example, networks that exist outside the confines of broadcast television allow for a broader spectrum when it comes to storytelling, whether in the form of violent or sexual images or just more complex, indirect narrative perspectives. With regard to violence, network television tends to avoid the topic, since network programs tend to be more accessible to younger audiences, and for this reason a debate about violence on TV and the impact it has on children has been going on since the 1950s (Fowles 1999, ix–x).

HBO was created in 1972 by Chuck Dolan. It was the first successful American subscription channel (Defino 2014, 4), and as a subscription service, HBO was exempt from the Federal Communications Commission's prying eye and control (Defino 2014, 4). Originally showing unrated comedians and R-rated films, HBO soon turned to creating its own programming that reflected cinematic and realistic R-rated film aesthetics (adult situations, language, nudity and sexuality, and violence), beginning with the prison series *Oz* (1997–2003). As Defino writes, "As the general public has become more tolerant of relaxed content standards—thanks in large part to the success of HBO original programming—we have seen something of a bleed-over into broadcast and basic cable" (2014, 5). This is reflected in Netflix's original programming. But Defino extends the "HBO style" to other television narratives as well: "the network has introduced a level of narrative, character, and thematic sophistication that has spread across the channel spectrum" (6). Elements such as unlikeable but watchable anti-heroes, "brooding strangeness," "mythical complexities," "existential darkness," postmodern feminism, steamy romances, manufactured crises, realistic villains who reflect people we know, dark comedy, tolerable affection, and grand, large-scale epics told through short-form storytelling are all elements that Defino sees as reshaping narratives across the board in the wake of HBO's move to original programming (6).

HBO's *The Sopranos* (1999–2007) is an example of a violent narrative on a subscription platform breaking barriers, the first in a line that can be drawn all the way to *Daredevil* and subsequently to *Jessica Jones*. David Chase, the writer behind *The Sopranos*, expressed how the series could only exist on a network like HBO, and not just in regard to portrayals of violence: "I had just had it up to here with all the niceties of network television. . . . I don't mean language and I don't mean violence. I just mean storytelling, inventiveness, something that really could entertain and surprise people" (McCabe and Akass 2008, 87).

This ability to tell a story that otherwise would not be told on network television extends beyond series like *Oz* and *The Sopranos*, or more comedic and "feminine" narratives like *Sex and the City* (1998–2004). Oscar-winning film director Mike Nichols attributes the success of his six-hour television miniseries *Angels in America* (2003) to HBO: "It has to do with HBO, it's simple as that. We loved the freedom that there is on HBO and the economic power . . . that affords us this freedom" (Edgerton 2008, 146). Says star Al Pacino: "[*Angels in America* would be] just too long, too artsy, too political, and too gay to be funded as a theatrical motion picture" (Edgerton 2008, 146).

Gary R. Edgerton agrees, stating that HBO—and I would include here Netflix's original programing as well—allow creators to take bigger risks because of "a business model that is different from selling tickets to a target audience where two-thirds of the cohort is between twelve and twenty-nine years old, like the movie studios do; or carrying spot advertisements and product placements for sponsors, like the broadcast and basic cable television networks" (2008, 146). What develops instead is a platform that allows for not just adult television but more nuanced storytelling as well. The darker settings, the adult stories, and even the "slow boil" narratives are all elements of the HBO style that were adopted by Netflix series such as *Orange Is the New Black* (2013–19), *Master of None* (2015–), or *The Crown* (2016–).

How Is *Jessica Jones* Different Than the Other Netflix Marvel Series and Their Characters?

Moving beyond the nuanced differences between Netflix and broadcast television, even within the realm of the MCU, the character Jessica Jones is real, she is brutal, and she is different. Her reality makes her story one of otherness within the MCU as the character connects more with the audience than the other superheroes, and much of that might have to do with her gender. The obvious point to make here is that Jessica Jones is the only female among the other male leads on Netflix: Daredevil, Luke Cage, and Iron Fist. But the analysis offered here is much more nuanced than that. Jessica Jones was the first female superhero to lead any MCU piece, whether on the big or small screen, surpassing already established characters like Black Widow or upcoming cinematic leads the Wasp and Captain Marvel. The fact that *Marvel's Agent Carter* premiered before *Jessica Jones* makes it the first solo female lead in the MCU; however, Agent Carter as a character is not definitively a superhero, even within the context of the MCU. Agent Carter has always been a spy of the Second World War and Cold War eras, and in this sense she is separate from both Black Widow and Jessica Jones. Black Widow is a spy from our own contemporary era. While Black Widow associates with the Avengers, Jessica Jones is more superhero than Black Widow, as she has special human abilities. In the series, Jessica's strength is obvious, and as a character she describes her ability to fly as more jumping and landing. Jessica is somewhat invulnerable (Ruscoe 2004, 86), but her brains are what sets her apart (even if the *Marvel Encyclopedia* would argue otherwise) (Ruscoe 2004, 86). As a private investigator, Jessica has an eye for uncovering the truth, using her brain over her fists to solve problems, though she can fight if need be.

Amanda D. Lotz explains that, prior to the rise of superheroine characters in the 1970s like Wonder Woman or the Bionic Woman, superpowered females exhibited traditionally feminine qualities. Shows such as *Bewitched* (1964–72) or *I Dream of Jeanie* (1965–70) tended to portray women in domestic settings regardless of their superhuman abilities (Lotz 2006, 68). By the 1990s, television series like *Buffy the Vampire Slayer* (1997–2003) and *Charmed* (1998–2006) were telling "women's stories instead of telling stories about superheroes who happen to be women[,] . . . construct[ing] narratives about characters with psychological depth, while acknowledging evidence that characters continue to be drawn for the fantasy of male audiences" (Lotz

2006, 69–70). Lotz argues that these roles remained problematic in that sexuality was often used to lure in male audiences (2006, 71). Further, female superheroines were written as role models, with their job being to explain how a modern, feminist female could both kick ass and be nurturing, which at times also proved counterintuitive to the narrative (Lotz 2006, 71). The modern woman is a "superwoman" able to do it all and do it well, regardless of the physical or mental toll it can take on her (Sumra and Schillaci 2015). Before third-wave feminism, women rarely could subvert this role; those who did were interpreted as failures or somehow lacking.

As a third-wave feminist character, Jessica Jones goes against all of this. Starting in the 1990s, female heroines tended to follow a third-wave feminism "girl power" trope of being "young, hip, and alluring" (Early and Kennedy 2003, 3). Imagine, if you will, the Spice Girls with magic powers, and you get a light interpretation of the sisters from *Charmed*. Yet Jessica Jones dismisses all of this: she isn't goodness and light incarnate; she doesn't even wear a costume. Like Luke Cage, her daily street clothes serve as her superhero uniform; there are no star-spangled, colourful suits, web-decorated bodysuit, or elaborate suits of armour here. Dressed in a leather jacket, jeans, and combat boots, Jessica stands in opposition to DC's feminized heroines (Wonder Woman and Supergirl have both worn more revealing costumes), or the sexualized and fetishized bodysuit of Marvel's Black Widow or *Watchmen's* Silk Spectre. Costume-wise, Jessica's closest female comparison is Agent Carter, who attires herself in work-appropriate dresses or skirts, pants, and shoes. Luke Cage wears casual clothes (hoodies, jeans, T-shirts) or work wear (Carhartts). Agent Carter, Jessica Jones, and Luke Cage are all working-class heroes (Kaveney 2008, 84); their costumes must be affordable within the confines of their daily wages. Lacking the means to create an Iron Man suit, the characters must work with the clothing at their disposal, most likely clothes in their regular wardrobes. An excellent example of this working-class hero in the cinema is Spider-Man. Peter Parker comes from a working-class home; he is a minor who still relies on his aunt's employment for income, and he only upgrades his homemade costume because Tony Stark gives him a new one. Returning to the character of Jessica Jones, Roz Kaveney explains that her lack of uniform makes her the "antithesis of the Good Girl" (2008, 70). Both her appearance and her actions go against the standard superhero qualities and visuals (Kaveney 2008, 70). Even in a homemade costume, we the audience still understand that we are looking at Spider-Man; but Jessica looks like an everyday hero in the same way that Agent Carter and Luke Cage do. On the surface, Jessica is one of us.

Further, Jessica never makes herself out to be a noble person: she drinks, acts and talks without a filter, does not care what people think about her, and is sexually active. While inherently good (we never question if she is a villain), Jessica is never as noble as other heroes in the MCU, such as the straightforward Captain America, or even the self-loathing Daredevil. At the end of season 1, Jessica has saved the day and defeated the villain; but it is Jessica's love for Trish that ultimately causes her to react and become a super-hero. Trish's safety and security needs to be called into question for Jessica to react. Jessica must be forced; she does not act on her own devices. Jessica is an anti-hero: she has the physical abilities to be a hero but lacks the mental drive.

The anti-hero as a character isn't new to literature, pop culture, or even superheroes. Entire series (e.g., *Watchmen* [1986–7]) revolve around morally ambiguous heroes. Batman, for example, has always had one foot in the dark, especially in the films. Christopher Knowles argues that post-9/11 comics and superhero films called for lighter *mise en scènes* and themes, and that characters who were violent (like Wolverine) or vigilantes (like the Punisher) were too unlikable or deplorable to be taken into popular culture (2007, 11–12). Daniel Chandler, on the other hand, suggests that since the 1970s, stories about villains have changed genres, such that stories that show unlikely or unlikable characters are now viable and capable of evolving the genre rather than being a detriment to it (2020). Yet the ambiguous anti-hero seems to create a more complex and interesting story for the audience. Jessica's complicated past and dark present make for an at times unlikable hero, but her evolution across the thirteen episodes of season 1 makes for compelling viewing. We see Jessica grow from a person who does not care to someone who does. Jessica's lack of drive or call to action—something most superheroes otherwise revel in—comes from a clear place of pain. She is not a terrible person, although many of her off-the-cuff reactions indicate she is moody. Rather, Jessica is a victim of a difficult childhood and an abusive past that she deals with through inaction. Jessica's passive-aggressive actions are meant to push people away, to keep them safe both from those who mean to hurt Jessica (such as Kilgrave) but also from Jessica herself. Jessica reacts instead of running away, but it takes time, especially when compared to others in the MCU who found their mission or call integral to their characters (see Captain America's "I don't like bullies" speech in Johnston 2011). Not all viewers will associate themselves with Jessica's past traumas, but they will likely relate to her passivity and even her negativity. Jessica has bad days, she acts poorly, or says the wrong thing. Jessica has sex—she doesn't just date or have love interests, she has sex. Elizabeth E. Lewis (2016) explains that this characteristic is also one of an urban fantasy heroine, while Roz Kaveney (2008, 78) writes that this is one of the human elements of Jessica's character. Jessica is human and this makes her story relatable to the audience.

Even the location of the Defenders on the New York City streets of Hell's Kitchen, contributes to this relatability. Kaveney likens Jessica Jones's comic book series *Alias* to early Scorsese films (2008, 77), most notably *Taxi Driver* (1976). My first response to *Daredevil* was that it exists within the MCU, but the Netflix series take place in the dirt, the grime; it is about the people we so often overlook during instances of big-screen destruction. It is a working-class tale, and a relatable one. The Defenders have nothing to do with the Avengers and S.H.I.E.L.D., but that does not mean the Defenders are not affected by their actions.

In episode 1.04 ("AKA 99 Friends"), Jessica is tasked with following a philandering husband. Suspicious of the accusing wife, Jessica takes the case anyways, only to discover the husband with his wife rather than another woman. It turns out the entire case was a set-up: the husband and wife know that Jessica has superpowers, and the wife has decided to kill Jessica. The wife's reasoning is that her mother was killed during the events depicted in the first Avengers film, and that being super-powered, Jessica is guilty by association.

At the climax of *The Avengers*, Loki opens a portal in the sky above New York City, thereby allowing hordes of aliens called the Chitauri to come to earth. The city is ravaged and many lives are lost. Beginning with the pilot of *Daredevil* (2015) the audience is told that the climax of *The Avengers* is referred to as "the incident," a shorthand for what has already happened. When accused with being associated with the Avengers merely because she has superpowers, Jessica responds by saying, "So go after the big green guy or the flag waver," before admitting that she was not even there the day of "the incident"—an event that Marvel Television head Jeph Loeb says inspired the inception of the Defenders universe as a whole (Li 2017, 29). After trashing the room Jessica, the husband, and the wife are in, Jessica makes a final point to the couple: she, too, has lost people and learned to live with it as best she can.

The Defenders represent a bridge between the more docile world of the MCU produced for the cinema and ABC and the more violent but human one of Netflix. Television allows for more complex and deep backstories than film since we are given the privilege of multiple hours and multiple seasons to discover characters' past and present. While film as a medium can often do this, the average two-hour time frame of the typical movie constricts how much can be seen of events taking place outside of the narrative proper. So, Jessica's home on Netflix allows for her role as an anti-hero to become more human and relatable as we delve deep into her traumatic past as well as her present. As an origin story, *Jessica Jones* reduces the stereotypical superhero backstory in exchange for the story of her real-world alter ego. Although not fully fleshed out by the conclusion of season 1, the character of Jessica remains more concrete than the origins of her superpowers, which are still quite opaque by the season finale. Her superhero persona is not part of Jessica Jones's identity. Indeed, Jessica moves beyond being a hero or even an anti-hero and is simply human, flaws and all, thereby bridging the fantasy world and the real.

NOTE

1   It should be noted that these actions predate Disney's acquisition of 20th Century Fox in March 2019.

References

Chandler, Daniel. 2020. "An Introduction to Genre Theory: Constructing the Audience." Visual-memory.co.uk, last modified September 12, 2020. http://visual-memory.co.uk/daniel/Documents/intgenre/intgenre3.html.

Coogan, Peter. 2013. "Comics Predecessors." In *The Superhero Reader*, edited by Charles Hatfield, 7–15. Jackson: University of Mississippi Press.

Cronin, Mary J. 2014. "Netflix Switches Channels." In *Top Down Innovation*, 25–35. New York: Springer.

Defino, Dean J. 2014. *The HBO Effect*. New York: Bloomsbury Academic.

Early, Francis, and Kathleen Kennedy. 2003. "Introduction: Athena's Daughters." In *Athena's Daughters: Television's New Women Warriors*, edited by Francis Early and Kathleen Kennedy, 1–12. Syracuse, NY: Syracuse University Press.

Edgerton, Gary R. 2008. "Angels in America." In *The Essential HBO Reader*, edited by Gary R. Edgerton and Jeffrey P. Jones, 135–48. Lexington: University Press of Kentucky.

Fowles, Jib. 1999. *The Case for Television Violence*. Thousand Oaks, CA: Sage Publications.

Grant, Barry Keith. 2007. *Film Genre: From Iconography to Ideology*. London: Wallflower Press.

Johnston, Joe, dir. 2011. *Captain America: The First Avenger*. Perf. Chris Evans, Sebastian Stan, Hayley Atwell, and Tommy Lee Jones. Los Angeles: Paramount Pictures.

Kaveney, Roz. 2008. *Superheroes! Capes and Crusaders in Comics and Films*. New York: I. B. Tauris.

Keyes, Rob. 2013. "Marvel & Netflix Confirm Deal For 4 TV Shows & 'Defenders' Miniseries." *Screen Rant*, November 7, 2013. http://screenrant.com/marvel-netflix-deal-tv-shows-daredevil-luke-cage-iron-fist-jessica-jones/.

Kiefer, Kitt. 2004. "Daredevil Movie Rewinds the True Believers." In *Marvel Encyclopedia*, vol. 5, *Marvel Knights*, edited by Jeff Youngquist, 25–30. New York: Marvel Comics.

Knowles, Christopher. 2007. *Our Gods Wear Spandex: The Secret History of Comic Book Heroes*. San Francisco: Weiser Books.

Legman, Gerson. 1948. "The Comic Books and the Public." *American Journal of Psychotherapy* 2 (1): 473–90.

Lewis, Elizabeth E. 2016. "To Hell and Back: Power, Violence, and Sexuality in Urban Fantasy." Master's thesis, University of Colorado, Boulder.

Li, Shirley. 2017. "The Defenders." *Entertainment Weekly*, January 20, 2017, 29.

Rotten Tomatoes. n.d. "Daredevil." Rotten Tomatoes, accessed June 18, 2017. https://www.rottentomatoes.com/m/daredevil.

Lotz, Amanda D. 2006. *Redesigning Women: Television after the Network Era*. Chicago: University of Illinois Press.

McCabe, Janet, and Kim Akass. 2008. "It's Not TV, It's HBO's Original Programming: Producing Quality TV." In *It's Not TV: Watching HBO in the Post-television Era*, edited by Marc Leverette, Brian L. Ott, and Cara Louise Buckley, 77–89. New York: Routledge.

Otto, Jeff, and Andy Patrizio. 2004. "*Daredevil*: Director's Cut." *IGN*, October 22, 2004. http://ca.ign.com/articles/2004/10/22/daredevil-directors-cut.

Ruscoe, Michael. 2004. "Daredevil, A to Z." In *Marvel Encyclopedia*, vol. 5, *Marvel Knights*, edited by Jeff Youngquist, 51–123. New York: Marvel Comics.

Sumra, Monika K., and Michael A. Schillaci. 2015. "Stress and the Multiple-Role Woman: Taking a Closer Look at the 'Superwoman.' " *PLOS ONE*, March 27, 2015. https://doi.org/10.1371/journal.pone.0120952.

PART 2

Portrayals of Masculinities,
Male Violence, and Entitlement

Portrayals of Masculinities, Male Violence, and Entitlement

Mary Grace Lao

The second part of the book focuses on the male characters in *Jessica Jones*. While the series is critically acclaimed for its representation of female characters, it is equally important to look at the many ways masculinity is portrayed as these choices reflect the highly gendered society within which the narrative situates itself. Evident in these chapters are the different ways toxic masculinity manifests at the intersection of white supremacy, entitlement, and rape culture. Toxic masculinity is inherently anti-feminist and misogynist, though contemporary toxic masculinity complicates traditional notions of dominant and hegemonic masculinities to include beta and geek masculinities, and those who identify themselves as being involuntary celibate (or incels) (Ging 2019). These non-dominant forms of masculinity use victimhood, mirroring feminist philosophies of gender and power imbalance (Banet-Weiser 2018), as a way to justify anger and feelings that "the world owes me" (Ging 2019).

In the first chapter in this section—which focuses on the range of masculinities portrayed in the series—Jessica Seymour argues that *Jessica Jones* follows a particular narrative in which hyper-masculinity is toxic and destructive. Seymour considers masculinities as a set of practices, echoing R. W. Connell (2005), who notes that masculinities are rooted in "processes and relationships through which men and women conduct gendered lives" (71) embodied in experience and culture. These practices, Seymour contends, are based on "popular conceptions of masculinity and femininity," and are thus key to understanding these popular conceptions from the perspective of the audience.

Brett Pardy's chapter on militarization again echoes Connell's (2005) writings, in which masculinity is often understood as being intertwined with violence. For Pardy, the militarized masculinity portrayed by Will Simpson reflects a romanticization of excessive violence as a necessary and even celebrated American tradition. Simpson's embodiment of the militarization of the police is all the more timely, as Pardy points out, given the recent intensification of police brutality against racialized communities. This is evident in the Black Lives Matter (BLM) movement that began in 2013, and more recently, in former US president Donald Trump's militarized response (Haas 2020) and the young white civilian men who have taken it upon themselves to attack BLM protesters (Allam 2020). Pardy argues that Simpson's embodiment of militarized masculinity reinforces the "bad apple" narrative, whereby individual police officers are blamed for losing control as a substitute for a deeper indictment of the institutional and systemic problems plaguing law enforcement.

The intersection of race and gender is also evident in the ways that Black masculinity is portrayed in the series. In her chapter, Seymour emphasizes the importance of seeing different representations of Black masculinity, not just for those in positions of privilege, but also for young Black men. This is true for both Luke Cage's and Malcolm Ducasse's Black masculine identities. Both characters' embodied masculinities are reminiscent of what bell hooks (2004) calls the "Black male cool . . . defined by the ability to withstand the heat and remain centered," a "willingness to confront reality, to face truth, and bear it not by adopting a false pose of cool while feeding on fantasy; not by black male denial or by assuming a 'poor me' victim identity. . . . [But by] daring to self-define rather than be defined by others" (138). For Luke, this is reflected in his well-cared-for bar and the unravelling story of his deceased wife, Reva, in season 1. We further learn about Luke in his own series, *Marvel's Luke Cage* (2016–18), where he becomes a celebrated figure in his local community—albeit reluctantly—as the so-called Hero of Harlem. Part of his role as the hero is to watch out for young Black men, to make sure that they do not fall into a life of crime while simultaneously working with law enforcement to combat organized crime.

Malcolm's masculinity, however, goes in a different direction. In particular, it stems from his efforts to overcome his drug addiction and hustle his way to working for Jessica at Alias Investigations in season 2, and eventually working for Jeri Hogarth in season 3. He never returns to his original career as a social worker, and the audience sees Malcolm's shift in masculinity, as he becomes more confident and assertive in his abilities, reflected through his clothing, which change from comfortable but clean T-shirt and jeans in season 2 to well-fitted power suits in season 3. We also see Malcolm's romantic and sexual relationships in more detail in the latter season, learning that he was once in a monogamous relationship with Nichelle in college prior to his run-in with Kilgrave and his becoming addicted to drugs. He also begins to have multiple sexual relationships, notably with Trish in season 2 and, in season 3, with Zaya Okonjo, a co-worker at Hogarth and Associates. In season 3, he ends up being Hogarth's "fixer," the antithesis of his earlier aspirations to becoming a social worker. He acknowledges that this line of work eats at his conscience when he says to Hogarth, "I just put an entitled drunk back on the road. I'm not sure that qualifies as good. . . . My job title is 'Investigator,' not 'Fixer' " (Lehman 2019). While Malcolm's ultimate goal in season 3 is to open his own firm as a private investigator, he must first play by a white woman's rules (Hogarth) and acquire her approval before he can forge his own masculine identity.

There is a stark contrast between the masculinities portrayed by Luke and Malcolm and those of Simpson and Kilgrave. Luke, Malcolm, and Simpson all wished to restore peace, though by different means: Luke and Malcolm by working with Jessica, and Simpson by way of a more vigilante approach, in this case killing those he deemed "in the way" of his goal. Like the white-supremacist men who attacked and murdered BLM protesters and were arrested without much struggle, Simpson, thanks to his privilege as a white, cisgender, heterosexual man with both social and financial capital, is "allowed" to express violence under the guise of "vigilante justice" with little consequence. Despite his violent outbursts in season 1, he somehow redeems himself in season 2, just before he is killed. Compare this to untold numbers of Black men who have been killed as a result of violent and excessive force, including Eric Garner and Tamir Rice in 2014, Philando Castille and Alton Sterling in 2016, and, more recently, George Floyd in 2020, among many others. Unlike the countless white men who are empowered to practise vigilante justice, these Black men are often criticized for not having "listened to the police," this claim then used to justify the violence inflicted upon them. In an echo of Judith Butler's (1988) notion of gender performativity, Black men are not allowed to express the same kinds of emotions and reactions as white men. Their gender performance must be calm at all times if they are to avoid "looking suspicious."

We also see in these chapters how expressions of a range of masculinities affect not only the male characters in *Jessica Jones* but also the other characters around them. Anastasia Salter and Bridget Blodgett focus on geek masculinity, once thought of as deviating from a hegemonic masculinity rooted in muscularity and physical strength (Connell 2004), and hyper-masculinity. For Salter and Blodgett, Kilgrave represents the ultimate geek man and embodies the ultimate "nerd power fantasy": good-looking, suave, and sensitive while simultaneously possessing mind-control abilities, he represents a white-supremacist entitlement that allows him to take and use what he sees. Kilgrave's toxic geek man reflects some of the ways that toxic geek masculinity has sought to delegitimize women and girls as "fake geek girls'" and "girl gamers" in comic, fan, and gamer spaces. We have seen the manifestation of these types of toxic entitlement in the 2014 Gamergate controversy, and more recently among incels, whose feelings of sexual inadequacy stem from the belief that they are entitled to have sex with women. They blame women and alpha males (Chads) for their lack of heterosexual relationships (Tolentino 2018).

This nuanced portrayal of the villain gives way to a different kind of relationship with the audience, one that is deeply rooted in gender and power. Mary Grace Lao's chapter challenges the viewer's relationship with masculinity, specifically that of violent men. Lao argues that the "active" role that the audience takes on in their "relationship" with Kilgrave highlights the myriad ways white men are often excused for their misogynistic behaviour. Both Salter and Blodgett's and Lao's chapters focus on Kilgrave's toxic masculinity through the example of Brock Turner, a cisgender, white, upper-class, educated, heterosexual man who was released from prison after serving three months for raping an unconscious woman behind a dumpster (*BBC News* 2016). Critics of Turner's highly flawed trial and sentencing have pointed to the news media's choice to publish his yearbook photos alongside headlines that tended to focus on his achievements as an "Olympic hopeful" (Sprankles 2016), rather than print his mug shot, which they see as evidence of a bias in favour of white men and a perpetuation of the "boys will be boys" trope evident in rape culture discourse. Kilgrave, like Turner, attempts to paint himself as an inherently "good" person who only became evil due to childhood trauma—someone capable of rehabilitation who therefore should not be judged for his indiscretions.

The chapters in this section harken back to Seymour's observation that the hyper-masculinity portrayed by men in the series has toxic consequences for others. Thinking about the key concepts of toxic masculinity, white supremacy, intersectionality, entitlement, and rape culture, this section attempts to show how toxic masculinity affects not only the individuals who embody it, but also the rest of us with regards to our interpersonal relationships, our cultural practices, and the gendered expectations we continue to confront in our day-to-day lives.

References

Allam, Hannah. 2020. "Vehicle Attacks Rise as Extremists Target Protesters." *NPR*, June 21, 2020. https://www.npr.org/2020/06/21/880963592/vehicle-attacks-rise-as-extremists-target-protesters

Banet-Weiser, Sarah. 2018. *Empowered: Popular Feminism and Popular Misogyny.* Durham, NC: Duke University Press.

BBC News. 2016. "Brock Turner: Stanford Sex Attack Swimmer Freed from Jail." *BBC News*, September 2, 2016. https://www.bbc.com/news/world-us-canada-37259537

Butler, Judith. 1988. "Performative Acts and Gender Constitution: An Essay in Phenomenology and Feminist Theory." *Theatre Journal* 40 (4): 519–31.

Connell, R. W. 2005. *Masculinities*, 2nd ed. Los Angeles: University of California Press.

Ging, Debbie. 2019. "Alphas, Betas, and Incels: Theorizing the Masculinities of the Manosphere." *Men and Masculinities* 22 (4): 638–57.

Haas, Benjamin. 2020. "Trump's Militarized Policing of Portland Has No Place in the US." *CNN*, August 7, 2020. https://www.cnn.com/2020/07/24/opinions/trumps-militarized-policing-of-portland-haas/index.html.

hooks, bell. 2004. *We Real Cool: Black Men and Masculinity.* New York: Routledge.

Lehman, Michael, dir. 2019. *Marvel's Jessica Jones.* Season 3, espisode 1, "AKA The Perfect Burger." Aired June 14, 2019, on Netflix.

Sprankles, Julie. 2016. "These Brock Turner Headlines Are beyond Tone Deaf." *Bustle*, June 6, 2016. https://www.bustle.com/articles/165164-8-brock-turner-headlines-that-totally-miss-the-point.

Tolentino, Jia. 2018. "The Rage of the Incels: Incels Aren't Really Looking for Sex. They're Looking for Absolute Male Supremacy." *New Yorker*, May 15, 2018. https://www.newyorker.com/culture/cultural-comment/the-rage-of-the-incels.

6

From Devils to Milquetoast Little Man-Boys

Jessica Seymour

The *Jessica Jones* TV series is a smorgasbord for gender theorists. Not only is there a range of exciting feminist themes, and a number of exciting and powerful female characters, but there are also several different representations of masculinity on display. When it comes to popular culture, particularly mainstream film and television, gender tends to be portrayed on a spectrum—with hyper-masculinity and hyper-femininity on either end and characters tending to fall somewhere in the middle. This is not a perfect system because it feeds into the expectation of a gender binary and does not include transgender representation (which is thin on the ground in mainstream media and virtually non-existent in the superhero genre). Using the hyper-masculine to hyper-feminine gender spectrum does not mean that this chapter is arguing *in favour* of a gender binary. It is just that viewers/readers are taught to associate certain personality traits with gender through repeated modelling by media, which is conceptualized as a binary more often than a spectrum. Identifying the hyper-masculine and the hyper-feminine as conceptualized in mainstream media is expedient for understanding how gender is generally performed.

There has been a strong tradition of the hyper masculine in superhero films and television, even though superhero *comics* offer much more diversity—in terms of gender, sexuality, and race (Kirkpatrick and Scott 2015). *Jessica Jones* draws from this comic tradition of diversity more explicitly than other offerings from the superhero genre in the television and film formats. *Jessica Jones* shows a nearly fifty-fifty split between male and female characters, and there is a diverse range of masculine personality traits on offer to viewers.

What is interesting from this chapter's perspective is that, while the male characters move across the spectrum between hyper-masculine and hyper-feminine, most traditionally hyper-masculine traits (violence, female objectification, and self-regarding behaviours) are portrayed as toxic and destructive. By contrast, caring behaviours associated with the female gender are viewed as more useful and healthier in the context of the narrative. This chapter focuses on the male characters' gender performance in the first season—specifically, those of Kilgrave, Luke Cage, Will Simpson, and Malcolm Ducasse—in addition to offering a brief exploration of masculine gender performance in the female leads.

The Theory

The fact that hyper-masculine behaviours have an overall negative impact on the *Jessica Jones* narrative is telling. Gender performance is a relational concept, and so male characters who are shown to complicate their relationship to traditional hyper-masculinity are interesting from a contemporary gender theory perspective. "Masculinity" is a term used to refer to a set of assumptions about what men are supposed to be like. These expectations are then repeated in media and projected onto young male characters.

Butler's (1988) theory of gender performance structures gender as a series of character traits that are culturally associated with a given gender. There are a range of masculinities that a male-identifying person can adopt, and some are more highly prized than others (Connell 1997a, 1997b; Reynolds 2002). Literature and popular culture often act as a method for "reaffirming or challenging cultural ideologies, including those of gender and masculinity" (Potter 2007, 28), so it is interesting to see how masculine characters are portrayed because this can be considered to reflect what the popular consciousness considers "masculine" at that point in time.

As discussed above, gender tends to be portrayed in media on a spectrum running from hyper-masculine to hyper-feminine. Romøren and Stephens (2002) developed a list of "masculine" traits that are typically associated with hyper-masculine gender performances, including

> be[ing] self-regarding, a physical or verbal bully, overbearing in relation to women and children, (over)fond of alcohol, violent,

short-tempered, neglectful of personal appearance, hostile to difference/otherness, actually or implicitly misogynistic, sexually exploitative, insistent upon differentiated gender roles and prone to impose these on others, classist, racist, generally xenophobic, sport-focused, insensitive, inattentive when others are speaking, aimless, possessive. (2002, 220)

Romøren and Stephens further argue that viewers are conditioned through repeated experience to associate most of these traits with a hyper-masculine gender performance. They claim that the presence of three or more of these traits in one character is generally an indication that they are performing hyper-masculinity. Female characters can also perform hyper-masculinity, particularly in *Jessica Jones*, which has so many diverse performances of female characters on offer. But that is beyond the scope of this chapter.

Popular conceptions of masculinity and femininity are very important in understanding how the average viewer might categorize or understand specific traits. In a video about Disney villains published by the website Cracked (2013), one of the featured panellists argues that Gaston, the hyper-masculine counterpart to the male protagonist in *Beauty and the Beast* (1991), should be considered a hero because the character is a masculine power fantasy. He is an arrogant fighter with bulging muscles, with women falling at his feet and a gun on his hip. The masculine power fantasy drives a lot of character design in superhero comics as well, so it would be expected that hyper-masculine traits would be glorified and celebrated in the genre. Popular culture helps reinforce conceptions of gender performance.

In *Jessica Jones*'s case, however, I argue that hyper-masculine traits are generally portrayed negatively—both in relation to characters and in the narrative as a whole. By contrast, the hyper-feminine trait of caring is portrayed positively. Jessica Jones initially does not like this aspect of her own character ("My greatest weakness? Occasionally, I give a damn"; ep. 1.02, "AKA Crush Syndrome"), and the characters who care are often taken advantage of by hyper-masculine characters displaying self-regarding behaviours. Nel Noddings (1998) argues that caring as a trait is often specifically connected with the concept of femininity, while Lindsey Averill (2012) builds on Noddings's thesis by arguing that female characters' ethics of care are frequently positioned in opposition to the hyper-masculine traits like self-interest and impartiality. But caring also acts as a catalyst for action. Noddings writes that "although philosophers have long denigrated emotions and put a high valuation on reason, most have recognized that emotions often motivate action" (2012, 135). In *Jessica Jones*, male characters who are portrayed in a positive light as developing caring relationships drive the plot, while more toxic, hyper-masculine behaviours have a clear negative effect on the plot and characters. These caring relationships lead male characters to move away from toxic, hyper-masculine behavioural indicators typically associated with the superhero genre.

The Toxic Masculine

Kilgrave's behaviour is typically hyper-masculine according to Romøren and Stephens (2002). He is a rapist, self-regarding (interested only in himself and his comfort), and he works steadily through the characters in the series, violating each one either physically, sexually, or mentally by getting into their heads and forcing them to comply with his desires. He incites physical violence (assault, murder, etc.) because he is not strong enough to be violent himself, using proxies like Jessica and Luke Cage. He also displays gaslighting behaviours, which are typical of emotional abuse.

Since Kilgrave is the main antagonist in the series, these examples of hyper-masculine behaviours on his part demonstrate how such actions should be viewed—that is, negatively. If the fact that he is the antagonist were not enough to indicate how these behaviours should be interpreted, the effect that his behaviours have on the narrative and on the other characters demonstrate the toxic, destructive nature of these traits.

The rape of Hope Shlottman is the catalyst for the narrative. Jessica Jones would have been ignorant of Kilgrave's return from the dead if it weren't for his violation of Hope. The narrative is driven by Jessica's desire to defend Hope from the legal ramifications of the things Kilgrave made her do while under his control. The act of rape also creates the embryo that Kilgrave's father, Albert Thompson, eventually uses to make his son more powerful later in the series, so his hyper-masculine behaviours create a continuing, self-reinforcing cycle of power, control, and destruction (ep. 1.13, "AKA Smile"). Hope becomes so disempowered by Kilgrave's behaviour that she decides the only way to regain her agency is to kill herself—an act that, in itself, is problematic because it requires her ultimate destruction. Hope's control over her own body is so limited at this point in the story that the most active choice she can make is to destroy herself quickly, rather than allow herself to be erased slowly through Kilgrave's manipulations. This behaviour robs Kilgrave of a bargaining chip, but that is the only direct consequence he suffers when Hope dies (Jessica's desire to stop Kilgrave is reinforced by this event, but it was already present before Hope's final act of autonomy). Without facing any direct consequences, Kilgrave has no reason to change his hyper-masculine behaviours. The more that Kilgrave thinks that he can benefit from these behaviours, the more he chooses to behave that way.

As his fight with Jessica in episode 1.09 shows, Kilgrave is not a fighter. Violence (both physical and non-physical, though in this case it is the physical that is Kilgrave's main limitation) is an element of hyper-masculinity, but since Kilgrave cannot exhibit this behaviour himself, he uses others—violating their minds and objectifying them so that they will perform in the way that he cannot. Jessica is his primary weapon before the events of the narrative. When she is able to break his control, he uses other proxies: the men and women in the police department, Luke Cage, and the people at the docks in episode 1.13. While Jessica is a strong opponent against Luke, when it comes to ordinary people, she is well out of their league because her care ethic prevents her from acting to her full potential. Kilgrave takes advantage of this by using ordinary people to fight each other and controlling Jessica through her caring instincts.

Luke Cage is almost certainly Kilgrave's most powerful weapon when he is unable to control Jessica, made doubly effective because using Luke violates Jessica sexually at the same time that it hurts her physically. As Kilgrave says in episode 1.12, while explaining that Luke had been under his control while Jessica and Luke had been looking for him, "Those tender moments, those sweet things he shared, it was all me. It was our sexual tension." Even when he cannot violate Jessica himself, he is able to use other men to do it.

Kilgrave is an actively antagonistic character from the beginning, so it makes sense that his hyper-masculine traits would have such a toxic influence on the narrative. Other male characters are more complex. Will Simpson is introduced to the viewer in episode 1.03 as one of Kilgrave's violated pawns, positioning him in the narrative as another victim and inciting sympathy from the viewer. This is supported further in episode 1.04, when he is shown to be desperate to see whether Trish Walker is alive or dead after Kilgrave's power wears off. The viewer, like Trish, takes his somewhat hyper-masculine approach to keeping her safe (trying to force his way into her apartment, giving her a gun, insisting that he help Jessica to take Kilgrave out) as a positive reflection of his caring personality—at least, at first.

Unfortunately, Simpson becomes more and more victim-oriented throughout the narrative, which leads him to rely on increasingly toxic behaviours in order to avoid the powerlessness that all victims of Kilgrave feel. After he is caught in an explosion during episode 1.08 (an attempt by Kilgrave to have him killed) and witnesses his fellow soldiers die, Simpson makes the transition to unbridled toxicity by aligning himself with his former regiment.

In episode 1.09, Simpson takes an unnamed medication from his former army doctor, Koslov, in order to heal quickly from his injuries. After this, however, he immediately becomes more ruthless, and he continues to take the medication to become physically strong and immune to pain. The medication is framed in the show as almost a hyper-masculine steroid that impedes Simpson's caring behaviours. He murders Detective Clemons because he has decided that the only way to protect himself is to kill Kilgrave, and Clemons's plan to jail Kilgrave will only create more victims. He also intends to murder Jessica because he believes that she will impede his plans.

Although Simpson's desire to neutralize Kilgrave is commendable, his approach is destructive because it victimizes other characters. It leads directly to the death of Clemons, the assault of Trish and Jessica, and (potentially, if his plans had worked) the life-long incarceration of Hope Shlottman. Jessica repeatedly emphasizes at crucial moments the need to keep Kilgrave alive in order to clear Hope's name, so the fact that Simpson's plan ignores that concern indicates that it is negatively aligned with the caring behaviours exhibited by Jessica. Simpson is more focused on removing Kilgrave and preventing further victimization than he is in helping the victims who have already been violated. Again, this is admirable but toxic: it places emphasis on pragmatic, aggressive prevention rather than caring for others.

Simpson's behaviour also triggers Trish's fear of helplessness—both when he almost kills her in episode 1.03, and when he has her and Jessica trapped in episode 1.11. Trish takes a military-grade stimulant to be able to fight Simpson. In an effort to meet his violence with equal strength, Trish nearly kills herself. Although Trish survives and wins the fight, the fact that Simpson's attack on her and her sister made her desperate enough to risk death is a telling element in the narrative; it shows that the hyper-masculine desire for complete power can lead to collateral damage in several different ways, especially when a character is forced to make themselves as hyper-masculine as their opponent in order to survive the confrontation. The fear that drove Trish is similar to Simpson's. She decides that the only way to survive and avoid victimization is to take performance-enhancing drugs. Interestingly, the narrative treats men's displays of hyper-masculinity as toxic to *others*, and women's displays of the same as toxic to *themselves*.

Masculinity and Intersectionality

Luke Cage initially appears to be hyper-masculine in his performance of gender. He is extremely muscular, the owner of a bar, sexually proficient, and non-monogamous. His behaviour during episode 1.06, when he intends to take revenge for the murder of his wife, could be considered hyper-masculine because he does not listen to reason, remains focused on his goal, and displays aggressive violence in his pursuit of the man he believes is responsible for his wife's death.

However, like Will Simpson, Luke Cage exhibits other traits that serve to develop his character as the series moves forward. Unlike Simpson, who started in the middle of the spectrum before moving toward hyper-masculine, Luke is located at the beginning of the series near the hyper-masculine end of the spectrum before moving toward a more neutral gender performance as the series progresses. His hyper-masculine behaviours are softened and rendered less destructive when he simultaneously performs more traditionally feminine behaviours such as caring and self-sacrifice.

When viewed from the perspective of traditional masculinity, Luke's performance of gender is important because it represents to the viewer the possibility of non-traditional masculinity despite expectations to the contrary. There is a racial element to this representation, of course, with contemporary feminist critics arguing that gender identity and race are inextricably linked because a society's expectations of gender are often affected by shared expectations of race. A white man, for example, may face different expectations than an Asian or Latin American man. This is called intersectionality, a term coined by Black legal scholar Kimberlé Crenshaw (1989) in her essay "Demarginalizing the Intersection of Race and Sex: A Black Feminist Critique of Antidiscrimination Doctrine, Feminist Theory and Antiracist Politics." It is unfortunate that stereotypes governing how African American men should comport themselves continue to be perpetuated in mainstream media, but Luke Cage subverts many of these expectations.

Luke is portrayed as forming several caring relationships. Specifically, he is portrayed in relationships—platonic or otherwise—that involve explicit caring behaviours such as taking responsibility for others' well-being, offering comfort, and maintaining honesty. He is portrayed as generally soft-spoken, as breaking up with a woman because she is married, and as engaging in the minimal amount of violence necessary to neutralize a confrontation in episode 1.02. This serves as an alternative representation of masculinity for mainstream audiences, one that is perhaps unexpected for a Black man with a history of jail time and an extremely muscular physique. These alternative representations of Black masculinity are important not only for privileged people, who may have stereotypical expectations without even realizing it, but also for young Black men who may feel that society does not have room for them to move away from these expectations. Characters like Luke Cage move across the gender spectrum by mixing hyper-masculine behaviours with caring behaviours, and their alternative performances of masculinity reflect positively on the narrative in which they are portrayed.

While Luke's masculine-coded behaviours are generally not destructive or toxic—either to himself or to the people around him—his obsession with vengeance does nearly cost him his life when, ignoring Jessica's advice to stay away from Kilgrave, he falls under Kilgrave's control in episode 1.11. Luke is then forced to destroy his bar, violate Jessica Jones by proxy, and eventually attempt to murder her. His violent, toxic need for vengeance puts him squarely in Kilgrave's path. Luke's love for his wife is commendable, but it leads to him behaving in reckless, violent ways, and this forces Jessica into the unenviable position of having to choose between harming Luke and allowing him to harm her.

At the last moment, however, we see Luke's caring nature overcome Kilgrave's mind control. At the conclusion of episode 1.12, when Jessica is holding the shotgun under Luke's chin, she says, "Please stop," to which he replies, "Do what you've got to do." This is self-sacrificing behaviour and creates a more empathetic approach to the hyper-masculine—or, rather, helps to alleviate some of the damage that Luke's (and Kilgrave's) hyper-masculine behaviour has caused. Because Luke is no longer in a position to control his actions, he gives permission to Jessica to do whatever she has to do to keep him from hurting her. This gives Jessica agency, and it also allows Luke to extend his care to her even though he is not in a position to actively protect her.

Of all of the male characters in *Jessica Jones*, I argue that the least hyper-masculine is Malcolm Ducasse. Before the events of the series, Malcolm was a social worker. This places him squarely between neutral and hyper-feminine in the gender spectrum because care-based jobs are traditionally and overwhelmingly held by women. After meeting Kilgrave, however, Malcolm is forced to become addicted to drugs—making him perform more self-regarding behaviours (such as spying on Jessica) in order to secure more heroin from Kilgrave. And yet, Malcolm exhibits caring behaviours even while he is high. When Jessica needs money, he offers her his TV unprompted and, apparently, without hesitation.

Malcolm is played by an Australian actor of Jamaican heritage, Eka Darville. Like Luke Cage's, Malcolm's performance of gender is portrayed as intersectional. In episode 1.03, his race and the expectations that come with it are actively addressed when Jessica uses him to break into the hospital and steel surgical-grade anaesthetic. This is prompted by a comment from Ruben, who had been carrying Malcolm back to his apartment: "If you see someone like Malcolm, you make a snap judgment." Later, Jessica takes Malcolm to the hospital under the guise of getting him treated for an injury, only to throw Malcolm into a nurse and incite fear by shouting, "Somebody help! . . . He just lunged at her!" (ep. 1.03, "AKA It's Called Whiskey").

This is an unfortunate but relevant narrative point because it treats Jessica's ability to get the drug she needs to stop Kilgrave as a direct result of the racism of which Malcolm is a victim. The scene ends with Jessica walking past Malcolm on her way out of the hospital. This scene is run in slow motion, with mournful music playing as Jessica and Malcolm lock eyes, and this shows that Jessica's use of Malcolm's race is meant to be read as toxic and wrong. Malcolm is the one to break eye contact, and Jessica's facial expression is meant to portray her guilt.

I would argue that Malcolm begins to exhibit more masculine behaviours after he kicks his drug habit in episode 1.05. But, again, these masculine behaviours are based in a caring instinct, so they are less destructive overall. When Malcolm is wavering over whether he wants to get sober, Jessica tells him, "Save me for once," in reference to her having saved him from a mugging before the events of the narrative. It is immediately after this conversation that Malcolm throws his drugs into the toilet, which creates a narrative link between Jessica's desire for protection and his own sober behaviours from that point onward. He puts himself between Jessica and Luke Cage in episode

1.06, even though Luke is significantly larger than him, because he seems to be under the impression that Jessica requires protection. This would generally be considered hyper-masculine—taking on a larger opponent in order to protect the female—but when Jessica tells him to back off, he complies, so the behaviour is less toxic and framed as stemming from his concern for her.

Malcolm is also shown to be resolute and pragmatic when Kilgrave murders Ruben in episode 1.07. Rather than allow Jessica to take the fall for the crime, Malcolm quickly decides that the best course of action is to destroy the body and hide all evidence so that Jessica can remain in a position to fight. In this sequence, Malcolm makes his decision quickly, reaches out to Trish, implements his plan, and does so in such a way that by the time Jessica returns home from her business that day there is virtually no indication that a man had been murdered in her home. In normal circumstances, the fact that Malcolm is able to so easily dispose of a dead body would be cause for alarm. But the narrative seems to imply that Malcolm would not consider this behaviour if Jessica's freedom were not on the line.

Malcolm performs care when he starts the support group for Kilgrave's victims, and he continues to care despite all of the horrors he has seen. He questions and gets frustrated ("Everything I learned in church, all the praying my mom did for the sick and dying, . . . all the community projects my dad worked on, basically everything that they taught me . . . it was all bullshit?"; ep 1.11, "AKA I've Got the Blues"), but he remains hopeful. He extends this care to Ruben's sister, Robyn, when he helps her put up fliers to find her brother, shows her the stretch of water where her brother's body has been hidden, and waits with her while she says her goodbyes.

Malcolm's strong caring instinct leads to him picking up the phone for Jessica in the final episode, when she is being contacted by potential clients and finds herself unable to do so herself. This act symbolically links the pair in a caring relationship (one that goes both ways, from carer to cared-for, and vice versa) and shows the viewer that Malcolm intends to continue supporting Jessica in her private investigator/crime-fighting lifestyle.

Other male characters of note include the thoughtful and protective Detective Clemons and the subservient and defenceless Ruben. These men also engage with the more feminized side of the gender spectrum, and they are both summarily murdered—Clemons by Simpson, and Ruben by Kilgrave. It could be argued that their murders can be read as a condemnation of feminine personality traits. Clemons was too trusting of Simpson; Ruben was too desperate to be loved by Jessica, allowing him to fall into Kilgrave's clutches.

These murders are narratively expedient. Ruben's death feeds into Jessica's desperation to stop Kilgrave, while killing Clemons is the line that Simpson crosses to show the viewer that he is moving beyond the point of redemption. Considering that neither of the victims could reasonably have been expected to stop their murderers, even if they had embodied hyper-masculine traits, the fact that they exhibit more feminine traits is more of a condemnation of destructive hyper-masculinity. These murders push the narrative forward at the same time that they demonstrate to the viewer how toxic the hyper-masculine characters are becoming.

Conclusion

The *Jessica Jones* TV series offers a range of exciting feminist themes for scholars and viewers to engage with. Popular culture often includes hyper-masculine traits in characters of both genders, but the *portrayal* of these traits and the effect that they have on the narrative in *Jessica Jones* is the primary factor for interpretation from this chapter's perspective. Simply put, how a male character's hyper-masculinity affects the narrative will determine whether it is toxic or healthy. Masculinity intersects with race in the characters of Luke Cage and Malcolm Ducasse, and I think that it is particularly telling and important that these men negotiate the gender spectrum so that their performance is more care-based than those of their white counterparts, Kilgrave and Will Simpson. Their race affects how people expect them to perform their masculinity, and by subverting these expectations *Jessica Jones* contributes to the positive representation of non-white masculine characters.

Hyper-masculinity is not entirely limited to male characters, though that has been the focus of this chapter. Hyper-masculine behaviours are just as toxic for the women in *Jessica Jones* as they are for men, and not just because they are victims of the masculine characters. Female characters who embody the hyper-masculine are, as discussed above, more *self*-destructive than generally destructive: Jessica Jones drinks in excess not because she is cool or reflecting the stereotypes associated with the character of the hard-boiled detective, but because she has PTSD. Trish Walker takes performance enhancers to make herself stronger, but they nearly kill her. Jeri Hogarth is self-regarding and attempts to use Kilgrave's power to force her ex-wife to sign divorce papers, but this leads to her current girlfriend killing her ex-wife. Hyper-masculinity is portrayed as toxic regardless of the gender of the character exhibiting the behaviour.

While the male characters in *Jessica Jones* move along the spectrum between hyper-masculine and hyper-feminine, most of the traditionally hyper-masculine traits (such as violent, self-regarding, and female-objectifying behaviours) are consistently portrayed as toxic and destructive not only to the characters in the story, but to the story itself. This is contrasted by the traditionally feminine caring behaviours, which are healthier and have a positive impact on the narrative as a whole, regardless of the gender of the character performing them.

References

Butler, Judith. 1988. "Performative Acts and Gender Constitution: An Essay in Phenomenology and Feminist Theory." *Theatre Journal* 40 (4): 519–31.

Connell, R. W. 1997a. "Gender Politics for Men." *International Journal of Sociology and Social Policy* 17 (1–2): 62–77.

———. 1997b. "Men, Masculinities and Feminism." *Social Alternatives* 16 (3): 7–10.

Cracked. 2013. "4 Disney Movie Villains Who Were Right All Along." YouTube, September 30, 2013. Video, 7:40. https://www.youtube.com/watch?v=IiGhALxbtK4&ab_channel=Cracked.

Crenshaw, Kimberlé. 1989. "Demarginalizing the Intersection of Race and Sex: A Black Feminist Critique of Antidiscrimination Doctrine, Feminist Theory and Antiracist Politics." *University of Chicago Legal Forum* 1:139–67.

Kirkpatrick, Ellen, and Suzanne Scott. 2015. "Representation and Diversity in Comics Studies." *Cinema Journal* 55 (1): 120–4.

Noddings, Nel. 1998. "Thinking, Feeling and Moral Imagination." *Midwest Studies in Philosophy* 22:135–45.

Potter, Troy. 2007. "(Re)constructing Masculinity: Representations of Men and Masculinity in Australian Young Adult Literature." *Papers: Explorations into Children's Literature* 17 (1): 28–35.

Reynolds, Kimberley. 2002. "Come Lads and Ladettes: Gendering Bodies and Gendering Behaviors." In *Ways of Being Male: Representing Masculinities in Children's Literature and Film*, edited by John Stephens, 96–115. Abingdon, UK: Routledge.

Romøren, Rolf, and John Stephens. 2002. "Representing Masculinities in Norwegian and Australian Young Adult Fiction: A Comparative Study." In *Ways of Being Male: Representing Masculinities in Children's Literature and Film*, edited by John Stephens, 216–33. Abingdon, UK: Routledge.

Will Simpson and the Failure of Militarized Masculinity

Brett Pardy

Jessica Jones (2015–19) uses the superhero genre as a vehicle through which to examine trauma. It is primarily an empathetic and complicated portrayal of Jessica's post-traumatic stress disorder (PTSD) after she was subjected to mind control by Kilgrave, who uses his victims to further his hedonistic life-style. Jessica's interactions while facing the source of her trauma, and working to prevent it from happening to anyone else, lead her into contact with other traumatized characters. One of these is New York City Police sergeant Will Simpson, who is sent, under Kilgrave's mind control, to kill Trish Walker (ep. 1.03, "AKA It's Called Whiskey"). Jessica manages to fool Simpson into thinking he has accomplished his task, and then saves his life when Kilgrave orders him to walk off a roof. When Simpson returns to a lucid state, he seems a potential ally. He is horrified thinking about what he has done, declaring, "I'm a goddamned monster" (ep. 1.04, "AKA 99 Friends"). To atone, he offers his "eight years special ops [experience] and an entire police force" (ep. 1.04, "AKA 99 Friends") to Jessica's cause against Kilgrave. Yet this supposed aid reveals he has his own traumatic past, not simply from his time controlled by Kilgrave, but also from the very training he presents as an asset.

Through engaging with Simpson's trauma, *Jessica Jones* deconstructs the conventional militarized masculine hero, interrogating how the trauma produced by militarism affects such men, rather than ignoring it as much of popular culture does. In many narratives, Simpson, a tall, muscular, white, cisgender man in the police with a background in the military, would be the idealized protagonist, mirroring how the soldier is often portrayed as the ideal citizen (Taber 2016). The military is celebrated as producing the ideal skills of the neoliberal citizen: self-reliance, discipline, the abilities to both take charge of a situation and to follow orders in a meritocratic hierarchy. This is not merely a conservative position, as Bacevich (2013) emphasizes: self-declared progressives see the military "not as an obstacle to social change but as a venue in which to promote it, pointing the way for the rest of society on matters such as race, gender, and sexual orientation" (25). This way of thinking was exemplified on the November 15, 2015, episode of *The Late Show* when liberal icon Stephen Colbert told two veterans, Jake Wood and Eric Greitens, working on reintegrating veterans into society through community service, "I think it would be wonderful if there were more people in government who had served in our military because they do have the training to organize and to lead people."

This type of thinking is what Cynthia Enloe (2016) defines as militarization, "a process by which a person or thing gradually comes to be controlled by the military or comes to depend for its well-being on militaristic ideas" (3). As neoliberal policies increase economic inequality in the United States, the military is promoted "to contrive a sentimentalized version of the American military experience and an idealized image of the American soldier. . . . They enable us to sustain the belief that . . . [America is] bringing peace and light to troubled corners of the earth" (Bacevich 2013, 97–8). This works to convince the population that the United States is the ideal model for the world, that everywhere else has worse conditions, and that the country is committed to improving everyone's lives. Of the fields that are celebrated for producing productive citizens, such as entrepreneurial business or science, technology, engineering, and mathematics jobs, the military is the most accessible. In a time when traditional labour jobs are disappearing, military recruiters intentionally target areas left economically distressed by the effects of globalization, offering the military as the path to a better life (Tyson 2005). At the same time, a trend Roger Stahl (2009) identifies as *militainment* has emerged, in which the increasingly privatized military is sold to the public as "state violence translated into an object of pleasurable consumption" (6), in contrast to the traditional propaganda, which sought to justify the military's actions.

The embrace of the soldier as idealized citizen comes with two serious costs. The first is that by emphasizing the supposed benefits of the military, it tacitly endorses various negative elements, such as the ability to view lives as expendable or to put the "mission" ahead of its human cost. While often unspoken, this results in a culture in which certain lives are, as Judith Butler (2009) says, not "grievable." This perfectly coincides with the logic of neoliberalism, whereby individuals are by default not valuable and must strive to justify their existence. As Olson (2012) argues, valuing lives must be minimized as "empathic motivations come to be seen as irrational, self-defeating, and existing beyond a neutral, immutable market logic" (48). The liberal discourse on the skills the military produces, coupled with the more traditional conservative celebration of military force, allows militarization to be a uniting factor in a fractured American culture.

But militarization is not only felt in foreign contexts. Simpson's post-military role, policing, is in many ways a continuation of his time in the military. Robin D. G. Kelley (2016) outlines how the "race riots" of the late 1960s were met with military surveillance and anti-guerilla tactics by the US government. This militarization was explicitly embraced in the so-called war on drugs launched in 1971. As predominantly racialized communities began to be seen as threats, and as urban decay intensified as a result of neoliberal policies, "state capacities [shifted] away from the production of social goods and towards 'security' concerns produced in their absence" (Camp and Heatherton 2016, 4). The militarized police became occupiers of space rather than protectors of people. The rise of the homeland security industry in the wake of 9/11 has escalated this, evidenced both in the police's ability to purchase great quantities of surplus military equipment and in the use of the threat of terrorism as a justification (Balko 2013). The militarization of the police has intensified police brutality against racialized communities, making the Black Lives Matter movement a necessary response to what has often been a publicly celebrated increase in militarization. Much like the military, policing has become a staple of American entertainment. Despite the human rights abuses perpetrated by police forces, pop-culture depictions of police usually mark "bad" cops through corruption rather than an embrace of excessive violence. The default position of American popular culture is to depict police as the moral champions of the modern city.

In addition to the external negatives of militarization, the celebration of soldiers also produces an internal one: trauma. As Kathleen Barry (2011) compellingly argues, not only does militarization make the lives of "enemies" ungrievable, but it also instills in men a conception that they must view themselves as expendable to the goals of state violence. She argues that if violent masculinity were natural, "society would not have to mount the powerful social pressure . . . it imposes on boys and expects from men" (13). This follows Pierre Bourdieu's ([1998] 2001) argument that masculinity is "a trap, and it has its negative side in the permanent tension and contention, sometimes verging on the absurd, imposed on every man by the duty to assert his manliness in all circumstances" (50). Though most men do not join the military, Barry contends that, much like their treatment as idealized citizens, soldiers provide the model boys are taught to emulate in all-male environments.

Barry (2011) argues that the most common coping mechanism used to combat expendable masculinity is emotional numbness. This begins with the standard socialization of boys not to express emotions, to "be men." But when boys join the military, this numbness is taken to an extreme. Military training seeks to dehumanize, to reshape a recruit's sense of humanity as extending only as far as their own unit. Soldiers are expected to unquestioningly follow orders and kill without hesitation. But Barry suggests that this dehumanization process, while undoubtedly damaging, is often incomplete. While collecting accurate statistics is difficult due to the number of unreported cases, the US Department of Veterans Affairs (2023) estimates that between 11 and 20 per cent of veterans—that is, hundreds of thousands of them—experience PTSD.

American genre fiction tends to largely elide trauma produced by militarized violence and the dehumanization of soldiers. Action "heroes" are able to witness atrocities and kill dozens with seemingly little effect on their emotional states. When genre fiction does deal with trauma, it typically occurs on the personal level, often in the form of revenge for the death of women, to which further violence is depicted as the answer. Sisco King (2011) shows that American narrative structures that privilege (straight, cisgender, white) men's trauma and vengeful sacrifice as redemptive emerge during times of social trauma, such as the post-9/11 period. She writes that despite retaliatory violence producing further trauma, it is the most common response, and that "by naturalizing masculinist constructions of the subject and privileging male bodies as both most vulnerable to trauma and most able to resolve its effects, sacrificial films reify the perceived importance of both violence and male subjects to the sustained life of the nation-state" (13). This conception suggests that the effects of trauma are best solved by their very causes, playing into the hands of militarized culture.

Jessica Jones disrupts militarization, not through a conventional "war is bad" approach, but by actually engaging with the effects of a militarized conception of masculinity. Jessica herself experiences PTSD resulting from her experiences with Kilgrave. But Kilgrave is not the only source of dehumanizing control lurking within society. The publicly celebrated military also produces great potential for destructive behaviour. Will Simpson's narrative arc rejects the mythology of redemptive violence, of using militarized masculinity to overcome trauma. Revenge here is not a force for healing; rather, it leads Simpson down a spiral of destruction.

Even when Simpson is helpful to Jessica by acquiring security camera footage for her to track down the source of Kilgrave's pictures, he displays the negative aspects of his militarized training. He is immediately suspicious of the hoodie-wearing Black man Malcolm Ducasse, roughing him up while accusing him of spying on them. There are also warning signs when he first seems to display emotional sensitivity, as he is distraught at the possibility that he could have killed Trish. Ominously, though he wishes to apologize to her, he believes the best way to do so is to give her an unlicensed handgun, tearfully telling her, "I just wanted you to feel safe" (ep. 1.04, "AKA 99 Friends"). Trying to convince the wary Trish to open the door to him, he tells her a story about burning his G.I. Joe action figure collection in a Barbie Dreamhouse he set alight (because he was "committed to the scenario"). He claims this is proof that "I've always been the guy saving people." In fact, it foreshadows how easily excessive violence is confused for necessity, further demonstrating how young boys internalize such messages.

Simpson quickly feels constrained by his helping role. The militarized masculinity he embodies leads him to expect deference from those around him. While in his military or police roles, he would follow orders, outside of these contexts he is unable to listen to a civilian, especially a woman, as if he is surprised to learn he is not the protagonist of the story. Simpson constantly assumes he is physically more capable than the superpowered Jessica. Feeling emasculated, he eventually asks Trish to tell him the specifics of her powers. His need for control is not limited to physical issues, however, as he also assumes himself to be the most knowledgeable about how to deal with Kilgrave. Overhearing Jessica explain to Trish her plan to stop Kilgrave, Simpson immediately interjects to explain why the plan will fail. His advice is to simply shoot Kilgrave, which follows the military logic of execution as the preferable solution. Jessica opposes this as she needs Kilgrave alive to clear Hope Shlottman's name.

Simpson is certain in his lethal approach to Kilgrave, derisively telling Jessica, "Whatever abilities you have, I'm guessing they don't include rendition, exfiltration, and isolation of enemy combatants" (ep. 1.05, "AKA The

Sandwich Saved Me"). Trish is taken by this, declaring "he's a war hero," echoing the common injunction to "support our troops," which assumes that soldiers are heroic regardless of their actions (Stahl 2009). The terms Simpson invokes here serve to obscure the worst human rights abuses of the "war on terror," and are hardly reflective of heroism: "rendition" refers to the practice of turning accused terrorists over to countries where US intelligence opera-tives knew they would be tortured (Mayer 2005); "exfiltration" is the kidnap-ping of "enemies"; while "isolation of enemy combatants" involves prisoners being held in solitary confinement in places like Guantanamo Bay without ever facing charges. This mirrors what Jessica plans to do with Kilgrave, but Simpson's choice to brag about his skills in these tactics gives us a new and murky definition of "war hero."

Simpson's efforts in aiding Jessica are not helpful; rather, they reveal the normalized brutality of his training. The plan to capture Kilgrave by drug-ging him with a dart fails due to the intervention of Kilgrave's hired private security contractors. In response, Simpson threatens to torture an injured contractor left behind in an effort to find out Kilgrave's location. Jessica prevents this by simply talking with the contractor, whom Kilgrave has told nothing. Yet Simpson is convinced he is holding back, which reveals one of torture's many problems: if the torturer believes there is a truth to find, they will not cease their violence until they hear what they want. Ironically, Jessica has to him of the motto of the police—"serve and protect"—in the process pointing out just how far Simpson's militarized behaviour is from the puta-tive ideals of policing.

However, Simpson remains convinced that his approach exhibits a sense of "realism." He tells Jessica, "everyone wants to be the hero, but now I see we can't be, because there's us and there's them. . . . It just means we can't always help. Not without getting hurt" (ep. 1.08, "AKA WWJD?"). He also tells Trish that "some people deserve to be removed from this earth" (ep. 1.07, "AKA Top Shelf Perverts"). This version of realism has infected the superhero genre since the 1980s with revisionist comics like Frank Miller's *Daredevil* (1979–83) and Alan Moore's *Watchmen* (1986–7), but it has intensified in the superhero's transition to film and television. As Will Brooker (2012) points out in a dis-cussion of the proclamation of realism in superhero films, "realism" tends to mean an angry, violent masculinity and an emphasis on technology. Through this adaptation, the superhero genre moved away from imagining alterna-tive forms of justice and instead entrenched certain patterns of state violence as inevitable. To make superheroes into a mass market property for adult audiences, superhero violence has evolved from the fantasy of excessive but non-lethal violence to superheroes who kill, as is the norm in the action-adventure blockbuster. *Jessica Jones*, a show clearly marketed for adults, represents a middle ground. The show treats killing as a drastic option. In keeping with this critical stance, Simpson's conception of realism does not lead him to be a celebrated anti-hero, but rather begins to clarify his position as an antagonist. This becomes the breaking point for Jessica, and their paths in seeking "justice" diverge from this point.

Simpson's first solution on his own is to bomb Kilgrave's house (ep. 1.08, "AKA WWJD?"). This is not dissimilar to American drone strikes, which are presented as targeted killings, but which are, in reality, indiscriminate (Ackerman 2014). Simpson's plan would have killed not only Kilgrave, but also several mind-controlled innocents as "collateral" death. The only person he considers rescuing is Jessica, who is in the house with her own plans to neutralize Kilgrave. Still needing him alive, she instead alerts Kilgrave to the bomb's existence. With the bombing thwarted, Simpson turns to another of the military's preferred methods of assassination, infiltration. That night he and two ex-army friends return to the house to murder Kilgrave. Instead, they find that he has been drugged by Jessica, who flies away with him before they have a chance to shoot. However, Kilgrave had a backup plan, using mind control to force his elderly neighbour to return the bomb to Simpson. This kills Simpson's two friends and leaves him gravely injured. His vengeance literally backfires on him, providing not healing, but setting him up for the most traumatic circumstances yet and killing his own team and an innocent woman.

Rushed to the hospital by Trish, Simpson demands to be taken to one Dr. Kozlov, whom the hospital staff do not know. Kozlov mysteriously arrives and Simpson, feeling emasculated by both his injuries and his inability to defeat Kilgrave, says, "I want back in." Kozlov vaguely refers to needing to alter protocol after "what happened in Damascus," grounding this operation in the ongoing American conflicts in the Middle East, but he is willing to take Simpson back into his program. He offers Simpson red (aggression), white (stabilizer), and blue (downer) pills. Simpson ignores orders and takes two red pills (ep. 1.09, "AKA Sin Bin"). Simpson's addiction to militarized masculinity is literalized in drugs coloured after the American flag. His trauma re-ignited by mind control and intensified by his injuries, he must return to what he imagined gave his life purpose.

The drugs reveal that Will Simpson is an adaptation of the Marvel Comics character Frank Simpson, code-named Nuke, a man driven insane by a failed experiment in the Weapons Plus program, the same one that had produced Captain America (see Miller 1986 for Nuke's introduction, and Morrison 2003 for his background in the Weapons Plus program). With his military buzzcut and the American flag tattooed on his face, the Simpson of 1986's *Daredevil* is a parody of Reagan-era American militarism and the belief that the military "wasn't given permission to win" in Vietnam (Reagan 1981). The renamed Will Simpson reimagines parody as tragedy. Up until this point, it has been emphasized that Simpson's trauma was produced by Kilgrave, and that his military training would provide the cure for this trauma, following the cliché that vengeance is curative. However, Kilgrave only re-ignited Simpson's deeper trauma, for the comment "what happened in Damascus" offers a hint that losing control to Kilgrave was not the first time Simpson has lost control. Simpson is one of many veterans suffering from unresolved trauma. But the military does not provide veterans with the tools for dealing with trauma (Barry 2011). Rather, they are expected to rely upon the self-reliance they were taught in the military. Unlike the fantasy that the military teaches veterans the skills to be successful in their post-military lives, having to be resilient and lacking support only deepens their trauma. Simpson left the military, but for a militarized job in policing. That drugs are used to cope with the trauma represents an apt symbol. Up to 13 per cent of veterans have a substance-abuse problem, primarily alcohol, and, as seen here in a hyperbolic form, prescription drug dependencies (Murphy 2023). But it also shows that militarized masculinity is an addiction, giving the short-term rush of power with the long-term effects of paranoia and emptiness.

High on his red pills (ep. 1.10, "AKA 1,000 Cuts"), Simpson arrives at the facility he had set up with Jessica to hold Kilgrave, only to find him already escaped. He is confronted by another police officer who has been reluctantly helping Jessica, Detective Oscar Clemons. Clemons relaxes when Simpson shows him his badge. Clemons reassures him they have all the evidence they need to put Kilgrave away. But that only re-inspires Simpson's belief that this will not work. He says, "maybe the system will be unable to contain him." It is here that Simpson identifies Kilgrave "as a terrorist, not a purse snatcher" (ep. 1.10, "AKA 1,000 Cuts"). As Lewis (2012) emphasizes, "terrorism is the word that makes any situation instantly dire" (232). Terrorism becomes a vague accusation that moves the individual beyond the criminal into the monstrous.

Similarly, the United States has used the term "unlawful combatant" as justification to ignore both constitutional safeguards and international human rights laws. Indeed, virtually any method has been justified in the "war on terror" (Konigsberg 2009). Reflecting his militarized training, Simpson sees terrorism as justifying any means of taking down Kilgrave. But militarization's black-and-white world view treats any questioning of authority as an allying with the enemy. In Simpson's warped view, Clemons, who simply believes in due process, is a barrier, and so, after getting the story from Clemons, including the location of Trish, Simpson shoots him in the head and torches the room. When Simpson arrives at the hotel, Trish notices his pupils are dilated and finds it unusual that he recovered quickly.

Simpson is suspicious of Dr. Albert Thompson, Kilgrave's father, who is working on a vaccine based on Jessica's DNA that will guard against Kilgrave's powers. Losing control, he assaults Dr. Thompson, thereby putting the vaccine at jeopardy. His violence once again compromises the possibility of systemic solutions. He calms down, but Trish is horrified and demands he leave, snatching away his pills. He tries to tell Trish the effects the drugs have on him: "everything turns red. It's good for battle, bad for people you care about" (ep. 1.11, "AKA I've Got the Blues"). While this is true, Simpson cannot even conceptualize a caring relationship outside of his control. Ultimately, his apparent honesty is but a ploy to manipulate Trish into telling him how to get at Jessica, who has become not just a competitor in bringing down Kilgrave, but an obstacle.

The addiction to vengeance at this point has rendered Simpson a villain. He barges into Jessica's apartment, resulting in a brutal fight with Jessica. She demands he "tell [her] you're Kilgraved," but the answer is far more horrifying—that traumatized militarized masculinity is similar in its effects to being Kilgraved; namely, the inability to deal with situations calmly, or with anything other than brute, mindless violence. Simpson is out of control, firing his gun wildly and throwing Jessica through a wall. Simpson tries to slash open the door to the bathroom, where Jessica and Trish have taken refuge, the scene shot in apparent homage to the image of Jack Nicholson chopping down a door in *The Shining* (1980), that classic tale of fragile masculinity as a route to madness. Eventually subdued, Kozlov repossesses Simpson, returning him to the military not as a person, but as a weapon. In his quest for justice, violence did not cure Simpson's trauma.

What makes Simpson a rare character is his role as an antagonist police officer who is neither corrupt nor fundamentally a bad person. Criticism of law enforcement is often presented through the popular notion that the frequent violence enacted by the police is the result of "bad apples" rather than structural issues associated with the rise of so-called broken windows–style policing, which seeks to control marginalized populations through harsh punishments for minor crimes (Camp and Heatherton 2016). *Jessica Jones* does not engage in this level of critique, nor does she emphasize that the violence of militarized policing is primarily aimed against racialized communities. But neither does the show engage in what Roland Barthes ([1957] 2012) called "the inoculation," where a small part of a system is criticized only to reaffirm that the good resulting from that system is worth its defects. The police, after the reluctant ally Clemons is murdered by Simpson, play no role in aiding Jessica. Instead, the show offers a middle ground, looking at how the militarized system of policing would produce "bad apple" cops through trauma. Simpson's trauma demonstrates how a militarized police force will continue to produce "bad apples" by encouraging certain forms of masculine dominance and violence to the point that these compromised individuals eventually lose control. Instead, Simpson believes he is doing good as he is following the route he has been taught. It is what militarization teaches that is the source of the problem.

This oppositional stance to militarization is refreshing in the context of the Marvel Cinematic Universe, which initially used the Strategic Homeland Intervention, Enforcement and Logistics Division (S.H.I.E.L.D) to tie together first the film franchise and then link it with their television properties, beginning with ABC's *Agents of S.H.I.E.L.D* (2013–present). The military was the glue holding together the universe's heroes, recruiting and moulding them into a functioning team. The masculinity modelled by the actual military is barely present in Marvel Cinematic Universe, where S.H.I.E.L.D. presents something of a liberal fantasy of the military, using force only when necessary and with a minimum of collateral damage. In fact, Simpson's two traits are present within *The Avengers* (2012), as Captain America is the product of military medicine and the Hulk's rage is harnessed, with its uncontrollability played as much for comedic effect as Simpson's is for horror. *Jessica Jones* instead shows militarized masculinity veering more closely to reality, a force both inwardly and outwardly destructive.

However, *Jessica Jones* ultimately privileges violence, defending it as a solution, though performed by Jessica rather than the military or police. As a last resort, she kills Kilgrave by snapping his neck. This seems to condone Simpson's solution, though Jessica is much more reluctant to enact such violence. The plot is constructed so that it could be argued that Simpson's desire to shoot Kilgrave, when they instead darted him, would have saved many people's lives. However, it will be up to future seasons to determine if Kilgrave's death is curative of Jessica's trauma, or if it will be another thing that haunts her.

Regardless, *Jessica Jones* demonstrates that militarized masculinity does not cure trauma. None of Simpson's actions have brought him peace—indeed, his efforts to face his trauma have seen him spiral out of control. His actions result in the deaths of innocent people, the destruction of his relationship, a crippling drug addiction, loss of personal freedom, and ultimately forestalls justice. This is not the fantasy world where trauma is overcome by "redemptive violence" (Sisco King, 2012). Rather, the show demonstrates that when society not only refuses to treat trauma, but valorizes the circumstances that produce it, justice is unattainable. Like the best superhero stories, *Jessica Jones* uses the hyperbole inherent to the genre to depict a very real crisis, showing that militarization produces not heroes but only further violence and trauma.

References

Ackerman, Spencer. 2014. "41 Men Targeted but 1,147 People Killed: US Drone Strikes—the Facts on the Ground." *The Guardian*, November, 24, 2014. https://www.theguardian.com/us-news/2014/nov/24/-sp-us-drone-strikes-kill-1147.

Bacevich, Andrew J. 2013. *The New American Militarism: How Americans Are Seduced by War*, updated ed. New York: Oxford University Press.

Balko, Radley. 2013. *Warrior Cop: The Militarization of America's Police Forces*. New York: PublicAffairs.

Barry, Kathleen. 2011. *Unmaking War, Remaking Men*. Santa Rosa, CA: Phoenix Rising Press.

Barthes, Roland. (1957) 2012. *Mythologies*. Translated by Richard Howard. New York: Hill and Wang.

Bourdieu, Pierre. (1998) 2001. *Masculine Domination*. Translated by Richard Nice. Stanford, CA: Stanford University Press.

Brooker, Will. 2012. *Hunting the Dark Knight: 21st Century Batman*. London: I. B. Tauris.

Butler, Judith. 2009. *Frames of War: When Is Life Grievable?* London: Verso.

Camp, Jordan T., and Christina Heatherton. 2016. "Introduction: Policing the Planet." In *Policing the Planet: Why the Policing Crisis Led to Black Lives Matter*, edited by Jordan T. Camp and Christina Heatherton, 1–14. Brooklyn, NY: Verso.

Enloe, Cynthia. 2016. *Globalization and Militarism: Feminism Makes the Link*, 2nd ed. Lanham, MD: Rowman and Littlefield.

Lewis, A. David. 2012. "The Militarism of American Superheroes after 9/11." In *Comic Books and American Cultural History: An Anthology*, edited by Matthew Pustz, 223–36. New York: Continuum.

Kelley, Robin D. G. 2016. "Thug Nation: On State Violence and Disposability." In *Policing the Planet: Why the Policing Crisis Led to Black Lives Matter*, edited by Jordan T. Camp and Christina Heatherton, 15–34. Brooklyn, NY: Verso.

Konigsberg, Peter Jan. 2009. *Our Nation Unhinged: The Human Consequences of the War on Terror*. Berkeley: University of California Press.

Mayer, Jane. 2005. "Outsourcing Torture: The Secret History of America's 'Extraordinary Rendition' Program." *New Yorker*. February 14, 2005. http://www.newyorker.com/magazine/2005/02/14/outsourcing-torture.

Morrison, Grant. 2003. "The Devil." *The New X-Men* 1, no. 145. New York: Marvel Comics.

Miller, Frank. 1986. "God and Country." *Daredevil* 1, no. 232. New York: Marvel Comics.

Murphy, Edmund. 2023. "Alcoholism, Drug Dependence and Veterans." *Recovered*, last modified June 1, 2023. https://www.ncadd.org/about-addiction/drugs/veterans-and-drugs.

Olson, Gary. 2012. *Empathy Imperiled: Capitalism, Culture, and The Brain*. New York: Springer.

Reagan, Ronald. 1981. "Remarks on Presenting the Medal of Honor to Master Sergeant Roy P. Benavidez." Ronald Reagan Presidential Library and Museum, February 24, 1981. https://www.reaganlibrary.gov/archives/speech/remarks-presenting-medal-honor-master-sergeant-roy-p-benavidez-0.

Stahl, Roger. 2009. *Militainment, Inc.: War, Media, and Popular Culture*. New York: Routledge.

Sisco King, Clare. 2011. *Washed in Blood: Male Sacrifice, Trauma, and the Cinema*. New Brunswick, NJ: Rutgers University Press.

Taber, Nancy. 2016. "Official (Masculinized and Militarized) Representations of Canada: Learning Citizenship." In *Gendered Militarism in Canada: Learning Conformity and Resistance*, edited by Nancy Taber, 63–82. Edmonton: University of Alberta Press.

Tyson, Ann Scott. 2005. "Military Recruiters Target Isolated, Depressed Areas." *Seattle Times*. November 9, 2005. http://www.seattletimes.com/nation-world/military-recruiters-target-isolated-depressed-areas/.

US Department of Veterans Affairs. 2023. "How Common Is PTSD in Veterans?" US Department of Veterans Affairs, last modified February 3, 2023. https://www.ptsd.va.gov/understand/common/common_veterans.asp.

#Kilgraved: Geek Masculinity and Entitlement in Marvel's Villains

Anastasia Salter and Bridget M. Blodgett

The Marvel Cinematic Universe (MCU) is one of the most powerful contemporary examples of the mainstreaming of so-called geek culture, with record-setting sales that make it "the most lucrative franchise in film history" (Hutchinson 2016). With the films' immense success and influence comes great responsibility: the titular male heroes of the franchise films offer iconic, hyper-masculine role models for a generation of consumers. They are strong, funny, and, most importantly, intelligent. While in eras past, the masculinity defined by Hollywood was of a vibrant physicality, the new man, as shown in the MCU, often relies more on his brain than his brawn. In *Iron Man*, Tony Stark—most recognizable through Robert Downey Jr.'s portrayal in the MCU—is a perfect forerunner for this new definition of masculinity, which takes the privileges of power and authority and subsumes them under a veneer of trauma and loss. This new man has suffered hardships and can often be painted as the underdog in his own story, fighting against oppressive forces using his ingenuity and unique skills. The depiction of masculine superheroes and villains within the MCU builds on a range of tropes, as Derek McGrath (2015) notes: "They are bonded by their individual understandings of the constraints of their masculine behaviors, marked by their ambiguous relationship to being human" (149). However, with the exception of a few minor characters (Black Widow, Scarlet Witch, and Wasp), there is no feminine equivalent of these representations: The MCU is decidedly centred on masculinity writ large. The first break from this trend came not from within the core MCU itself, but through an offshoot show on Netflix, *Jessica Jones*.

Compared to the other MCU properties, *Jessica Jones* is part of a set of shows produced with a more mature audience in mind: while it acknowledges the main narratives of the MCU, it is mostly self-contained, introducing superhero turned private investigator Jessica Jones, a sarcastic, bitter, heavy-drinking woman with superpowered strength and healing abilities. As Brown (2016) argues, "the basic formula at the core of most superhero narratives is an allegory for adolescent puberty and a male wish-fulfilling fantasy of becoming a pinnacle of hegemonic masculinity, but *Jessica Jones* breaks with genre conventions to construct an allegory for physical and psychological abuse" (58). Jones is shown not only as an adult within the story but as someone who is dealing with the very salient consequences of her relationships and history.

However, the character who truly rejects the typical wish-fulfillment narrative of superhero-dom within the narrative is not actually Jessica Jones but, rather, the show's supervillain, Kilgrave, who presents the most meaningful challenges to hegemonic masculinity. Kilgrave is not a traditional supervillain. He is not after totemic objects of power in a universe where nearly every other villain is obsessed with the Infinity Stones, which represent various forms of control and mastery. He is not seeking wealth or fortune—he can acquire those things at a moment's notice, which makes them meaningless to him. Instead, he is particularly obsessed with Jessica herself, and presents the viewer with a chilling and compelling model of a superpowered stalker. In a unique take on the villain, Kilgrave is interested in completely possessing and subsuming another person under his control, and he has focused this intent on a woman who managed to exhibit the one trait he did not desire: independence from him.

Kilgrave is the ultimate example of a toxic geek man: his presence is a repudiation of comic fanboys and a critique of existing fan gender discourse, which heavily favours masculinity while othering women as outsiders and "fake geek girls." His methods even mirror those wielded with such effectiveness by geek men in recent outbreaks of cultural conflict, such as Gamergate, a dispute over what some men saw as the attempts of "social justice warriors" to diversify gaming; Sad and Rabid Puppies, a set of campaigns aimed at "reclaiming" the Hugo Awards for "real" science fiction fans; and ongoing disputes over conventions, cosplays, and other traditionally male-dominated spaces of fandom. Much like the members of these movements, Kilgrave paints himself as a valiant hero fighting against injustices imposed upon him by outsiders. Thus, *Jessica Jones*, as a show helmed by and primarily starring women, inevitably became a contested media object for its representations of gender within the superhero space. In this chapter, then, we examine the reactions to *Jessica Jones* and its portrayal of entitled, suave villain Kilgrave in terms of geek masculinity.

Toxic Geek Men as Villains

The geek villain emblematic of toxic masculinity has made several appearances on screen over the last few years. In the *Ghostbusters* (2016) remake, a reboot widely criticized by male fans of the franchise who saw the all-woman cast as a betrayal of the original, the isolated and awkward Rowan North brings terror to New York City by getting ghosts to attack those who have rejected him. In a mockery of Rowan's angst that simultaneously reinforces hyper-masculine norms, a dead Rowan possesses the body of Chris Hemsworth (best known for his portrayal of Thor within the MCU) and remarks that he definitely should have spent more time at the gym while alive. The movie even includes a self-referential scene in which a video of the team encountering a ghost is posted on YouTube and draws hateful misogynist comments such as "Ain't no bitches gonna hunt no ghost." Rowan is cast as a fan turned villain: he owns a copy of the book written by the two professors on the Ghostbusters team, which he uses to plan his attacks. The movie is an emblematic example of gendered conflict, with male-identifying reviewers consistently downvoting the film on IMDB even before its release (Hickey 2016). The campaign against *Ghostbusters*, which particularly focused on Twitter harassment of star Leslie Jones, is the perfect example of entitled male outrage over the perceived violation of traditionally male institutions—even though, in this case, the institution is fictional. The decision to cast a white male geek as the villain of the narrative is clearly intentional, and a marked departure from the original film's narrative, which did not include any active human agent as a villain.

Ghostbusters is not the only iconic geek franchise to acknowledge the toxicity of white male geek villains: *Star Wars: The Force Awakens* (2015) features perhaps the ultimate example of a fanboy gone bad, Kylo Ren. Kylo Ren at first appears to be similar to Darth Vader, with an imposing mask and control over the dark side of the Force. But when his mask is removed, he is revealed to be an emo fanboy, and shown having a temper tantrum and destroying machinery to no productive end. He keeps the burnt mask of Darth Vader in a disturbing shrine, and ultimately the narrative suggests that his combination of hero worship and father issues have led him to absolute darkness (which he demonstrates by killing his father, Han Solo). Critics have noted in Kylo Ren's descent a reflection of current geek masculinity: "the patriarchy's chief drone of the film remains on the dark side—Kylo Ren's arc and his struggles to conform to the dark ways of the Force are a spot-on metaphor for the toll of toxic, performative masculinity" (TMS Contributors 2016). Ironically, there is a powerful moment within the film, centred through this analytical lens, where Ren begins pounding on a wound to attempt to make himself stronger, a wound he gained through adherence to this ideal of a dark lord. This is shortly before he is defeated through an effort of co-operation and caregiving by the movie's protagonists.

There is increasing critical awareness of this form of toxic masculinity within popular media, but much of this discourse is still couched in terms that leaves room for denial, rather than clear support for a cultural dialogue. Kilgrave's presentation, however, leaves less ambiguity as to the creators' intent in adding a villain that matches these characteristics.

Kilgrave vs. Killgrave: Comparing Versions of Villainy

Jessica Jones's Kilgrave at first glance does not resemble these other villains: he is clearly an adult, not an arrested adolescent like Kylo or Rowan. His suave appearance and fondness for suits do not read so immediately as markers of geekdom, and his status as a fan is not so clearly marked. However, his association with toxic masculinity is even stronger, and reflects a dramatic change from his origin in the comics. Kilgrave's reimagining for streaming media includes several dramatic departures from his comic book predecessor, including the replacement of his trademark purple skin with more subtle, purple-themed accessories, and the iconic casting of *Doctor Who*'s David Tennant. These changes play an important part in reinventing Kilgrave as a personification of the entitled, angry fanboy: throughout the series, Kilgrave's powers are focused on the mental manipulation and emotional abuse of a thoroughly modern predator simultaneously unable to see himself as the villain of the story.

The original Killgrave of the comics is known as Purple Man. He is a far cry from the suave character portrayed by David Tennant: most notably, he is actually a deep shade of purple, which stands out in a crowd and reflects the damage he sustained from his exposure to the same chemicals that gave him his mind-control powers. The comic version also goes by a less subtle name (Killgrave, with two *l*s), and includes a horrific rape storyline in which he forces a woman he meets and takes a fancy to, Melanie, to marry him. They have a daughter, Kara Killgrave, who becomes a super girl who goes by several names, including Purple Girl, Purple Woman, and the apt Persuasion. In her first appearance—*Alpha Flight* vol. 1, no. 41 (Mantlo 1986)—a flashback shows the circumstances of Kara's birth and Melanie's horror when she realizes the powers have passed to her daughter after Killgrave released her from his mental hold. While Melanie's trauma and fear over Killgrave's potential return in their lives is occasionally shown, it is not emphasized in the narrative. Killgrave's actions are portrayed as no worse than any other form of villainy.

In *Alias*, the Purple Man's perversions and abuse are explored more fully through his relationship with Jessica Jones. However, the story unfolds very differently from the Netflix adaptation: as the superhero Jewel, Jessica Jones is under Purple Man's thrall, and he sends her to kill Daredevil for him. However, the Avengers stop her, and Jean Gray implants a psychic control to allow Jessica Jones to resist Purple Man in the future. Unlike the Netflix version, Jones is now aware she can resist, and still decides to leave behind her previous life to become a private investigator rather than remain a superhero. She fights Purple Man later, but does not kill him, and Purple Man continues to be a threat through her relationship with Luke Cage and in a number of later storylines. *Alias* does not revolve around her relationship to Purple Man: only one section of the series, the Purple Man storyline (depicted in nos. 24–8), involves the confrontation.

Killgrave makes appearances in a few other adaptations of Marvel narratives, including an episode of *The Avengers: Earth's Mightiest Heroes* (2010–12). In the 2012 episode "Emperor Stark" (ep. 2.19), Killgrave possesses Tony Stark, declaring, "For so long, I've been able to take anything I wanted. But I wasn't enough. I should have been able to rule the world with my power! And through you, Stark, that's exactly what I'm doing" (Kirkland 2012). The adaptation puts a similar emphasis on Killgrave's compelling voice as the new Netflix series, calling on voice actor Brent Spiner (better known as Data from *Star Trek: Next Generation* [1987–94]) to play the role. The episode downplays the sexual nature of Killgrave's compulsion, but keeps the emphasis on self-hatred and the potential for devastating trauma in the aftermath:

Purple Man: I want you to feel this. I want you to know exactly what I'm making you do!

[Iron Man turns his repulsor on Cap but tries to stop himself from using it]

Purple Man: You're mine, Stark, forever! No matter how hard you resist you'll never be free! The most you'll ever be able to do is wiggle your finger when I'm next to you! Now finish him! (ep. 2.19, "Emperor Stark")

Rather than embodying hyper-masculine tropes, Kilgrave in *Jessica Jones* represents a different breed of toxic geek masculinity. And the directors of the series have chosen the right actor to play this part. David Tennant is not only a skilled actor but one who is immediately recognizable as one of the big faces in geek fandom. Tennant's portrayal of the Doctor in the long-running series *Doctor Who* (1963–89, 2005–present) helped to bring that show worldwide success after its 2005 relaunch. Tennant himself is acknowledged by his peers for the unique perspective he often brings to his characters. Commenting on Tennant's work as an actor, Russell T. Davies, former *Doctor Who* showrunner, says, "I think what sets him apart from just about every other man on the screen, actually, is a lack of boring machismo with him. He skates over stuff, he dances over stuff, he's so nimble and light and clever" (National Television Awards 2015). Although Davies is not talking here about Tennant's acting in *Jessica Jones*, it is noticeable that when casting for the role of Kilgrave, the directors of the series selected someone who presents a very different type of masculinity.

The version of Kilgrave depicted in *The Avengers: Earth's Mightiest Heroes* sets the formula for Tennant's performance in *Jessica Jones*, but the latter character is decidedly updated for a different era. The presentation for the Netflix series is meant to blend in more subtly with the universe that the creators of the *Jessica Jones* series were building. As Tennant describes it, "This iteration of him . . . you wouldn't notice him walking down the street. He's very sharply dressed, but beyond that there's . . . nothing to give away what is ticking inside" (*Digital Spy* 2015). Building on the more recognizably human nature of the villain within the series, the characteristics that were chosen for Tennant's performance add further subtlety to the character. The Kilgrave of *Jessica Jones* is explicitly a fanboy. Indeed, at one point, in response to Jessica's question about whether he seeks to model himself on the *Star Wars* character Obi-Wan Kenobi, Kilgrave answers in the affirmative, adding, "But cooler" (ep. 1.08, "AKA WWJD"). He enjoys having others see and appreciate the knowledge that he has cultivated. To him, Jessica is important for reflecting his worth at knowing this back to him in a positive light. Additionally, it allows him the ability to define his own identity and worth by then building on a positive impression of the fan character.

The show represents the relationship between Kilgrave and Jessica as being necessary for the villain to survive as a person. Kilgrave suggests that he is in desperate need of Jessica to serve as his conscience: "I can't be a hero without you," he says. Without her there to act as a mirror, he quickly loses control of his own actions and his sense of self. *Jessica Jones* even suggests that Kilgrave believes that he is in a love story:

Jessica Jones: You have been ruining my life—

Kilgrave: You didn't have a life.

Jessica Jones: . . . as a demented declaration of love?

Kilgrave: No! Obviously, I was trying . . . to show you what I see. That I'm the only one who matches you. Who challenges you. Who'll do anything for you. (ep. 1.07, "AKA Top Shelf Perverts")

His romantic declarations are perverse but seem sincere: "You were the first person I ever wanted that walked away from me. You made me feel something I never felt before. Yearning. I actually missed you" (ep. 1.07, "AKA Top Shelf Perverts").

One thing that remains salient about these interpretations of Kilgrave's character is his inability to see people beyond the realm of things that will help or hinder his personal goals. People serve as chess pieces used to advance his desires in the physical realm, or as emotional mirrors to reflect what he sees as his strengths back at him with a sheen of admiration he clearly desires. Tennant, in a promotional tour for the show's release, talked to Seth Meyers about Kilgrave's power and how that shapes the character's psychology:

He doesn't think he's a villain. No. . . . He's got this thing where, from childhood, anything he says becomes fact. So he has no way of knowing what's appropriate and what isn't. . . . Clearly he has done some pretty reprehensible things. But he doesn't understand that. He's locked in the curse of his own ability. (*Late Night with Seth Meyers* 2015)

This viewpoint helps to humanize the main villain, something rare in many comic book stories. Unlike the older Marvel villains, who could be defeated in an epic fight scene, the new villains are more like regular people. They might not act in ways that the audience considers appropriate, but they also do not deserve simple physical abuse because of their actions. This leads to a more nuanced engagement with what Kilgrave has done and what could be considered appropriate responses to his actions.

Reading Kilgrave as Men's Rights Activist

When *Jessica Jones* arrived on the scene, it followed in the wake of several controversies surrounding geek masculinity. These conflicts—such as Gamergate and Sad Rabid Puppies—centred on perceived ownership of geek content in the face of its growing mainstream popularity and the increasing visibility of diverse voices among both fans and authors. Similar online fights have emerged cyclically over the last ten years as geek-centred media has become accepted in the mainstream entertainment market and as Internet-enabled platforms have allowed for the formation of identity-based sub-communities focused on these media products (e.g., sites for feminist nerds, queer *Star Trek* fans, etc.). Common themes can be traced among these various conflicts, many of them tied to similar movements in the offline world, such as the rise of men's rights activism. In particular, the efforts of diverse authors and fans to "destroy" the presence of traditionally powerful social groups are invoked by many of these movements to support their arguments and tactics and to defend against the backlash that results from their actions. These are all themes that the writers of *Jessica Jones* have included and analyzed within the narrative arc of Kilgrave and Jessica's relationship.

One notable thing about *Jessica Jones* is its positioning in the timeline of these real-world events. Unlike the larger, big-budget movie presentations of the MCU, *Jessica Jones* allows for a more niche and overtly political discussion of present cultural tensions. The show's debut in 2015 allowed the creators to engage in social commentary within the framework of the show. As one writer put it, "Jessica Jones is our first identifiably post-Gamergate thriller" (Chu

2015). The reduced need to perform like a blockbuster movie meant that the show could delve into topics that were currently impacting members of the Marvel fandom and comment upon their morality and the impact they may have upon the lives of fans.

Through the lens of a serial drama, the writers could deconstruct the political conflicts happening within nerd communities and look at the motivations behind different factions' behaviour. Viewed in this context, Kilgrave presents an excellent character study of the type of mentality that can arise within geek spaces and lashes out in the type of gatekeeping and control seen during the events that preceded the show's creation. As Chu says about Kilgrave's status as nerd power fantasy: "Kilgrave's power is an analog, low-tech, 'meatspace' version of a power that some men in the Gamergate crowd seem to dream of having: the power to be anyone, be anywhere, and do anything without social repercussions. It's a power that, in our world, can be acquired by any determined troll with basic computer skills and an Internet connection" (2015). Kilgrave has the ability to be immediately recognized as a somebody. He is important and powerful and will receive the accolades that he feels he is due. But with this power, he also does not have to face the negative consequences of his actions. In a similar way, participation in online harassment provides the abuser with a sense of power and control over what their target does both on- and offline.

The character of Kilgrave has created an elaborate story about his life, and within it he has set Jessica up as both his inevitable love interest and his main antagonist. The writers were quite clever in having Kilgrave draw upon meta-commentary related to popular culture to serve as the base for his own story. As Nussbaum notes about Kilgrave's self-narrative in relation to Jessica,

> It's a particularly effective form of gaslighting, since he has cast her in a popular narrative, one that shows up in many forms these days, in books and movies, and particularly in stories aimed at and embraced by female audiences. Is it really such a reach for Kilgrave to insist that Jessica will succumb to him in the end? Tweak Kilgrave's banter, and he'd be a wealthy vampire who desires Jessica above any other woman, a man who is literally irresistible, as in "Twilight." Wrench it again, and they'd be role-playing "Fifty Shades of Grey." (Nussbaum 2015)

Of interest here is not just the fact that Kilgrave draws upon these stories for inspiration, but also his insistence that he is really doing what is best for Jessica. It allows him to cast himself as the selfless victim if his advances are unappreciated by his target. He is giving her everything that popular culture says a woman really desires in life and love. Any rejection of him or his advances can be used to paint Jessica as heartless or cruel since she is ignoring the sacrifices Kilgrave has made.

While the writers did a thorough job of dressing Kilgrave in the signifiers that would lead to a sympathetic portrayal in other media, they do not support his decisions within the narrative structure, and indeed make efforts to show the monstrous impacts of his choices:

> Throughout *Jessica Jones*, the audience is invited to sympathize with the survivors of Kilgrave's abuse, not with Kilgrave. Other than a couple short moments in which Kilgrave explains that he believes himself to have been abused and wronged, the majority of the show focuses on his crimes against others—about which Kilgrave feels zero remorse. We learn about these survivors' lives and perspectives; we see their support groups, their struggles. We don't see exploitative or romanticized depictions of rape or abuse; the show seems to have made the intentional choice not to display those scenes, focusing instead on the aftermath felt by the survivors. (Myers 2015)

This narrative rejection of Kilgrave as a sympathetic figure is a crucial counterpoint to the typical narratives of rape culture in popular media, where accused rapists (such as the infamous Brock Turner, who served a short sentence after raping an unconscious woman) are more likely to be shown in smiling swim team photos and graduation gowns than in mug shots, and where questions focus on their futures and lives rather than on the trauma and suffering of their victims (Zutter 2015). Or, indeed, the alternative, which plays up the vulgarity of the trauma that occurs to titillate audiences rather than express the horror of such actions.

Part of what makes Kilgrave such an intriguing villain is the inescapable nature of his interactions with Jessica. Using his abilities, he is able to integrate himself into her surroundings and habits such that, even if he is not seen by her, he is nearby. The show portrays this beautifully in the first few episodes by having Kilgrave use those around Jessica to photograph her without her knowing. For the audience, this begins the conflict between the two by establishing both an existing history between the characters as well as Kilgrave's nebulous presence within Jessica's life. "But *Jessica Jones* isn't just about a survivor getting retribution for her rapist's crimes; it also presents us with her rapist, over and over, and his belief that he did nothing wrong" (Zutter 2015). With each interaction, Kilgrave refuses to show real awareness or growth regarding his relationship with Jones. Her responses are like those of real-world victims of abuse and harassment: she is looking to appease her attacker and take back some small measure of control over her life.

Kilgrave's deeply disturbing monologue in the final episode of the season suggests his need to be desired and to affirm his value, which goes hand in hand with his desire to see Jessica suffer:

> Dear God, I would do anything to see the look on her face when she realizes she's helpless. I'd make her want me, then reject her. Devastate her over and over and over until she wants to die. . . . No, I won't give her that, either. She'd wither away like someone dying of thirst or starvation. Be a certain ring of hell, designed specially for her. . . . Or maybe I'll just kill her. (ep. 1.13, "AKA Smile")

Kilgrave's fixation on her, his replaying in his mind her torture and suffering, is a direct acknowledgement of his desire for control over her. To be able to rescind momentarily her pain or potential death, only to watch her suffer again and again at his whim, is central to how he sees himself. It is a nod to the power that he has while still framing the entire relationship as a result of her actions. It allows him to paint himself as the victim of a cruel woman who refused to acknowledge his personal needs.

Conclusion

The move within popular media to begin criticizing the negative consequences of male entitlement, and a portrayal of how that entitlement can play out in different subgroups, represents an opportunity for change within fan spaces. From Kilgrave's development as a character across the various Marvel media properties to his deliberate presentation in the *Jessica Jones* series, the audience is meant to understand the changing nature and threat that he represents, and to learn to identify those habits within their own environment.

Kilgrave represents some of the most toxic aspects of male entitlement and privilege found within geek and online communities. The particular characteristics he exhibits—his need to control Jessica, the nebulous nature of his presence in her life, his portrayal of himself as the aggrieved party—are all instantly recognizable as themes found in the different hate movements that have arisen within fan communities. While he is the villain of the story, he is not portrayed as totally heartless. Overall, his development shows how he could potentially make changes to improve himself and grow beyond the limitations of his current path. The show's creators allow for a clear damnation of Kilgrave's actions while still leaving open a chance for hope. In this portrayal, Kilgrave is not just the embodiment of entitlement—he is also something of a moral lesson, trying to show others the potential consequences of their harmful tactics.

The show does not let Jessica off lightly in the moral department either. "Ironically, Jones is only able to overcome Kilgrave by embracing her similarities to him, setting up an elaborate sting in the finale that is predicated on understanding his dark mental workings and being willing to sacrifice innocent people to his machinations" (Thury n.d., 6). Jessica herself even acknowledges the darkness of her actions: "They say everyone's born a hero. But if you let it, life will push you over the line until you're the villain. Problem is, you don't always know that you've crossed that line" (ep. 1.13, "AKA Smile"). However, when Jessica ultimately snaps Kilgrave's neck, we cannot help but see this as a moment of victory, as she throws his (and untold numbers of street harassers') favourite line in his face: "Smile." While the show is significantly more sympathetic to Jessica's struggles as a victim, it also warns against using the same tactics against your opponents. The show presents Jessica with the same chances to rise above while cautioning the audience to take a more fruitful path.

References

TMS Contributors. 2016. "Resistance, Caring, & 'Mask'ulinity: The Feminist Message of the Dudes in *The Force Awakens*." *Mary Sue*, January 19, 2016. http://www.themarysue.com/masculinity-the-force-awakens/.

Brown, Jeffrey A. 2016. *The Modern Superhero in Film and Television: Popular Genre and American Culture*. New York: Routledge.

Chu, Arthur. 2015. "Marvel's Jessica Jones and Gamergate: How the Netflix Series Absorbed the Anxieties of the Online Movement." *Slate*, November 24, 2015. http://www.slate.com/articles/arts/television/2015/11/marvel_s_jessica_jones_and_gamergate_how_the_netflix_series_absorbed_the.html.

Digital Spy. 2015. "David Tennant 'I'd Never Heard of Jessica Jones!'" YouTube, November 11, 2015. https://www.youtube.com/watch?v=HXBTg5XAVSU.

Hickey, Walt. 2016. "'Ghostbusters' Is a Perfect Example of How Internet Movie Ratings Are Broken." *FiveThirtyEight*, July 14, 2016. https://fivethirtyeight.com/features/ghostbusters-is-a-perfect-example-of-how-internet-ratings-are-broken/.

Hutchinson, Sean. 2016. "Why the $10-Billion Marvel Cinematic Universe Can't Be Killed." *Inverse*, May 16, 2016. https://www.inverse.com/article/15723-why-the-10-billion-marvel-cinematic-universe-can-t-be-killed.

Kirkland, Boyd, dir. 2012. *The Avengers: Earth's Mightiest Heroes*. Season 2, episode 19, "Emperor Stark." Aired September 16, 2012.

Late Night with Seth Meyers. 2015. "David Tennant Talks Playing Jessica Jones' Charming Villain." YouTube, November 24, 2015. https://www.youtube.com/watch?v=vlq_c9czohc.

Mantlo, Bill. 1986. "It's Not Easy Being Purple." *Alpha Flight* 1, no. 41. New York: Marvel Worldwide.

McGrath, Derek. 2015. "Some Assembly Required: Joss Whedon's Bridging of Masculinities in Marvel Films' *The Avengers*." In *Screening Images of American Masculinity in the Age of Postfeminism*, edited by Elizabeth Abele and John. A. Gronbeck-Tedesco, 135–54. London: Lexington Books.

Myers, Maddy. 2015. "Let's Talk about the Fandom for Kilgrave." *Mary Sue*, December 2, 2015. http://www.themarysue.com/kilgrave-fandom/.

National Television Awards. "David Tennant's NTA Special Recognition—His Reaction." YouTube, March 12, 2015. https://www.youtube.com/watch?v=Li_WIjv53pI&index=2&list=RDvlq_c9czohc.

Nussbaum, Emily. 2015. "Graphic, Novel." *New Yorker*, December 21 and 28, 2015. http://www.newyorker.com/magazine/2015/12/21/graphic-novel-on-television-emily-nussbaum.

Thury, Eva M. n.d. "Marvel's Jessica Jones as a Female Trickster: Reformulating the Contemporary Superhero." Accessed arch 29, 2024. https://www.yumpu.com/en/document/view/57778165/thury eva-super2-dpaper.

Zutter, Natalie. 2015. "What Rape Apologists Need to Learn from Jessica Jones." *Reactor*, December 1, 2015. http://www.tor.com/2015/12/01/jessica-jones-kilgrave-consent-rape-culture/comment-page-1/.

Undeniably Charming, Undeniably Wicked, and Our Shameful Kilgrave Crush

Mary Grace Lao

In a 2015 *Yahoo! News* article about *Jessica Jones*, Mookie Loughran writes, "As the manipulative villain of *Marvel's Jessica Jones*, Kilgrave's wish is your command. No really, he's a master of mind control. On paper, he's undeniably wicked, but in person, he can be undeniably, well, charming." Loughran's "Seven Stages of Your Shameful Kilgrave Crush" outlined the mixed feelings that fans (likely cis-heterosexual women) are apt to experience in the following order: disgust, curiosity, swooning, hope, pity, anger, acceptance. The oscillation between feelings of disgust and curiosity, hope and anger, alludes to a dissonance that the audience experiences, jumping between Kilgrave as sociopathic serial killer and rapist and Kilgrave as misunderstood but charming villain. Loughran argues that by the end of season 1 "Kilgrave's hold over you has worn off. You're exhausted from trying to make this relationship work. You don't root for him on the dock during his last twisted attempt to make Jessica love him, and you're relieved when it's finally over." The discussion surrounding fans' fascination with Kilgrave unsurprisingly was met with backlash, and with good reason, with some arguing that it romanticizes an abusive relationship.

Like Loughran, I experienced the same cycle of disgust, curiosity, swooning, hope, pity, anger, and acceptance as I watched Kilgrave. Numerous times throughout the first season, I asked myself, "Why am I so fascinated with this white man?" Guided by this question, this chapter examines how the Marvel Cinematic Universe (MCU) constructs the supervillain and how these constructions normalize heterosexual relationships between men and women that perpetuate a rape-supportive culture. I want to focus specifically on the following key terms that stood out as I read Loughran's article: "undeniably charming," "undeniably wicked," and "shame." Kilgrave's development as the "undeniably wicked" yet "charming" villain is reminiscent of some of the rape culture[1] narratives that continue to be perpetuated in mainstream popular culture, since his ability to manipulate his victims is invisible to law enforcement and the public. To understand shame, I look to affect theory, initially put forward by Silvan Tomkins (1962), who argues that affect is connected to our bodies, thoughts, and ideas. Building on this, Shelley Budgeon (2003) argues that rather than thinking of embodiment as a form of mind/body dualism, whereby women are seen only for their bodies and men for their minds, we should consider bodies "as *events* that are continually in the process of becoming—as multiplicities that are never just found but are made and remade" (50; emphasis in original). These emotions, Sara Ahmed (2014) argues, shape both individual and collective bodies, and in so doing create communities and affect political discussions. This culmination of "undeniably charming" and "undeniably wicked" leads to our feelings of shame that arise from watching David Tennant's portrayal of Kilgrave, which reminds us that women and survivors of sexual violence live with shame individually. In addition, we must also consider that this shared shame is a reflection of society's tendency to not believe women and survivors. Through a close reading comparing Kilgrave to similar "misunderstood" supervillains, I argue that creating a nuanced villain with a complex past addresses and challenges previous notions of who abusers and rapists are. The series brings to light important issues pertaining to the experiences of sexual violence survivors, and the raw emotional reactions to a villain, one whom others may not necessarily see as heinously evil or even "capable" of such an indiscretion.

Undeniably Charming

The MCU villains contrast with those of Marvel's parent company, Disney, whose classic villains have historically been portrayed as non-white with racially coded voices, while "good" characters tended to have American or British accents (Rabison 2016). By contrast, the MCU villains are portrayed in the more traditional Hollywood mould, with the charisma and good looks usually attributed to leading white men. The MCU also changed Kilgrave's origin story: In this series, he was formerly Kevin Thompson, who, as the result of a degenerative brain disease, was subject to painful treatment at the hands of his scientist parents. The treatment cured his disease but resulted in Kevin's mind-control abilities (ep. 1.09, "AKA Sin Bin"). This new origin story is markedly different from the comic book version, where Zebediah Killgrave is a Yugoslavian-born communist spy introduced to readers in *Daredevil* no. 4 (1964), which appeared at the height of the Cold War. Zebediah Killgrave was subject to experimental nerve gas, which gave him his powers and his purple skin. Killgrave's Yugoslavian background and his purple skin fed into the fears many Americans had of the communist other at that time. Netflix's new origin story sets the stage for a British Kilgrave, replacing his purple skin with well-fitted, expensive purple suits and an affinity for fine dining. Tennant's portrayal of Kilgrave reflects similarities with his portrayal of the Tenth Doctor of the BBC's *Doctor Who* series, including adopting the same English accent, an accent that Lalwani, Twin, and Li (2005) argue is seen as more professional, affluent, and credible.

Kilgrave's characterization as charming, affluent, and credible perpetuates the rape-culture discourse of who constitutes an abuser and a rapist. This rhetoric is salient in light of #MeToo, where the question of credibility often falls on the victims and survivors rather than the perpetrator. For example, Brock Turner, who raped an unconscious woman behind a dumpster in January 2015, is a prime example of white male privilege: affluent thanks to his family's fortune, a (former) student at Stanford University, and an athlete and one-time Olympic hopeful. Julie Sprankles (2016) of *Bustle* wrote that various news headlines "focus on his accomplishments prior to his actions . . . which have no bearing on his actions that night," framing Turner as, for example, an "all-American swimmer" rather than an accused rapist during his trial. CBC's Lauren O'Neill (2016) argues that the way Turner was treated by the press would be different had he been Black, and she highlights the various Twitter users who criticized the press for posting his yearbook picture rather than a mug shot.

In addition to Kilgrave's changed origin story, the audience also sees, if only briefly, that he had the ability to be rehabilitated. We see this as he looks on uncomfortably when Jessica watches a video clip of his parents subjecting him to experimental treatments as a child (ep. 1.08, "AKA WWJD?"). This initial glimpse into his traumatic past gives Jessica the idea that Kilgrave may not be an inherently evil person, and perhaps even has the potential to be a hero. In episode 1.08 ("AKA WWJD"), Jessica tries to convince Kilgrave that he is not an evil person, and she tries to get him "to do the hero thing." Jessica brings him to the scene of a domestic dispute they saw on television with the hope that Kilgrave would use his powers for good and intervene without causing any deaths. Even Kilgrave seemed surprised at how good he felt upon returning to Jessica's childhood home, saying, "The look on that woman's face, the genuine awe and gratitude for me. Is that why you did the whole superhero thing?" The tone in which Kilgrave asks this question sounds positive and seemingly innocent.

This reimagining of Kilgrave's origins follows the MCU's tradition of misunderstood villains, generally played by suave British men. For example, in *Marvel's Thor* (2011), Loki (played by Tom Hiddleston), the adopted son of Odin, eventually falls from grace as a prince of Asgard upon discovering that he is a descendant of Laufey, the king of the Frost Giants of Jotunheim. The audience is meant to feel empathy for Loki, who had so much self-hatred as an outsider in Asgard that he sought to destroy a realm into which he had been welcomed into. Confronted with both Kilgrave and Loki, the audience feels a level of relatability, as both are misunderstood by their parents and both exhibit a pre-existing condition that made them different. In that sense, they became villains as a result of their circumstances.

The redemption narrative was also evident in Brock Turner's trial, at which his father, Dan Turner, presented a letter on behalf of his son. The letter pleaded for leniency, focusing on the accused's childhood aspirations in an attempt to frame him as someone who is remorseful for his actions. The letter claimed that Turner will be "deeply altered forever . . . for 20 minutes of action" (quoted in Gray 2016). Dan Turner, along with his letter, were heavily criticized as a prime example of rape culture (Gray 2016). As various people have pointed out on social media, Turner's past behaviour, coupled with his portrayal of himself as a non-violent individual, inherently overshadowed and erased the violent nature of his crime. Similarly, Dan Turner's claim that his son will be "deeply altered forever" suggests that this one action should not carry any consequences for his son, essentially framing rape as a mere misdeed or mistake—the "boys will be boys" excuse. In a similar vein, portraying Kilgrave's particularly traumatic childhood as the reason for his nefarious actions focuses on the needs of the rapist, rather than those of the survivors and victims of rape. It is therefore a form of gaslighting, as it reinforces the rapist and abuser as inherently good, despite a few "misdeeds."

Undeniably Wicked

The construction of the villain works in tandem with the development of the hero/heroine. In the comic book canon, the supervillain serves as a foil to the superhero, and their respective roles are more explicit. For example, the relationship between Professor Charles Xavier and Magneto in the *X-Men* series makes it clear that the traits evident in one are absent in the other. Although they are long-time friends who advocate for mutant rights, their approaches to this shared goal are markedly different. While Professor X seeks to create an allyship between mutants and non-mutants through non-violent means, Magneto believes that mutants must be allowed to live in peace "by any means necessary" (Singer 2000), even if that means destroying humans or anyone Magneto sees as a threat to mutants. Magneto's violent approach is undeniably wicked, and the trail of harm that ensues can be traced directly to him.

In *Jessica Jones*, the audience is made aware that Kilgrave is an evil individual, but we only see snippets of his wickedness throughout the first season. As Andrew Smith (2013) writes, "For many arch-villains, a hero is someone onto whom they can project their failures or who can be used as an excuse for less-than-meritorious actions" (104). Robin Rosenberg (2013) calls this kind of villain the vengeful villain: "the thwarted criminal whose actions stem from a personal vendetta" (108). We learn that, while Jessica had been purposely avoiding any confrontation with Kilgrave at the start of the series, Kilgrave had in fact been tracking her. In the course of that pursuit, Kilgrave leaves a trail of destruction, manipulating innocent people so that he can find Jessica. We see this at the police station, where Kilgrave forces the officers to point their guns at each other. While Jessica makes it clear that her relationship with Kilgrave was abusive, Kilgrave believed he was doing this out of love: "no, obviously, I was trying to show you what I see. That I'm the only one who matches you, who challenges you, who will do anything for you" (ep. 1.07, "AKA Top Shelf Perverts").

We see this confusion of love and dependence as Kilgrave's main reason for wanting to find Jessica. Upon looking more closely at his attempt at "the superhero thing" (ep. 1.08, "AKA WWJD"), we see not only Kilgrave's inability to differentiate between right and wrong, but also that his intentions are misguided and selfish. In this scene, Jessica and Kilgrave go to a family's house where the father, Chuck, is holding his family hostage. Jessica manages to get Chuck's family out of the house to prevent any injuries or casualties. Once the rest of Chuck's family is safe, Kilgrave proceeds to try and convince him to "put the barrel of the gun into [his] mouth." While Jessica insists that they cannot kill him, Kilgrave justifies it by saying that "the man's clearly insane. He is never gonna be a productive member of society," even calling him a burden to taxpayers should he go to prison. Eventually, Kilgrave follows Jessica's orders by convincing Chuck to turn himself in to the police, albeit grudgingly. Although Jessica herself is a reluctant superhero, she is still bound by morality and a responsibility to protect the vulnerable (see Stang's chapter in this collection). Kilgrave's inability to empathize with a man in distress, and his quick judgment of Chuck as never being a productive member of society, reflect his lack of morality and his unwillingness to take responsibility.

As mentioned earlier, Kilgrave seemed pleased with himself after seeing that the woman and children he saved were grateful for his actions, leaving us to feel some glimmer of hope that he could potentially be a good person. However, these feelings were immediately suppressed when he put the onus on Jessica to help him become a hero:

> Kilgrave: The look on that woman's face, the genuine awe and gratitude for me. Is that why you did the whole superhero thing?
>
> Jessica: I don't know.
>
> Kilgrave: Or was that about balancing the scales? All that survivor's guilt you carry around, because of—
>
> Jessica: It doesn't work like that.
>
> Kilgrave: Why not? You're so outraged by all the people I've affected. Do the moral maths. How many more lives do you think I'd have to save to get back to zero?
>
> Jessica: Saving someone doesn't mean un-killing someone else.
>
> Kilgrave: Well, even so, we should do this more often. Think of all the people we could help, all the crimes we could stop. We'd be a hell of a dynamic duo.
>
> Jessica: You don't need me to do that.

Kilgrave: Are you kidding me? That man almost blew his brains out, which I genuinely thought was the right thing to do. I can't be a hero without you.

Jessica: My God. You're right. (ep. 1.08, "AKA WWJD?")

Rosenberg (2013) calls this kind of villain the sadistic supervillain: one who "induce[s] the superhero to wrestle with his or her conscience about what can be sacrificed for the greater good" (111). A notable example includes the Joker (from *The Dark Knight* [2008]), who did not have any other motives behind his actions other than to wreak havoc and derive pleasure from the suffering of others. Like the Joker, Kilgrave uses the people around him for personal pleasure. Kilgrave's use of emotional blackmail makes Jessica (and the audience) realize that he will blame Jessica for any future evil deeds because he is unable to differentiate between right and wrong. This, in addition to the initial confrontation at the police station, indicates that while Kilgrave may not be using his superpowers to control Jessica, he remains in control of her by manipulating the people around her, making her choose between her own safety and the safety of innocent people, "to protect them. Not out of choice," as he says (ep. 1.07, "AKA Top Shelf Perverts).

Shame

Kilgrave, as both unbelievably charming and unbelievably wicked, plays into the ways in which white men are portrayed when it comes to issues of sexual violence. On the one hand, there is the invisible trauma: the trauma that survivors of sexual violence experience, but which is not necessarily visible to the rest of the world. It is only when others fall victim to Kilgrave's manipulation that they can finally empathize with Jessica and the other women in the series. On the other hand, there is the treatment of love as a form of control over women's bodies. The persistent myth that rape is a crime of passion rather than a crime of violence and power continues to circulate in public discourse. It is deeply embedded in our culture, where young girls are taught that boys who push them or pressure them do so because such behaviour comes from a place of love.

Recalling Loughran's claim that "Kilgrave's hold over you has worn off. You're exhausted from trying to make this relationship work. You don't root for him on the dock during his last twisted attempt to make Jessica love him, and you're relieved when it's finally over," it is worth asking, Why, then, do we feel shame? Perhaps the reason why it is shameful to watch or love Kilgrave in the way that fans of villains do is because we are not "supposed to like the villain." This experience of our shameful Kilgrave crush is one in which we recognize that it is wrong not in the sense of being a perpetrator, but as the viewer. Ahmed (2014) argues that emotions are less psychological states than the result of a shared set of social and cultural practices. Shame is an affective bodily experience that involve the deforming and re-forming of our bodily and social spaces (Ahmed 2014; Budgeon 2003), hence shame and identity "remain in a very dynamic relation to one another" (Sedgwick 2003, 36). For Ahmed, "If we feel shame, *we feel shame because we have failed to approximate 'an ideal' that has been given to us through the practice of love*" (2014, 106; italics in original). This "icky" feeling is in fact the feeling of shame itself, but we also feel it because Loughran "called us out," so to speak.

I am reminded of Janice Radway's *Reading the Romance* (1980), which analyzes the process whereby women sought out ideal romances to explore and understand the misogyny they experienced in the real world. In Radway's analysis, women who read romance novels in which the female heroines are put in positions of weakness do so because it echoed their real-world experience of weakness. Using Radway's analysis, we might also claim that the audience sees themselves in Jessica for similar reasons. We are meant to shoulder some of Jessica's invisible emotional labour. This strikes an all-too-common chord for women, whose own responsibilities when it comes to employment, house chores, caregiving, and providing emotional support for family and friends is often overshadowed by the effort and work of men. We are now simultaneously Jessica and ourselves: It is *our* relationship with Kilgrave and *our* purpose is to save him. *We* save him by giving men like him the benefit of the doubt as *we* attempt to convince ourselves that he is not inherently bad, but is merely reflecting his own childhood trauma and can therefore be reversed or rehabilitated. Here, I use *our* and *we* to refer not only to individuals composed of you or I, but to the audience and the bystanders as well.

Focusing on Loughran's keywords, "undeniably charming, "undeniably wicked," and "shame," I come back to my initial question: Why am I so fascinated with Kilgrave? I am fascinated because his portrayal mirrors what we often see in women's own daily lives, one that is inherent to a patriarchal society? Not only is Jessica herself forced to perform immense emotional labour when interacting with Kilgrave when he reappears in her life in season 1, but she continues to deal with the aftermath of killing Kilgrave in season 2, as she is haunted by him through her own guilt. This experience of guilt culminates in episode 2.11, "AKA Three Lives and Counting," in which Jessica is shown alone and curled up on the floor immediately after killing Dale, the correctional officer who had been abusing Alisa, her mother. Her internal voice says, "You killed him. He's dead. You took a life. You're going to jail. You have to run, he would've killed you. Can't hide. You have to take the blame" (Lynch 2018). All of this occurs as a purple light gradually shines on her face and her internal voice is eventually replaced by Kilgrave's. The purple light and Kilgrave's voice are symbolic of the control that he continues to have over her, even after his death. Eventually, Jessica begins to "see" and speak to Kilgrave, as if he is her conscience.

The killing of Kilgrave serves as a metaphor for the killing of an abusive relationship, and it is the survivor who must now deal with the aftermath. As the audience, we may not feel the shame that we initially felt in season 1, but we can now empathize with the guilt Jessica endures throughout season 2 as she questions whether she is becoming a monster. Like Jessica, the survivor goes through a similar experience after being subjected to the abuse and gaslighting not just of their abuser, but also of the police, friends, and family who are skeptical, as well as media images that blame them because of the way they dress and behave. Confronted on all sides, they begin to wonder if they are the ones who are at fault, if there is something wrong with them, or if they should have acted differently.

Chris Deis (2013) argues, "superhero genre stories are political commentary, and the relationships of the characters—the superhero and the supervillain in this case—are examples of how popular culture can inform readers and audiences about deeper questions regarding identity, values, and politics in a society" (97). Though Deis's claim is based on the notion that the superhero and supervillain are fixed and "real" categories, in *Jessica Jones*, as in real life, the question of what is and is not moral is not as clear-cut as other television or comic series might have us believe. This is *Jessica Jones*'s political commentary: it challenges the ways in which abuse and gender-based violence are depicted and normalized in popular culture. And it does so by evoking our feelings of shame. By making obvious our shameful Kilgrave crush, series creator Melissa Rosenberg challenges us to think about the ways we (as a collective society complete with cultural practices) create and reinforce the narrative that men who are charming, credible, and affluent would never be capable of emotionally and sexually abusive behaviour, and if they do exhibit such toxicity, it is simply a "one-time mistake." It is easier, after all, to picture rapists and abusers as people who deviate from the standard definition of the attractive, middle- or upper-class, cisgender, white heterosexual man. The shame we feel does not come from this Kilgrave crush, then; rather it is a shared shame stemming from our own tendencies to disbelieve women's stories of abuse and violence.

Acknowledgements

I would like to thank Steve Jankowski for providing feedback on an earlier draft of this chapter.

NOTE

1   Rape culture is defined by Buchwald, Fletcher, and Roth (1993) as that in which "both men and women assume that sexual violence is a fact of life, inevitable as death or taxes. This violence, however, is neither biologically nor divinely ordained" (vii).

References

Ahmed, Sara. 2014. *The Cultural Politics of Emotion*. Edinburgh: Edinburgh University Press.

Buchwald, Emilie, Pamela Fletcher, and Martha Roth, eds. 1993. *Transforming a Rape Culture*. Minneapolis, MN: Milkweed Editions.

Budgeon, Shelley. 2003. "Identity as an Embodied Event." *Body and Society* 9 (1): 35–55.

Deis, Chris. 2013. "The Subjective Politics of the Supervillain." In *What Is a Superhero?*, edited by Robin S. Rosenberg and Peter Coogan, 95–100. New York: Oxford University Press.

Gray, Emma. 2016. "This Letter from the Stanford Sex Offender's Dad Epitomizes Rape Culture." *HuffPost*, June 6, 2016. https://www.huffingtonpost.ca/entry/brock-turner-dad-letter-is-rape-culture-in-a-nutshell_n_57555bace4b0ed593f14cb30?ncid=other_twitter_cooo9wqtham&utm_campaign=share_twitter.

Lalwani, Ashok, May Lwin, and Kuah Leng Li. 2005. "Consumer Responses to English Accent Variations in Advertising." *Journal of Global Marketing* 18 (4): 143–65.

Loughran, Mookie. 2015. " 'Marvel's Jessica Jones': The 7 Stages of Your Shameful Kilgrave Crush." *Yahoo! News*, December 1, 2015. https://ca.news.yahoo.com/netflix-kilgrave-david-tennant-213413111.html.

Lynch, Jennifer, dir. 2018. "AKA Three Lives and Counting." *Marvel's Jessica Jones*. New York: Marvel Television and ABC Studios.

O'Neil, Lauren. 2016. "Status and Race in the Stanford Rape Case: Why Brock Turner's Mug Shot Matters." *CBC News*, June 11, 2016. https://www.cbc.ca/news/trending/brock-turner-mugshot-stanford-rape-case-images-sex-assault-1.3629147.

Rabison, Rebecca. 2016. "Deviance in Disney of Crime and the Magic Kingdom." In *Debating Disney: Pedagogical Perspectives on Commercial Cinema*, edited by Douglas Brode and Shea T. Brode, 199–210. Lanham, MD: Rowman and Littlefield.

Radway, Janice A. 1984. *Reading the Romance: Women, Patriarchy, and Popular Literature*. Chapel Hill: University of North Carolina Press.

Rosenberg, Robin S. 2013. "Sorting Out Villainy: A Typology of Villains and Their Effects on Superheroes." In *What Is a Superhero?*, edited by Robin S. Rosenberg and Peter Coogan, 107–11. New York: Oxford University Press.

Sedgwick, Eve Kosofsky. 2003. *Touching Feeling: Affect, Pedagogy, Performativity*. Durham, NC: Duke University Press.

Singer, Bryan, dir. 2000. *X-Men*. Hollywood, CA: 20th Century Fox.

Smith, Andrew. 2013. "Supervillains Who Need Superheroes (Are the Luckiest Villains in the World)." In *What Is a Superhero?* edited by Robin S. Rosenberg and Peter Coogan, 101–6. New York: Oxford University Press.

Sprankles, Julie. 2016. "These Brock Turner Headlines Are Beyond Tone Deaf." *Bustle*, June 6, 2016. https://www.bustle.com/articles/165164-8-brock-turner-headlines-that-totally-miss-the-point.

Tomkins, Silvan S. 1962. *Affect Imagery Consciousness*, vol. 1. New York: Springer.

PART 3

Surviving Trauma

Surviving Trauma

Pree Rehal

The third and final part of this collection looks at trauma, interpersonal relations, and race. Trauma narratives are a main theme in the *Jessica Jones* series; however, this section takes an interdisciplinary approach rather than one centred on trauma theory. Beginning with how trauma has been depicted in recent years, and the impacts of off-screen rape in *Jessica Jones*, chapter 12 dives into the ways in which trauma narratives are represented in the series. In chapter 10, Keira Obbard analyzes how abusive dynamics like rape impact characters in the long term, and how rape is demonstrated by its aftermath rather than its onscreen portrayal. Obbard inspects how Kilgrave continuously terrorizes Jessica after the fact through violations of consent and boundaries, while noting the way the series allows her to take control of her narrative even as trauma impacts her memory and Kilgrave continuously gaslights her. And how does our society stop serial rapists? The series gives us a non-carceral example that widens the narrative of trauma and rape in society.

Michelle Johnson uses Laban movement analysis (LMA) to unpack how trauma, gender performance, bodily movement, and somatic experiences are linked. Johnson explains that "LMA is strongly connected to the idea of personal style and expressivity, understanding that everyone has their own particular movement tendencies and that there are often deep connections between psychology and movement patterns." Johnson employs LMA concepts in order to create meaning with characters' bodily movement and to demonstrate how the series represents binary power relations, including between abuser and victim, masculine and feminine, attractive and unattractive, and before and after trauma.

Tracey Thomas delves into the significance of Jessica and Trish's friendship. Their sisterhood is driven by the platonic femme love they developed in childhood, and they continue to protect each other from their abusers, including Trish's mom and Kilgrave, in their adulthood. Thomas contrasts Jessica's superpowers and flawed heroism with Trish's natural heroic prowess. The chapters for this volume were originally developed between 2017 and 2020, and one of the major historical events of this period, also mentioned in the introduction to part 2, was #MeToo. As the movement gained virality in the interim period, its Black creator, Tarana Burke, was often left out of the picture. In this section about trauma, it feels necessary to acknowledge and highlight the work that Burke has been doing for over a decade. In her chapter, Thomas argues that "Whether it is 'saving' the other, or just being there, Jessica and Trish embody strong female protagonists who do not let their lives revolve around their past and/or male-driven traumas."

As Dreama G. Moon and Michelle A. Holling (2020) point out in " 'White Supremacy in Heels': (White) Feminism, White Supremacy, and Discursive Violence," "yet another example of (white) feminism's penchant for marginalizing women of color is the whitening of #MeToo and #TimesUp, evident in their popularization and visibility extended to white women's victimage. Only later was the founder of Me Too, Tarana Burke, a Black woman acknowledged, while testimonies of black and Latina actresses were ignored" (255). In Me Too International's first *Impact Report* (2019), Burke explains that she "set out to bring healing to the Black and Brown girls in my community while raising awareness about the trauma they faced, and the lack of protections made available to them" (3). That a Black movement, by and for Black women, was subsequently co-opted by white women is unsurprising and reminiscent of the ways that both academic and activist communities have been employing the buzzword "intersectionality" within feminist contexts. Crenshaw (1991) writes, "Although racism and sexism readily intersect in the lives of real people, they seldom do in feminist and antiracist practices" (1242), and she coined the term "intersectionality" to identify the dual violence faced by Black women experiencing intimate-partner violence and violence from police.

Sorouja Moll reminds us in her chapter that women have always been discredited as she unpacks the etymology of the word "hysteria" and the ways it has been weaponized against women both historically and in the present-day, providing examples from US politics and the series itself. In chapter 14,

Pree Rehal and Caitlynn Fairbarns decode how the audience consumes rape and violations of consent within the series. This chapter extends beyond considerations of gender to also analyze racial violence through the vehicle of white feminism in *Jessica Jones*. Similar to Jessica Seymour in her chapter "From Devils to Milquetoast Little Man-Boys," Rehal and Fairbarns turn in the latter half of their contribution to Luke Cage, though here in an effort to unpack the impact of anti-Black racism and issues of consent on the show, rather than gender and Black masculinities.

Arun Jacob and Elizabeth DiEmanuele inspect place, space, and trauma in the series through the lens of urban revanchism. As a society, much of Turtle Island suffers from revanchism, a strategy that displaces the most oppressed: " 'Revanchism' means 'revenge,' but what marked the city of the late 1980s into the 1990s was not so much revenge as a broad-based vengefulness" (Mitchell quoted in Lawton 2018, 867). And theorist Neil Smith, who coined the term, argued that "the concept of the revanchist city has captured the tense relationship between the remaking of urban space via gentrification and the experiences of those social groups side-lined by such processes" (quoted in Lawton 2018, 867). Analyzing Jessica's domain and surroundings, Jacob and DiEmanuele thus ask, appropriately, "Who is more threatening to such an ideal than Jessica Jones, a woman who can lift cars, hold her own in a bar fight against a group of rugby players, and sleep in an apartment with a broken door, despite living in a densely populated, threatening city?"

References

Crenshaw, Kimberlé. 1991. "Mapping the Margins: Intersectionality, Identity Politics, and Violence against Women of Color." *Stanford Law Review* 43 (6): 1241–99.

Me Too International. 2019. *Me Too. Impact Report 2019.* https://metoomvmt.org/wp-content/uploads/2020/01/2019-12-09_MeToo_ImpactReport_VIEW_4.pdf.

Moon, Dreama G., and Michelle A. Holling. 2020. " 'White Supremacy in Heels': (White) Feminism, White Supremacy, and Discursive Violence." *Communication and Critical/Cultural Studies* 17 (2): 253–60.

Lawton, Philip. 2018. "Situating Revanchism in the Contemporary City." *City* 22 (5–6): 867–74.

"Tell Us Which One of Us Was Truly Violated": Disrupting Narratives of Trauma, Rape, and Consent

Kiera Obbard

In 2016, North American culture bore witness to unprecedented discussions of sexual assault and consent on social media, in news outlets, and in popular culture. From the portrayal of rape on shows such as *Game of Thrones* (2011–19), *Orange Is the New Black* (2013–19), and *Outlander* (2014–present), to major media coverage of the trials of Jian Ghomeshi and Brock Turner, social discussions of sexual assault—including what constitutes sexual assault and how it is portrayed in popular culture—have never been more relevant or necessary (Opam 2015). Against the backdrop of a post-feminist era in which "the media has become the key site for defining codes of sexual conduct" (McRobbie 2009), Western society is experiencing a resurgence of feminist discourse in popular culture, an increase in celebrities identifying as feminist, and a surge of online communities who hold the film and television industries accountable for their portrayals of rape. In the midst of these sexual assault trials and depictions of rape that make a spectacle of sexual assault, these communities encourage conversations about rape, consent, and trauma in society and in popular culture, and demand better from the industries providing popular entertainment. Situated within this cultural context is *Jessica Jones*, a Netflix original program that took the world by storm for its refusal to portray rape on screen and for appropriately addressing rape and rape culture in Western society (Opam 2015; Sarkeesian 2015; Young 2015). In the series, Jessica's rape is never shown—neither in the act nor in flash backs. Rather, the show focuses on how Jessica copes with life following her traumatic experiences.

In *Jessica Jones*, we first meet Jessica in a world she later describes as "after Kilgrave." Kilgrave, played by David Tennant, is a villainous man from Jessica's past who can control minds; when he meets Jessica, he becomes enthralled by her superhuman strength and takes control of her mind, forcing her into a relationship with him and, as we learn, raping her over and over again until she breaks free from his control. As a woman with superhuman strength, however, Jessica is not physically weaker than Kilgrave; rather, she is vulnerable to Kilgrave's power of mind control. Throughout the series, the show uses this initial disruption of normative conceptions of the limits of the human body to push the conversation beyond notions of "fighting back" to interrogate and question common narratives of trauma, victimization, and consent, and to create space for new conversations on trauma, rape, and victimhood in society. Additionally, through discussions of rape and trauma found within the series—in particular, in episodes 1.07, "AKA Top Shelf Perverts," and 1.08, "AKA WWJD?," with Kilgrave telling Jessica in the latter episode, "Watch this and tell us which one of us was truly violated!"—*Jessica Jones* creates space within which common narratives of trauma, consent, and violation in Western society can be critiqued, unpacked, and restructured. Ultimately, the representation of Jessica's body and Kilgrave's mind control, and the juxtaposition of Jessica's and Kilgrave's traumatic experiences, create space for discussions of consent (and consensual "grey areas"), trauma, and definitions of violation—contributing to a widening of cultural narratives and understandings of rape, consent and trauma in North America.

Jessica Jones: A Hard-Drinking, Short-Fused Mess of a Woman

When the audience first meets Jessica Jones, she is a heavy-drinking (arguably alcoholic) and short-tempered woman working as a private investigator at Alias Investigations, which she runs out of her home office. Jessica wears the same grungy clothes every day, she has no friends of note except Trish Walker—a child TV star whose mother adopted Jessica as a publicity stunt after Jessica's family died in a car crash—and she suffers from post-traumatic stress disorder (PTSD) as a result of being held captive and repeatedly raped by Kilgrave. Jessica sees hallucinations of Kilgrave on the subway and in her apartment; to calm herself during these traumatic flashbacks, she recites the street names surrounding her childhood home: "Birch Street, Higgins Drive, Cobalt Lane." Jessica repeats the phrase numerous times throughout the season. A coping technique provided to Jessica by a therapist she used to see, this is "a grounding mechanism that Jones relies on to pull her back to reality, to quell the trauma that still haunts her. Yet it is also a persistent reminder that she's a woman who has unwillingly come undone" (Edwards 2015). This depiction of Jessica's trauma and her attempts to survive each day show a refreshingly honest image of the long-term effects of sexual violence. Jessica drinks too much, she cannot sleep, and she experiences flashbacks, all harsh realities that many survivors of sexual assault must endure. Jessica is, as Luke Cage says, a "hard-drinking, short-fused mess of a woman" (ep. 1.06, "AKA You're a Winner!"). She is, however, a mess of a woman who possesses superhuman strength and who used to be a superhero.

The audience first witnesses Jessica's superhuman strength in the first episode, which occurs in the world "after Kilgrave." In the episode, Jeri Hogarth, a lawyer for whom Jessica works on a freelance basis, hires her to serve a summons to a strip club magnate named Spheeris. Jessica follows Spheeris as he leaves a club without his security guards and gets his attention by asking for directions, and then keeps him from leaving by lifting the back end of his car with one hand when he tries to drive away (ep. 1.01, "AKA Ladies' Night"). Jessica successfully serves Spheeris with his summons and even threatens him with her laser eyes (a power she does not actually possess). Within the first twenty minutes of the season, then, the audience is aware of Jessica's physical prowess and her ability to defend herself against cars, let alone predatory men. In contrast to centuries-long debates about evolutionary gender differences, and women's putative status as the physically (and mentally) weaker gender, Jessica Jones is a force to be reckoned with (Heyward, Johannes-Ellis, and Romer 1986; Miller et. al 1993). Further enforcing this point, Jessica lives alone in New York, often without a functioning door—something Hope Shlottman's father comments on when hiring Jessica to find Hope, who has been kidnapped by Kilgrave—and she is fully capable of defending herself and others.

When Kilgrave first meets Jessica, as depicted in a flashback, Jessica is using her superhuman strength to save Malcolm from a group of muggers (ep. 1.05, "AKA The Sandwich Saved Me"). The scene opens in the present day with Jessica stopping Malcolm's drug dealer from shooting him, and Malcolm yelling at Jessica, "You can't save me again." The scene fades into a flashback in which Jessica walks down the street and witnesses two muggers assaulting Malcolm while demanding his wallet. "Just end it, bro," the first mugger says.

"He saw our faces." Jessica intervenes by throwing the first mugger across the sidewalk, fighting off the second mugger, who is brandishing a knife, and then fighting off the first mugger again, who is now charging at her with a lead pipe (ep 1.05, "AKA The Sandwich Saved Me"). Jessica displays feats of immense strength in the scene as she throws one mugger over a car and the second one through a door of a nearby building.

Clearly, Jessica Jones is superhuman and quite possibly a superhero; most definitely, her body and her abilities do not conform to societal narratives and definitions of human bodies, let alone (argued to be weaker) female bodies. Even the category "superhuman" suggests that Jessica is something more than human. In season 2, her powers are revealed to have come from experiments conducted on her by IGH, a secret research laboratory and genetic technology clinic that conducts illegal human experimentation. Jessica Jones's body is a hybrid—part human, part genetic technological experimentation—and this hybridity places her body in a "grey area" in which she cannot be classified as entirely or only human. Jessica could be considered a cyborg, an identity that is "predicated on transgressed boundaries" such as those between human and superhuman (or, more traditionally, non-human) (Balsamo 1996, 32). The genetic experiments Jessica undergoes work to transgress not only the boundaries of the human body writ large, but also the boundaries of normative representations of female-gendered bodies more specifically. Instead of a woman who is physically weaker than (and thus succumbs to) her attacker, we are presented with a superhuman who could easily fight off Kilgrave in a physical altercation but who cannot fight off his mind control. Other than Kilgrave's ability to control her mind, Jessica's superhuman strength means she is not normally vulnerable to physical attacks by humans. Thus, Jessica's superhuman body transgresses boundaries and exists outside of normative narratives of the human body and female-gendered bodies.

Jessica's immense physical strength not only positions her as superhuman and outside normative narratives of female-gendered bodies, but it is also what first makes her attractive to Kilgrave. When Jessica attempts to check on Malcolm after she has fought off the muggers, Kilgrave appears in a scene flanked by three beautiful women. Kilgrave claps and commends Jessica on how amazing she is, commenting, "Here I am, just debating where to eat and then, bam! There you are, performing feats of heroism. . . . You're a vision, hair, skin . . . appalling sense of fashion, but that can be remedied. And underneath it all the power . . . just like me" (ep. 1.05, "AKA The Sandwich Saved

Me"). This scene, in which Kilgrave refers to Jessica as a collection of those parts of her body of which he approves (hair, skin), is the moment in which Jessica's violation begins. Kilgrave takes control of Jessica's mind and free will. The fact that Kilgrave has taken control of Jessica is evident in her changed disposition: she goes from fighting off two muggers to ensure the safety of a stranger, to snapping to Kilgrave's attention and going for Szechuan with him, leaving Malcolm lying injured in the street. Because of our prior knowledge of Jessica's physical strength, the audience can presume that if Kilgrave did not have Jessica under his powers of mind control, she could successfully fight him off, stay with Malcolm, and, later on, prevent Kilgrave from committing rape. This fact, in itself, works to disrupt the normative script of sexual violence and helps push the conversation past conceptions of what it means to fight back. The question then becomes not whether Jessica physically fought off her attacker—a question commonly posed to survivors of sexual assault— but whether Kilgrave's use of mind control and manipulation to force himself on Jessica *counts* as rape (Campbell and Raja 1999; Maier 2008). To Jessica, the answer is a resounding yes; to Kilgrave, the answer is not quite as clear.

Inside Kilgrave's Head: Top Shelf Perverts

In episode 1.07, "AKA Top Shelf Perverts," Jessica has become so traumatized by Kilgrave's relentless attacks on the people she cares about that she resolves to take matters into her own hands: she enters a police station and claims to have manually decapitated Ruben, one of the twins from her apartment complex. In truth, Kilgrave has forced Ruben to commit suicide out of jealousy because Ruben admitted his (unrequited) feelings for Jessica when he caught Kilgrave in Jessica's apartment. Now, Jessica is using Ruben's dead body to have herself committed to a supermax prison. Once inside, Jessica hopes to gain video evidence of Kilgrave using his powers to reach her through the multiple levels of security. However, Kilgrave, who has been monitoring Jessica's movements, comes to the station and uses his powers to prevent the police from arresting her. In their first face-to-face meeting in the series, Kilgrave tells Jessica he has only been trying to make her see the obvious: that their becoming a couple is inevitable.

> Kilgrave: I have absolutely no intention of controlling you. I want you to act on your own accord.

Jessica Jones: Act how? Suicide? Is that why you've been torturing me?

Kilgrave: [*Laughing*] Oh my god. Jessica, I knew you were insecure but that's just sad. Torturing you, why would I? I love you.

Jessica Jones: You have been ruining my life—

Kilgrave: You didn't have a life.

Jessica Jones: . . . as a demented declaration of love?

Kilgrave: No! Obviously, I was trying . . . to show you what I see. That I'm the only one who matches you. Who challenges you. Who'll do anything for you.

Jessica Jones: This is a sick joke. You have killed innocent people.

Kilgrave: Well, that . . . that . . . milquetoast little man-boy? He interrupted me while I was leaving you a present, which apparently you didn't even find. Come on! You cannot pretend he didn't irritate you too. I wanted to slap him after thirty seconds! [*Leans in close*] I know. I realize this will take time. But I'm going to prove it to you. (ep. 1.07, "AKA Top Shelf Perverts")

In this exchange, Kilgrave employs a number of tactics often used by perpetrators of domestic violence to control women. Firstly, by following Jessica's every move and appearing at the police station where she is trying to confess to murder, Kilgrave is displaying his significant power over Jessica: no matter where she goes, Kilgrave will be following closely behind. Secondly, by breaking into Jessica's apartment and leaving a "present" for her, he is engaging in stalking and harassment, and he violates the one place Jessica is supposed to feel secure—her home. Thirdly, by insisting that he is going to prove the inevitability of their love to Jessica, Kilgrave is reminding Jessica that he will pursue her until she succumbs to his advances. Kilgrave removes any prospect of a safe space for Jessica: he is everywhere, at all times, he can reach her through anyone, and he is relentless in his pursuit of her. As writer Arthur Chu notes, Kilgrave "may be just one man, but he can act through an army of servants, of which he has a limitless supply" (2015). Just like many women experiencing violence today, there are no safe spaces or safe people for Jessica Jones (Sarkeesian 2015). Anybody and everybody could be, as Jessica calls it, "Kilgraved."

Taking this one step further, by laughing at Jessica's analysis of the situation, calling her insecure, and questioning her recollection of events, Kilgrave engages in gaslighting. As Kate Abramson frames it, the term "gaslighting" refers to "a form of emotional manipulation in which the gaslighter tries (consciously or not) to induce in someone the sense that her reactions, perceptions, memories and/or beliefs are not just mistaken, but utterly without grounds" (2014, 2). Instead of genuinely listening to what Jessica has to say, Kilgrave dismisses her complaints as a sign of her own insecurity. In doing so, he absolves himself of any wrongdoing and places the blame for Jessica's trauma on her. The key message here is that if Jessica were only confident in herself, she would be able to see that Kilgrave's actions are declarations of love and not forms of abuse. This undermines Jessica's ability to think rationally and positions her not just as the token "madwoman in the attic" in need of a mental health practitioner, but also as someone who is ruled by her emotions and in need of Kilgrave's rationality to properly understand the situation (Munford and Waters 2014). Consciously or not, Kilgrave's dismissal of Jessica's account positions her as misremembering and misidentifying events, unjustifiably reading his actions as abusive, and failing to see that they are living in a love story—she just has not realized it quite yet.

Kilgrave's repositioning of events works to cast doubt on Jessica's memories of abuse—memories that are already subject to intense cultural scrutiny. Women who experience domestic violence or sexual violence are often called upon to accurately narrate their traumatic experiences, whether in the courts, to police, or to friends and family. As psychoanalytic clinician and feminist Janice Haaken notes, however, trauma can disrupt memory formation by way of "both intrusive remembering—often described as 'flashbacks'—and amnesia for overwhelming events, accompanied by emotional numbing" (1996, 1070). This disruption of memory formation is evident in Jessica's life. Indeed, the audience has witnessed Jessica's flashbacks throughout the series: apparitions of Kilgrave appear in Jessica's apartment, on the subway, following her wherever she goes. Trauma, and sexual violence in particular, can disrupt our experiences of past, present, and future; trauma "halts the flow of time, fractures the self, and punctures memory and language" (Schwab 2010, 42). The effects of trauma on memory formation often make narrating events in a chronological, linear manner difficult; for those who experience sexual violence, piecing together the details of the traumatic event can be challenging, to say the least (Brison 2002; Schwab 2010). In this scene, the audience already knows that Jessica is suffering from PTSD and flashbacks, suggesting some potential disruptions in her memory formation. By calling Jessica's memory into question, Kilgrave casts doubt on Jessica's version of events—did it really happen the way she claims, the audience is persuaded to question, or is Jessica simply so insecure she is unable to accurately read the situation, thus inflicting trauma on herself over nothing?

Not only does Kilgrave's repositioning of events cast doubt on Jessica's account, but the workings of trauma place Jessica's rape in a grey area—one that typically is not depicted on television and that is, paradoxically, a far more accurate depiction of many women's lived experiences of gendered violence. After all, Kilgrave is not a stranger hiding in a bush, and he does not use physical force to rape Jessica—both common tropes of rape portrayed on television; rather, he uses mind control to keep her in a relationship and to force himself on her. Furthermore, their interactions after Jessica breaks away from Kilgrave's control could complicate external understandings of what occurred between them. Indeed, as Emily Nussbaum, television critic for the *New Yorker*, states,

> Kilgrave raped Jessica, but since he did so using mind control, rather than physical force, the scenario emerges as a plastic, unsettling metaphor, a violation that produces a sense of collusion. Jessica hates Kilgrave, so why, when he requests a selfie of her smiling, does she send him one? She has strategic reasons. But to the world it looks as if she were flirting—and that's what he keeps telling her, too. (2015)

Jessica's decision to appease Kilgrave and send photos of herself, while done to save Malcolm, may cause the audience to question whether her claims about Kilgrave are legitimate. After all, why would Jessica send photos of herself to the man she claims raped her and forced her into a relationship? In the midst of these circumstances, the audience is left to ask: Did Kilgrave rape Jessica? Do their interactions count as rape, even if Kilgrave believes he truly loves Jessica?[1]

Returning to the police station scene, immediately following Kilgrave's claim about Jessica's insecurities, Jessica's depiction of Kilgrave and his actions are reaffirmed: a phone rings at a police officer's desk, sending Kilgrave into a rage and causing him to threaten that the next person whose phone rings will have to eat it. Having such a minor inconvenience set Kilgrave into a violent rage shows his inability to regulate his emotions and appropriately engage in social interactions, and it confirms for the audience that Kilgrave's perception of reality is not quite right. This positions Jessica's perception of Kilgrave and their interactions in a more believable light, leaving the audience wondering how Kilgrave sees his "relationship" with Jessica. Jessica then attempts to save the police officers, who are still pointing their guns at each other. Jessica agrees to go with Kilgrave, an offer he rejects, stating, "Oh please, I am new to love but I do know what it looks like! I do watch television!" (ep. 1.07, "AKA Top Shelf Perverts"). Here, it becomes evident that Kilgrave's understanding of love is grossly underdeveloped. If the audience can take Kilgrave's word as truth—that he has developed his perception of love based on what he has seen on television—then his actions in the series, although inappropriate, illegal, and twisted, begin to make sense. As children, we rely in part on television and other forms of media to create schemas and rules about the social and physical world around us (Strasburger and Wilson 2002). In the series, then, Kilgrave is simply mimicking the narratives of love that are displayed on television—and, unsurprisingly, they look eerily similar to women's accounts of rape and harassment. Indeed, as Nussbaum asks, "Is it really such a reach for Kilgrave to insist that Jessica will succumb to him in the end? Tweak Kilgrave's banter, and he'd be a wealthy vampire who desires Jessica above any other woman, a man who is literally irresistible, as in 'Twilight.' Wrench it again, and they'd be role-playing 'Fifty Shades of Grey' " (2015).

This mirroring of normative relationship narratives in popular culture is significant. First, it points to the importance of accurate depictions of healthy and unhealthy relationships in popular culture to the formation of societal narratives concerning love, consent, and sexual assault. Second, it identifies Kilgrave's perceptions of love, consent, and sexual assault as severely distorted by the television industry—an industry that, time and time again, packages stalking, harassment, and sexual assault as the epitome of romance (Brown 2009; Kahlor and Eastin 2011; Reenen 2014). In this moment, the audience comes to understand the vast differences between Kilgrave's and Jessica's accounts of their interactions. Just as many individuals in society do not identify their actions (or the actions of loved ones, beloved celebrities, etc.) as rape, Kilgrave is unable to categorize his actions as anything but declarations of true love. Kilgrave's continued erratic behaviour and obvious lack of mental or emotional development—particularly, his inability to display love and affection in a healthy manner—leads the audience to rethink Kilgrave's dismissal of Jessica's memory, and to begin to understand the depths to which Kilgrave will go to prove his love for Jessica and to disprove that he raped her.

Who Was Truly Violated—AKA WWJD?

If Jessica is, at first, stunned into silence by Kilgrave's distorted perception of reality in episode 7, she quickly recovers from this and continues to hold Kilgrave accountable for rape throughout the remainder of the season. In the next episode, Jessica, having found the "present" Kilgrave left at her apartment, has joined him at her childhood home (ep. 1.08, "AKA WWJD?"). Now legally owned by Kilgrave and refurbished to look exactly as it did when Jessica lived there with her now deceased family, Jessica's childhood home is the one remaining place that contained happy memories for her. Kilgrave has now violated even Jessica's trauma therapy as he physically infiltrates Birch Street, Higgins Drive, and Cobalt Lane—whose names provide the grounding mechanism Jessica uses to keep her trauma at bay. Left with no coping strategy for her PTSD, Jessica is forced to play her role in Kilgrave's twisted fantasy—recreating her happy memories with him—and yet, she still manages to maintain some semblance of power and control. When Jessica agrees to live with Kilgrave at her childhood home, she does so under one condition: that Kilgrave not touch her. Kilgrave breaks this condition by placing his hand on Jessica's one morning during breakfast, to which Jessica responds by yelling at Kilgrave not to touch her. In the scene that follows, Jessica repeatedly speaks out against Kilgrave's abuse and names it for what it is—rape:

> Kilgrave: Come on, Jessie—
>
> Jessica Jones: Don't call me that!
>
> Kilgrave: We used to do a lot more than just touch hands.
>
> Jessica Jones: Yeah, it's called rape. (ep. 1.08, "AKA WWJD?")

This strong and straightforward identification of Kilgrave's actions as rape removes any notion of a consensual grey area from their interactions. When

Jessica finally and actively names Kilgrave's actions as rape, she "invokes [the word "rape"] over and over, explaining to him that by revoking her ability to consent, he violated her in a profound way that he can never make up for, nullifying any 'kind treatment' during that time" (Young 2015). In this scene, Jessica again pushes the normative conversation beyond the concept of physically "fighting back" and holds Kilgrave accountable for removing her ability to fight back. Here, Jessica's words show the audience that the absence of a physical struggle is not the same as obtaining consent.

Although Jessica clearly identifies Kilgrave's actions as rape and directly speaks out about it, this is not enough to create change. In response to Jessica's assertion of rape, Kilgrave attempts to place the blame back on Jessica, to remove his culpability because of his kind treatment of Jessica, and to force her to misremember events to better suit his narrative:

> Kilgrave: What part of staying in five-star hotels, eating in all the best places, doing whatever the hell you wanted, is rape?
>
> Jessica: The part where I didn't want to do any of it! Not only did you physically rape me, but you violated every cell in my body and every thought in my goddamn head.
>
> Kilgrave: That's not what I was trying to do.
>
> Jessica: It doesn't matter what you were trying to do. You raped me, again and again and again.
>
> Kilgrave: How was I supposed to know?! Huh?! I never know if someone is doing what they want or what I tell them to!
>
> Jessica: Oh, poor you.
>
> Kilgrave: You have no idea, do you? I have to painstakingly choose every word I say. I once told a man to go screw himself. Can you even imagine? I didn't have this. A home, loving parents, a family.
>
> Jessica: You blame bad parenting? My parents died! You don't see me raping anyone!
>
> Kilgrave: I hate that word. (ep. 1.08, "AKA WWJD?")

By actively naming their sexual encounters as rape, despite Kilgrave's insistence that it was not his intention to rape her, Jessica reinforces the important nuances in the concept of consent. It is not enough for Kilgrave simply to not have *intended* to rape Jessica; Kilgrave needed to have Jessica's enthusiastic consent without means of manipulation, coercion, or mind control. Here, Jessica's refusal to let Kilgrave misname his actions and her rejection of his claims to ignorance regarding her consent makes "plain text of the subtext of rape culture" (Young 2015). It is not enough for Kilgrave to believe he did not rape Jessica; it is irrelevant that Kilgrave took Jessica to the best hotels and restaurants; it does not matter that Jessica did not physically fight back. Regardless of every other factor, Kilgrave raped Jessica.

When faced with this fact, Kilgrave attempts one more time to sidestep responsibility for his actions by blaming his parents for his behaviour. Kilgrave shows Jessica a video of his parents performing experimental procedures and cerebral spinal fluid extractions on him as a young child, stating, "Watch this and tell us which one of us was *truly* violated" (ep. 1.08, "AKA WWJD?"; emphasis added). In this dialogue, Kilgrave attempts to position his wrongdoing as a byproduct of his own experiences of trauma. He tells Jessica that, firstly, he never intended to rape her and, secondly, that because he was so traumatized as a child and grew up without parents, he never learned how to interact with others in a healthy manner. Indeed, as Kilgrave previously disclosed, his idea of love comes from television. If Kilgrave has only learned about love through television, which often includes problematic depictions of love, how is he supposed to understand complex concepts such as consent and rape? Thus, Kilgrave attempts to make excuses for his behaviour and to diminish Jessica's trauma—situated within expensive hotels and restaurants—in comparison with his own childhood trauma in a sterile, cold, and harsh-looking laboratory. The video clip showing the young Kilgrave being experimented on is horrifying and difficult to watch, and it certainly helps to humanize Kilgrave. It reminds us that "Kilgrave is a victim, too; his powers were forced on him by his parents . . . and he has no idea how to live life without making people do his bidding" (Opam 2015).

However, as Jessica notes, his childhood trauma does not remove Kilgrave's culpability for the trauma he inflicted on her—and it also does not diminish the severity of Jessica's trauma. Rather, despite Kilgrave's arguments, Jessica continues to hold Kilgrave accountable for his actions: no matter his intentions, the abuse he experienced as a child, or his ignorance on the subject, he removed Jessica's ability to consent and therefore raped her. By naming Kilgrave's actions as rape, by refusing to shy away from the word "rape" despite the negative connotations associated with it, *Jessica Jones* works to narrate Jessica's personal experience of rape in popular culture. This strategy has long been used by the movement against sexual violence, which "works to expose the reality of rape culture through the narration of women's experiences in the public sphere in speakouts and through the media" (Heberle 1996, 63). In one sense, this "speaking out," or what Alcoff and Gray refer to as the "strategic metaphor of 'breaking the silence,' " broadens the discourse about sexual violence and creates space for a more diversified public narrative of sexual violence (1993, 261). In this case, we as audience members add a narrative of rape due to mind control to our cultural understandings of rape, sexual assault, and consent. After all, with her superhuman strength, Jessica was not vulnerable to physical attacks from humans, and yet she was still raped by Kilgrave. Jessica's body does not conform to normative narratives of the female body; likewise, her traumatic experiences do not conform to normative narratives of rape in popular culture. By making room for different narratives of rape—ones that do not necessarily include a physical "fighting back" narrative, or the intention to commit rape—and by relentlessly identifying this particular experience of mental manipulation as rape, *Jessica Jones* creates space for further discussions of what counts as rape.

However, scholars have long noted the existence of a sort of double effect in which "survivor discourse has paradoxically appeared to have empowering effects even while it has in some cases unwittingly facilitated the recuperation of dominant discourses" (Alcoff and Gray 1993, 263). Despite Jessica's attempts to confront Kilgrave for his actions, to make clear that what he did counts as rape regardless of his intentions, her efforts are to no avail. Although the show doesn't fall into the trap of sensationalizing or exploiting survivor stories by showing graphic rape scenes, Jessica's act of speaking out is ultimately futile (Alcoff and Gray, 1993). As Alyssa Mercante states, "For Kilgrave, he saved Jessica and 'gave her everything she wanted.' For Jessica, Kilgrave mentally and physically raped her, invading her mind and holding it hostage" (2015), and this glaring discrepancy in their accounts is never settled. Thus, it would seem that the act of speaking out or narrating one's experience of sexual violence does not necessarily bring about the end of sexual violence (Alcoff and Gray 1993; Heberle 1996). For Kilgrave, Jessica's version of his actions is incompatible with his own view of himself. However, the larger significance of Jessica's speaking out lies within the plot of the show itself. In the end, *Jessica Jones* exactly mirrors Heberle's argument: instead of continuing to use "the reality or truth of women's pain as a *political* strategy to authorize further action," or make Kilgrave admit he raped her, Jessica does "what is intuitively and understandably expected, that is, making men stop raping and beating women" (1996, 68). In other words, she makes Kilgrave stop raping and assaulting women the only way she can: by killing him. In this moment, Jessica transcends the tradition of narrating women's experiences of sexual violence in the hopes of effecting change, reclaims power over her body and control over her mind, and implements positive change in her own world. Kilgrave is ultimately held accountable for his actions, and Jessica ensures he will never again be able to inflict trauma on others.

A Widened Cultural Narrative of Trauma, Consent, and Rape

In a cultural context in which sexual assault trials hinge on the "grey areas" of consent and popular television shows depict graphic, titillating rape scenes as mere plot devices and/or elements of character development, the alternative depiction of trauma, consent, and rape in *Jessica Jones* is immensely significant. The show's audience bears witness to a piece of popular culture and a strong female lead who insist on believing women's memories of sexual violence, on requiring enthusiastic consent before engaging in sexual activity, and on holding men solely accountable for their actions. If, as Angela McRobbie states, the media "has become the key site for defining codes of sexual conduct," and "casts judgement and establishes the rules of play," (McRobbie 2009, 15) then *Jessica Jones* works to disrupt the normative narratives of trauma, consent, and rape that currently exist in popular culture and in society more broadly.

Instead of relying on onscreen portrayals of rape, *Jessica Jones* focuses on the aftermath of rape to engage in critical discussions of why such violations happen. Notably, although the show does not depict the inciting trauma inflicted on those whom Kilgrave assaults, it dedicates a considerable amount of time to showing the characters' efforts to deal with the effects of this trauma. The audience witnesses Jessica's attempts to "cope with being violated on such a profound level, [and to] grapple with [her] own feelings of guilt and culpability" in being assaulted (Young 2015). We bear witness to the gritty, complicated aftermath of Jessica's trauma, we watch as she attempts to regain some power and control over her life, and we stand with her as her strategies for coping with this trauma are violated, and as she ultimately confronts and overcomes her abuser. Watching *Jessica Jones* is an emotional experience that works to put the audience in Jessica's shoes, without ever depicting her rape. The show explores the concepts of rape, trauma, and consent with immense sensitivity (Young 2015), and is "unafraid to confront the trauma and victimization of the protagonist without falling into a pit of bad stereotypes" (Edwards 2015). The result is a community of viewers who believe Jessica Jones's claim to being sexually assaulted without ever needing to witness it onscreen—and a renewed emphasis on believing women's stories of sexual assault, without requiring the sharing of titillating details. The exploration of Kilgrave's defences against rape—that he did not know Jessica had not granted consent, that he has only garnered knowledge of love through depictions on television—encourages critical analysis of portrayals of love in popular culture and the concept of consent, and delivers a new narrative of consent into Western society: one in which a physically strong woman is (perhaps unintentionally) raped by a man with a twisted conception of love and the power of mind control. In *Jessica Jones*, then, we witness a widening of cultural narratives and understandings of rape, consent, and trauma in North America. In the end, the audience is left with depictions of consent as something that is actively requested and enthusiastically given, trauma as a complex, long-term effect of sexual violence that manifests in innumerable ways, and rape as something that does not always include a physical struggle and that is committed by friends, strangers, and would-be boyfriends alike, against even the strongest of female leads.

NOTE

1   Notably, these questions echo ones often asked of individuals who claim they were raped: Why did you have the accused's number saved in your phone? Why did you agree to a date? Why did you contact the accused following the alleged assault? As witnessed during the trial of Jian Ghomeshi, survivors of sexual assault who do not conform to societal conceptions of "good victims" are often subject to intense scrutiny (Pazzano 2016).

References

Abramson, Kate. 2014. "Turning Up the Lights On Gaslighting." *Philosophical Perspectives* 28 (1): 1–30.

Alcoff, Linda, and Laura Gray. 1993. "Survivor Discourse: Transgression or Recuperation?" *Signs* 18 (2): 260–90.

Balsamo, Anne. 1996. *Technologies of the Gendered Body: Reading Cyborg Women.* Durham, NC: Duke University Press.

Brison, Susan J. 2002. *Aftermath: Violence and the Remaking of a Self.* Princeton, NJ: Princeton University Press.

Brown, Caitlin. 2009. "Feminism and the Vampire Novel." *The F-Word*, September 8, 2009. https://www.thefword.org.uk/2009/09/feminism_and_th/.

Campbell, Rebecca, and Sheela Raja. 1999. "Secondary Victimization of Rape Victims: Insights from Mental Health Professionals Who Treat Survivors of Violence." *Violence and Victims* 14 (3): 261–75.

Chu, Arthur. 2015. "How Jessica Jones Absorbed the Anxieties of Gamergate." *Slate*, November 24, 2015. http://www.slate.com/articles/arts/television/2015/11/marvel_s_jessica_jones_and_gamergate_how_the_netflix_series_absorbed_the.html.

Edwards, Stassa. 2015. "Netflix's Jessica Jones Is a Complex Portrait of a Woman Undone." *The Muse*, November 23, 2015. http://themuse.jezebel.com/netflixs-jessica-jones-is-a-complex-portrait-of-a-woman-1744182340.

Haaken, Janice. 1996. "The Recovery of Memory, Fantasy, and Desire: Feminist Approaches to Sexual Abuse and Psychic Trauma." *Signs: Journal of Women in Culture and Society* 21 (4): 1069–94.

Heberle, Renee. 1996. "Deconstructive Strategies and the Movement against Sexual Violence." *Hypatia* 11 (4): 63–76.

Heyward, Vivian H., Sandra M. Johannes-Ellis, and Jacki F. Romer. 1986. "Gender Differences in Strength." *Research Quarterly for Exercise And Sport* 57 (2): 154–9.

Kahlor, Leeann, and Matthew S. Eastin. 2011. "Television's Role in the Culture of Violence Toward Women: A Study of Television Viewing and the Cultivation of Rape Myth Acceptance in the United States." *Journal of Broadcasting & Electronic Media* 55 (2): 215–31.

Maier, Shana. 2008. " 'I Have Heard Horrible Stories . . . ': Rape Victim Advocates' Perceptions of the Revictimization of Rape Victims by the Police and Medical System." *Violence against Women* 14 (1): 786–808.

McRobbie, Angela. 2009. *The Aftermath of Feminism: Gender, Culture and Social Change.* Thousand Oaks, CA: Sage.

Mercante, Alyssa. 2015. "Jessica Jones: 'AKA Noir Feminist Fodder.' " *Criminal Element*, December 16, 2015. http://www.criminalelement.com/blogs/2015/12/jessica-jones-aka-noir-feminist-fodder-marvel-kilgrave-defenders.

Miller, A. E. J., J. D. Macdougall, M. A. Tarnopolsky, and D. G. Sale. 1993. "Gender Differences in Strength and Muscle Fiber Characteristics." *European Journal of Applied Physiology and Occupational Physiology* 66 (3): 254–62.

Munford, Rebecca, and Melanie Waters. 2014. *Feminism and Popular Culture: Investigating the Postfeminist Mystique.* New Brunswick, NJ: Rutgers University Press.

Nussbaum, Emily. 2015. "Graphic, Novel: 'Marvel's Jessica Jones' and the Superhero Survivor." *New Yorker,* December 14, 2015. http://www.newyorker.com/magazine/2015/12/21/graphic-novel-on-television-emily-nussbaum.

Opam, Kwame. 2015. "On Jessica Jones, Rape Doesn't Need to Be Seen to Be Devastating." *The Verge,* November 23, 2015. http://www.theverge.com/2015/11/23/9786180/jessica-jones-game-of-thrones-rape-consent-television-2015.

Pazzano, Sam. 2016. "Judge Rips Testimony of Women in Acquitting Jian Ghomeshi." *Toronto Sun,* March 24, 2016. http://www.torontosun.com/2016/03/24/jian-ghomeshi-verdict-expected-on-sexual-assault-charges.

Reenen, Dionne Van. 2014. "Is This Really What Women Want? An Analysis of *Fifty Shades of Grey* and Modern Feminist Thought." *South African Journal of Philosophy* 33 (2): 223–33.

Sarkeesian, Anita. 2015. "Some Thoughts on Jessica Jones." *Feminist Frequency,* December 1, 2015. http://femfreq.tumblr.com/post/134336278616/some-thoughts-on-jessica-jones.

Schwab, Gabriele. 2010. *Haunting Legacies: Violent Histories and Transgenerational Trauma.* New York: Columbia University Press.

Strasburger, Victor C., and Barbara J. Wilson. 2002. *Children, Adolescents, and the Media.* Thousand Oaks, CA: Sage.

Young, Cate. 2015. "Rape, Consent and Race in Marvel's 'Jessica Jones.'" *Bitch Flicks,* December 11, 2015. https://btchflcks.com/2015/12/rape-consent-and-race-in-marvels-jessica-jones.html.

Before Kilgrave, After Kilgrave: The Choreographic Effects of Trauma on the Female Body

Michelle Johnson

The tough but reluctant heroine with a tragic past is at this point a well-explored trope in television and film. She defies gender expectations, doesn't take any guff, and is more than capable of handling herself (often thanks to the skills or lessons learned from said tragic past). We recognize this heroine in Buffy Summers from *Buffy the Vampire Slayer* (1997–2003) Emma Swan from *Once Upon a Time* (2011–18), and the titular characters from *Veronica Mars* (2004–19) and *Wynonna Earp* (2016–present). Like many of these female protagonists, Jessica Jones attempts to separate herself from her past, to harden her shell and sharpen her edges as a defence against further pain, a strategy supplemented by her particular brand of alternate femininity. Though there is little doubt that Jessica is a badass, she inhabits and displays her traumatic experiences not with grace and aplomb, but with a sustained sense of "barely keeping it together." Her past is not a prop to give her an air of mystery, trotted out on occasion to show the soft, vulnerable girl under the cold exterior; on the contrary, Jessica's traumatic experiences are constantly present as the underlying focus of the series. In this chapter, I focus on physical movement as a means of conveying this trauma and Jessica's relationship with it as the underlying foundation of her daily life.

I approach the representation of trauma in *Jessica Jones* through Laban movement analysis, a methodology used for observing and interpreting movement. Analyzing Jessica's movement preferences and contrasting them to those of other female characters, I argue that bodily movement plays a key role in the show's presentation of trauma and performed femininity (or lack thereof), both as individual elements and in the intersection of the two. The series features a wide range of female characters, each of whose movement tendencies demonstrate the possibility for both multiple femininities and divergent reactions to trauma. Elements such as posture, gait, use of limbs, and interactions with others work together to contribute to Jessica's alternate femininity, which in turn becomes part of her unique way of reacting to and dealing with trauma. Jessica's physical approach to coping can then be compared to that of other female characters, such as Hope Shlottman and Trish Walker.

About Laban Movement Analysis

Laban movement analysis (LMA) is a system of observing and analyzing movement created by Austro-Hungarian movement theorist Rudolf von Laban in the early twentieth century. Laban's initial work has been developed, expanded, and codified over time to include systems such as Labanotation (a detailed, symbol-based method of recording movement sometimes likened to musical notation), Irmgard Bartenieff's movement fundamentals (Bartenieff and Lewis 1980), Judith Kestenberg's movement profiles (Kestenberg Amighi, Loman, and Sossin 2018), and other analytical approaches to movement and the human body. While primarily associated with dance, dance education, and movement therapy, LMA's uses are wide-reaching, and early applications of Laban's system found use in more pedestrian settings, such as diagnosing movement patterns and related inefficiencies in industrial workers (Davies 2001). LMA is strongly connected to the idea of personal style and expressivity, understanding that everyone has their own particular movement tendencies and that there are often deep connections between psychology and movement patterns (Fernandes 2015).

LMA consists of four overarching categories for analyzing movement: body, effort, shape, and space.[1] Each category is always present in movement, but an individual may operate with a greater emphasis within one or more categories, either in their movement in general or in the context of a particular circumstance or movement sequence. Elements of the body category include concepts such as breath and core support, body connectivity and organization, initiation and sequencing, and body attitude. The last of these, body attitude, is referred to throughout this chapter and describes an individual's underlying preference for how they hold their body. I will describe the four body attitudes—wall, ball, pin, and screw—as they arise in relation to Jessica and other female characters throughout my analysis.

Effort, which deals with dynamic movement qualities such as quick versus sustained and strong versus light, is described as expressing an individual's "internal attitude" (Fernandes 2015, 143) through external movement. Effort is often studied by actors and used as a tool to explore and express a character's inner landscape, making it useful in this context from an analytical standpoint. Shape deals with how the body moves and adapts in relationship to others, itself, and the environment, with qualities such as advancing and retreating, rising and sinking, and spreading and enclosing. Finally, the space category deals with directions in space through elements such as kinesphere (the space around one's body that is accessible without shifting weight, akin to the concept of personal space), pathways, and reach space.

Many LMA terms are fairly intuitive and easy to understand without explanation, such as the effort qualities: quick versus sustained (time effort), strong versus light (weight effort), free versus bound (flow effort), and direct versus indirect (space effort). Shaping movement in the vertical, horizontal, and sagittal planes[2] is also relatively straightforward, though it is important to understand that these terms refer not to actual movement through space, but rather to the shaping of the body in relation to the environment (or itself): rising/sinking (vertical), enclosing/spreading (horizontal), and advancing/retreating (sagittal) (Newlove and Dalby 2004). Rather than provide a lengthy explanation or glossary, I will define these and other terms requiring explanation as they appear throughout the chapter.

Introducing Jessica Jones

The audience first encounters Jessica Jones as a voice—that of a jaded narrator spilling truths while an anonymous man and woman give in to their bodily desires on the screen. She is soon revealed to be an observer in this opening scene, a film noir–esque sequence capturing an illicit affair through a partially subjective camera angle. She is there, presumably, but separate from the action. The viewer never sees her. As she continues to establish her perspective through voice-over, the scene shifts, bringing us teasingly closer to identifying our heroine: Jessica is now part of the scene as she deals with an angry male client (the cuckold in the aforementioned affair), but only the client's murky silhouette is visible through the door of Jessica's office. We still do not see Jessica herself. Already Jessica Jones is disrupting our expectations of her as a conventional television protagonist by existing behind the camera instead of in front of it, as well as disrupting the male gaze[3] by establishing a female perspective through her narration without providing a female body to be viewed and consumed.

After two minutes of this voice-over, Jessica finally makes a physical appearance. She dispatches her belligerent client by shoving him through the pane of glass in her office door, and the camera then cuts to Jessica walking down the streets of New York. Several of Jessica's habits of movement and spatial relation immediately present themselves in this short sequence. During the scuffle with her client she maintains a small kinesphere, keeping her limbs relatively close to her body so that the fight does not extend beyond the frame of the doorway. Her limbs continue to occupy near reach space[4] as she walks down the sidewalk with her hands deep in her pockets and her chin tucked down, giving the impression that she is attempting to make herself compact and unseen, avoiding interaction with the world around her unless absolutely necessary.

Jessica does not, however, project an air of timidity. While she has made her kinesphere small, she occupies it assertively, and the conflicting impression given by her movement is also present in her body attitude, a combination of ball,[5] with her rounded shoulders, and screw,[6] as her body twists, particularly apparent when in motion. While LMA does not ascribe meaning to specific movements, the rounded posture of ball body attitude may be associated in Western culture with passivity or protecting oneself, while a common example of screw body attitude is the "supermodel walk," an image associated with confidence and assertiveness. Thus, combining these two body attitudes lends to the complex, and in many ways contradictory, nature of Jessica's character.

After the violent encounter with her male client, Jessica's next interactions on screen are with the women of the law firm Hogarth, Chao & Benowitz. Jessica's appearance serves to immediately demonstrate how different she is from these women: their hair is neatly styled, in contrast to Jessica's Hollywood non-style (messy but not unattractively so), and they wear form-fitting dresses and heels, as opposed to Jessica's androgynous jeans, boots, and leather jacket. However, her movement also sets her apart. As Jessica walks beside Jeri Hogarth, no-nonsense, middle-aged attorney and managing partner of the firm, there is a clear difference in movement quality between the two. Although both incorporate elements of screw body attitude, with exaggerated movement of the hips and rotation between upper and lower body while walking, Hogarth's upper body is not at all rounded—her secondary qualities appear closer to pin body attitude.[7] There two women also exhibit a subtle distinction in terms of their hip movements: while Jessica's has a bouncing, forward-moving quality, Hogarth's hips sway from side to side with each step, complementing her form-fitting skirt and heels and emphasizing her feminine silhouette in spite of her cropped, masculine hairstyle—and the typically male-occupied position of power she holds in her company. Interestingly, Jessica and Hogarth both perform different combinations of femininity and masculinity, often in distinct opposition to each other.

The series takes care to present Jessica as feminist but not conventionally feminine, and at the same time tomboyish but not overly masculine. Even her former neighbour, Mrs. De Luca, describes a young Jessica as "the strangest tomboy," wearing "princess dresses with high-tops" (ep. 1.08, "AKA WWJD?"), her masculine tendencies strategically tempered with a feminine element. As an adult, shades of this delicate balance, echoed in the contrasting movement qualities discussed above, remain present in her appearance: she dresses androgynously but keeps her hair long, not even pulling it back into a practical ponytail; she curses, drinks, and fights. And yet in the privacy of her apartment, Jessica is often shown wearing nothing but underwear and a tank top, clearly displaying her female figure to the audience. These contrasts could be interpreted as signifying gender fluidity in Jessica's character, or they may be an attempt on the part of the show to "pull back" when she is at risk of becoming "too masculine."

Gender theorist Jack Halberstam (1998) observes that, whether displayed by males or females, "excessive masculinity" is stereotypically associated with working-class bodies[8]—an interesting distinction when contrasting Jessica, with her derelict apartment and struggling business, to other female characters such as Jeri Hogarth and radio personality Trish Walker, who both have lucrative careers and upper-class lifestyles, and who both present as more feminine than Jessica. Jessica demonstrates an acute awareness of her lack of stereotypical femininity and uses her ability to perform varying levels and types of femininity as a tool in her PI business. She employs different vocal qualities and word choices when pretending to be someone else, accompanied with changes in body language, even when she is speaking on the phone and the individual she is attempting to deceive cannot see her (as seen in ep. 1.01, "AKA Ladies' Night," and ep. 1.06, "AKA You're a Winner!"). These mini-performances demonstrate Jessica's perception not only of different types of femininity, but of herself as separate or different from these femininities, as her method of embodying them represents a drastic shift from her own vocal and movement patterns. It is never stated outright whether or not Jessica looks down on the female stereotypes she employs. A slight eye roll and head shake after the aforementioned phone conversation in episode 1.01 could be simple exasperation at the naïveté of the person she just duped, or it could be interpreted as derision, Jessica viewing herself as superior to the role she has just played due to her own less stereotypically feminine or "girly" performance of gender—the internalized misogyny of "I'm not like other girls." In the words of Halberstam, "sometimes female masculinity coincides with the excesses of male supremacy, and sometimes it codifies a unique form of social rebellion" (1998, 9). At first glance Jessica might appear to be all social rebellion, but perhaps there is more at play, both in the writing of her as a character and the complexities of her relationship with her own femininity due to her trauma at the hands of Kilgrave.

Trauma and (Un)Femininity

Rather than presenting Jessica's non-normative female behaviour solely as an independent inherent or learned trait, the show suggests a correlation between it and her trauma. Through a series of flashbacks, Jessica is shown to become more abrasive and less stereotypically feminine as each traumatic experience unfolds: losing her family in a car crash, discovering her superpowers as a teen, and finally being controlled and abused by Kilgrave. Halberstam (1998) suggests that the "tomboy phase" experienced by many young girls is generally accepted by society as normal, so long as girls grow out of it once they reach adolescence. In this context, Jessica's failure to "grow out of" the dark, tomboyish edge she is shown to have as a young adolescent (supported by Mrs. De Luca's reminiscing in ep. 1.07, "AKA Top Shelf Perverts"), and to do the opposite instead, is perhaps used to demonstrate that something has disrupted her normal development—the aforementioned traumatic experiences, beginning with losing her family in a car accident during this early adolescent tomboy phase.

In conjunction with each trauma, Jessica's movement tendencies shift slightly over the course of her teen and young adult years as she becomes the Jessica Jones introduced to us at the beginning of the series. While teen Jessica only appears a handful of times, several movement patterns can be established. Her ball body attitude is present, although the elements of screw body attitude are not yet developed. Additionally, the rounding associated with ball body attitude is more exaggerated in flashback scenes taking place after the car accident in which she lost her family, suggesting a possible correlation to this first traumatic experience. Before this trauma, and to an extent after it (but still before she comes under Kilgrave's control), Jessica exhibits relatively direct space effort,[9] or single-focus attention on her surroundings. Present-day Jessica's space effort is much more indirect—a multi-focus attention to her environment that suggests her desire to be constantly present and aware of her surroundings in the wake of being controlled, raped, and held against her will for an extended period of time.

Further flashbacks to Jessica's adult life before her experience with Kilgrave continue to demonstrate the effects of her trauma—as she states in episode 1.05, "there's before Kilgrave, and there's after Kilgrave." There is no attempt to exaggerate this division by portraying pre-Kilgrave Jessica as bright, naive, or bubbly; she is still sarcastic and cynical, just slightly less so— and perhaps a bit more good-humoured about it, particularly with Trish, her best friend and adopted sister, and someone with whom she is shown to have a strong relationship. As a result, the changes Jessica exhibits after Kilgrave are subtle, allowing the audience to see how deeply she has been affected and how the impact of trauma may not always manifest in obvious ways. In a flashback scene in episode 1.05 that echoes her first appearance in the pilot episode, Jessica is shown walking down the street before coming upon a man (later revealed to be her future neighbour, Malcolm) being attacked by a pair of muggers. Compared to the first walking scene in the pilot, where Jessica appears guarded and closed-off, this Jessica is much more open: she holds her head higher, exhibits less ball body attitude, and her indirect space effort projects a sense of casual interest in her surroundings, rather than wariness.

In terms of body attitude in particular, compared to both present-day Jessica and post-accident teen Jessica, pre-Kilgrave adult Jessica does not display the same ball body attitude, suggesting through this physical shorthand that she is in a better place mentally and emotionally during this time; she has healed somewhat from the previous trauma of losing her family, but has not yet been exposed to Kilgrave's manipulation and imprisonment. Other movement tendencies also suggest positive growth and healing in the time between these two events, such as a shift in shaping from enclosing and retreating to the opposite, spreading and advancing—another pattern that is reversed in the post-Kilgrave period, as present-day Jessica once again has a tendency to enclose with her torso. She also demonstrates greater asymmetry in her postural movements (particularly during the bar scene in episode 1.05), hinting at the shift from pure ball body attitude to the ball-screw combination she eventually adopts. It is almost as if present-day Jessica's body attitude reflects the multiple layers of her personality or an integration of specific elements of her past selves: the defence/protection of her teenage ball body attitude, but not the vulnerability; the projected confidence of her more recent asymmetry/screw body attitude, but not the openness. However, Jessica's present-day movement habits often seem to indicate a preference for postural symmetry, with her weight distributed evenly between both legs, suggesting an exaggerated need to feel stable and grounded that perhaps did not exist before—in addition to integrating her previous experiences and personality traits, her body and habits continue to layer in new ones.

Flashbacks are frequently juxtaposed with present-day scenes to further highlight these and other changes in Jessica's movement tendencies: there is a particularly striking cut between scenes in episode 1.05, from Jessica sitting cross-legged in a flashback to the same position in the present. In the past, Jessica sits casually on Trish's couch, eating chips and chatting about becoming a superhero. She is open and relaxed, her head is up, and she leans back on the couch for support. The scene cuts to the present, and Jessica sits in the exact same position on her desk, alone in her empty apartment. She is closed off from the world, head down and shoulders hunched. She holds tension in her torso and limbs, and she leans forward with her elbows on her knees, supporting herself rather than being supported by her environment.

Hope Shlottman, a victim of Kilgrave's who pulls Jessica back into his world at the start of the series, is used in combination with Jessica's flashbacks to further demonstrate the effects of trauma and its aftermath on bodily movement. Hope's very name both suggests the possibility for redemption and catharsis for Jessica and reminds her of who she was before Kilgrave: someone who, despite her previous traumas and her acute sense of sarcasm, still had hope of her own. Accordingly, Jessica first sees photos of pre-Kilgrave Hope, showing her open posture, lifted chin, and wide smile, before meeting post-Kilgrave Hope. In contrast to her past self, and foreshadowing what the audience eventually sees of Jessica's own movement transformation, this Hope displays enclosing shaping in her torso, with her chin tucked down and a look of despair on her face. This is only her first trauma, however, and she maintains some of her openness and positivity, demonstrated when she hugs not only her parents but Jessica, too, before turning to leave after her rescue in episode 1.01.

Tragedy follows this brief optimistic moment, as Hope enters the elevator behind her parents and pulls out a gun to shoot them, still under Kilgrave's control. It is interesting to note that, right before the doors close and the gun goes off, Hope and her parents are facing each other head-on in the elevator. In the following shot of Hope, after the elevator has opened to reveal her dead parents, not only is Hope's body angled away when she speaks to Jessica, but the camera has shifted from a centred, balanced shot of the elevator to a tilted Dutch angle shot, marking this moment as a significant transition point for Hope.

Throughout the following episodes, Hope's movement preferences gradually become more like Jessica's as she loses optimism and, ironically, hope. During a conversation between Jessica and Hope at the prison in episode 1.02 (Hope's first scene after her parents' murder), Jessica faces Hope directly and leans forward with advancing shaping—uncharacteristic actions to accompany her rare display of earnest support. In contrast, Hope leans back and looks away from the conversation, much more "Jessica-like" and closed off with her retreating shaping and indirect space effort. The conversation turns when Hope says that Jessica should kill herself, prompting Jessica to put her metaphorical armour back on: she leans back in her seat and angles her upper body, switching from her previous encouragement and comfort to her usual sarcastic, glib responses. Jessica has gone from open to closed, both physically and emotionally, and a shot showing both women facing each other across the table demonstrates how Hope's physicality mirrors Jessica's when the latter reverts back to her regular defensive state.

Hope's new movement preferences have other similarities to Jessica's as well, such as the way Hope tilts her head to the side when she looks up at Hogarth during their first meeting later in episode 1.02, or her phone interview with Trish in episode 1.03. During the interview, Hope advances with her torso when she leans forward over Hogarth's phone as she makes herself vulnerable, telling not only Trish but anyone listening to the live broadcast about her time under Kilgrave's control. The scene recalls her conversation with Jessica in the previous episode, in which Jessica was likewise opening herself up (both physically and emotionally) to Hope when she advanced. For both of these characters, advancing signifies engaging with others and allowing themselves to be vulnerable, while retreating becomes a mechanism for closing themselves off, shoring up their defences—and indeed, Hope retreats as she leans back slightly when Hogarth surprises her by using the interview to dismiss Hope as a lunatic.

Finally, when Jessica visits Hope in prison in episode 1.05, we see Hope's transformation reach its peak through her tilted head and the saunter displays as she walks away from Jessica, her dismissal accompanied by a flippant "I'll hold my breath" in response to Jessica's reassurances that she is close to catching Kilgrave. The quality of both her movement and speech in this scene chillingly mirrors Jessica's signature tendencies, a parallel made especially striking as the scene is immediately followed by flashbacks of past Jessica transforming into present Jessica.

What are the movement preferences that make up "present Jessica"? Her ball-screw hybrid body attitude has been established, as has her preference for enclosing shaping. She has a tendency to lower her chin and often tilts her head when she speaks to someone; when her temper or emotions flare, this habit turns into increased movement in her head and neck while speaking, as seen when she is in a car with Officer Simpson in episode 1.05. She gravitates toward bound flow effort,[10] indirect space effort, and strong weight effort.[11] Various combinations of two out of these three effort factors—flow, space, and weight—form the following effort states:[12] stable state (weight and space), which might evoke feelings of concentration, balancing, or determination; remote state (flow and space), within which the combination of bound and indirect might suggest searching; and dream state (weight and flow), of which a strong and bound combination may call to mind senses of frustration or heaviness. While these associations are by no means definitively prescriptive of these effort states, they do suggest a connection with many of Jessica's behaviours and coping strategies, including her mistrust of others, aggression, and a general misanthropy.

In addition to tilting her head, Jessica frequently angles her entire body when interacting with others; what is noteworthy here is not that she always orients herself in this way (she regularly faces people head-on as well), but rather the circumstances in which she does so. In the pilot Jessica shies away from front-facing conversations, establishing this positioning as an element of her character, until her encounter at the restaurant Niku (ep. 1.01, "AKA Ladies' Night") cements her understanding that Kilgrave is back. At this point in her investigation, she shifts so that her entire body fully faces the restaurant's maître d', perhaps to signify that she has finally accepted that she must face her past head-on. Of course, it takes some time for her to abandon her plans to flee New York and fully embrace this decision, but this interaction marks the first time that she knows for certain that Kilgrave is back and that she must react in some way.

The contrast between direct versus indirect facing (not necessarily linked with direct and indirect space effort) is employed in various ways throughout the series, primarily related to Jessica's emotional comfort. Early in the series, Jessica shifts to a direct facing whenever she grows openly agitated about Kilgrave: the aforementioned encounter at Niku, confronting Hope's parents after connecting her disappearance to Kilgrave, and certain points during her conversation with Trish in episode 1.01. It is also used to demonstrate Jessica's level of comfort versus wariness, as situations such as approaching an unknown location or speaking to someone she does not know well often involve an indirect facing (e.g., approaching the hotel where Hope is hiding in episode 1.01, or talking to her neighbour Ruben at her apartment door in episode 1.05), while conversations with people she trusts (more common in later episodes) are more likely to occur head-on.

This distinction allows us to observe the growth in Jessica's relationship with Trish as the two women reconnect and learn to give and accept help from each other. In early episodes there is often asymmetry in their conversations: if one is directly facing, the other (often, but not always, Jessica) is angled slightly away. Somewhat humorously, this dynamic is alluded to before the two women even interact on screen. In a scene in episode 1.01, Jessica comes upon a poster for Trish's talk show and leans against it, her body angled away from the image of Trish, who faces the camera (both the one that took the picture for the ad and the one through which the audience views the scene) directly. Once Jessica and Trish do begin to interact on screen, their inability to face each other continues to be shown even when they are not physically present in the same space: in a scene in episode 1.04 featuring a phone conversation between the two women, Trish faces toward the camera, while Jessica is angled away not only from the camera, but from the scene she is observing through a window across the street as well. As the series progresses, however, Jessica and Trish gradually open to each other and engage in more mutually direct-facing conversations. A flashback to teenage Jessica and Trish shows a similar pattern in the aftermath of Jessica's childhood trauma as well, as she directly faces Trish, whom she still feels close to in this pre-Kilgrave scene, but speaks at an angle to Trish's abusive mother, with whom she has no such closeness.

Trish serves in many ways as a foil for Jessica, yet due to her own experiences she is not portrayed as the bright, bubbly blond one might expect to contrast Jessica's darkness. Trish herself has experienced trauma as well, as a child celebrity at the hands of her abusive mother. Particularly as an adult, Trish's position as a celebrity makes her both more capable (trained as a child star to control how people see her) and more conscientious of concealing her traumatic experiences and preventing them from playing out on her body. Additionally, as an adult she appears to have taken more steps to confront and move past her trauma, partially due to the fact that her traumatic experiences are significantly further in the past than Jessica's time under Kilgrave's control. It is no coincidence that Trish also presents herself more femininely than Jessica, further demonstrating the show's tendency to correlate female trauma with ambiguous or deficient femininity.

Despite her relative "success" in coping (at least compared to Jessica), the audience is given glimpses of the effects of Trish's past, both in present-day scenes and in flashbacks. In episode 1.12, Trish's estranged mother visits her hospital room. Taken by surprise, Trish's body posture immediately shifts from the confidence she felt while on the phone with Jessica moments earlier: she retreats and encloses, her movements become less quick[13] and direct, and a sudden increase in bound flow effort is accompanied by held tension throughout her body. Later, in her apartment, when she is no longer caught off guard, she manages to regain her composure; in her comfort zone and no longer vulnerable, she returns to her less defensive physical patterns.

Flashbacks also show Trish's reaction to trauma, through both similarities and differences with Jessica. In a confrontation between the two teens in episode 1.11, whereas Jessica advances and engages in more shaping in general, Trish remains more neutral, potentially indicative of her constant need to perform and contain, as both a child star and a victim of abuse. Both girls cross their arms in front of their chests when talking to each other, but while Jessica tends to keep her arms crossed for a length of time, establishing a stable defence, Trish crosses and uncrosses her arms frequently, seemingly more comforted by the action than the held position. Jessica's habit hints at her future coping strategy of turning her body into protective armour against the outside world, with her small kinesphere, ball body attitude, and enclosing shaping. These differences are reflected in the strategies both women employ to protect themselves from the world around them in the present: where Jessica has made her body into a fortress, Trish, with no superpowers, has closed in on herself by turning her home into her fortress, complete with doorman, security system, and bulletproof glass. The role of the home for each of these women highlights the role of their bodies and creates a form of symmetry between them: just as Trish's body cannot do the things that Jessica's can (despite intense Krav Maga training), Jessica's home, with its broken door and non-existent security, cannot protect her, and so her body is her shield.

Conclusion

Ironically, Jessica's superhuman body is both the cause of and defence against her trauma at the hands of Kilgrave, having led to his initial interest in her but also allowing her to finally defeat him. However, as I have discussed, Jessica's superpowers are not the only way in which she uses her body to defend herself from the world around her, as her movement habits also serve to protect and distance her from the world. In this chapter I have used Laban movement analysis to uncover how Jessica's trauma affects her movement and how her movement is used in turn as both a signifier of her trauma and a coping mechanism in its aftermath. Further, Jessica's alternate femininity is shown to be linked to her past experiences, with her evolving mental and emotional state being expressed through her movement tendencies.

Of course, the portrayals in *Marvel's Jessica Jones* are fictional dramatizations. The series shows multiple causes of trauma, including childhood abuse, loss, major life changes, rape, and coercion, and demonstrates variances and commonalities in individual responses to such experiences over time. Even so, we know trauma as experienced in real life to be infinitely varied and complex, and the movement patterns of the characters analyzed in this chapter are not universally indicative of the range of reactions or coping mechanisms that may be found.[14] Perhaps most significantly, post-traumatic stress disorder and gender presentation do not necessarily correlate, and unconventional approaches to femininity need not be signifiers of any sort of underlying traumatic experience or mental health concern.

In this context, LMA does, however, provide a deeper understanding of how trauma and gender performance are linked through movement in *Jessica Jones*, not only in Jessica herself, but in Trish and Hope, as well as in Jessica's relationships with them and other characters. Bodily movement is a significant means of conveying gender in Western media, changing through time as societal gender ideals change. Contemporary femininity is in many ways housed in the body, with bodily movement serving as just one method of transmission. Fans and critics of various media often discuss a female character's empowerment versus objectification in terms of costuming, camera angles, and storyline, but the role of movement is somewhat less discussed. Phenomena such as the Hawkeye Initiative[15] have begun to take elements of character posing into account in addition to costuming and facial expression, bringing awareness to the significance of the body in terms of static positioning. Observing bodies in motion serves as a useful accompaniment to these other elements—by examining how a character moves within their environment, the viewer gains a new perspective on how that character relates to their world.

In addition to its value in observing and analyzing moving bodies, LMA can be applied to still forms and images as well, and it may in fact be a useful tool in exploring how comic book characters such as Jessica Jones are adapted to live-action film and television. Further research on this topic might include a comparison between the Jessica Jones of the Marvel Cinematic Universe and the original Jessica Jones of various Marvel Comics series. By considering elements such as body attitude, shaping, use of space, and even how effort is conveyed in the static images of the comics, the reader/viewer can gain an understanding of how aspects such as backstory, plot lines, characterization, and the general shorthand of the medium are translated and modified through choices related to movement and the body. In this way, Laban movement analysis provides insight into how meaning is produced, rather than simply what meanings can be found.

NOTES

1   LMA terminology is typically capitalized, in part to avoid confusion between LMA-specific concepts and common English words or phrases. In keeping with the publisher's preferred style conventions, all movement analysis language has been made lowercase throughout this chapter. For the purposes of this work, many LMA terms can be generally understood based on their English-language definitions; however, I will provide more detailed explanations when necessary.

2   These three dimensions can be likened to the x, y, and z axes of the Cartesian coordinate system. "Vertical" refers to upward/downward movement and spatial pulls, "horizontal" to side-to-side actions, and "sagittal" to forward/backward.

3   A term introduced by film critic Laura Mulvey in her article "Visual Pleasure and Narrative Cinema" (1975), which addresses the prioritization of the male point of view and consequent female objectification in film and other media.

4   Reach space has to do with where in one's kinesphere (the space around the body that can be accessed without shifting weight) a gesture takes place. Near reach movements take place closest to the centre of the body, far reach furthest away, and mid reach in between.

5   Ball body attitude: rounding of the spine and shoulders either forward or, less typically, backward.

6   Screw body attitude: a way of shaping or carrying the body that emphasizes contralateral movement by twisting in a spiralling fashion.

7   Pin body attitude: a narrow, vertical way of holding the body. An example of a pin body attitude might be found in the stereotypical image of a ballerina.

8   Halberstam also argues that notions of excessive or insufficient masculinity and femininity are strongly connected to race. I have focused here on the class associations as all main female characters in *Jessica Jones* are white, an observation that in itself merits discussion beyond the scope of this chapter.

9   Space effort describes one's focus or attention in space/environment. Direct space effort describes attention that is concentrated on a single point or focus, while indirect space effort diverts attention toward multiple foci at the same time.

10 Flow effort relates to muscular tension, having either fluidity (free) or restraint (bound) in movement.

11 Weight in LMA terms has nothing to do with an individual's measurements in pounds or kilograms, but rather with changes in force used to move. Strong weight involves increasing force or pressure, while light weight involves decreasing it.

12 Effort states occur when two effort factors (space, time, weight, flow) combine to create expressive, meaningful movement.

13 Time effort describes the dynamic quality of time, not how many seconds, minutes, or hours an action takes. A movement is quick when it gradually becomes faster and sustained when it gradually becomes slower.

14 As mentioned briefly at the beginning of this chapter, LMA has found frequent application in somatic and movement-based therapies, including approaches to trauma. Although the aim of this chapter is to use LMA as a tool to observe and analyze how movement is used in *Jessica Jones* to convey trauma, and not to discuss the realities of trauma survivors or offer therapeutic solutions, this connection bears mentioning. Some key names in the field of somatic and body-centred approaches to trauma therapy include Babette Rothschild, Bessel van der Kolk, Peter Levine, and Stephen Porges.

15 An online project started in 2012, the Hawkeye Initiative encourages fans to submit parody drawings featuring male superheroes in the hyper-sexualized poses in which female characters are often drawn. The purpose is to highlight the female objectification prevalent in comic books, video games, and other media. See the project's Tumblr page is available at https://thehawkeyeinitiative.tumblr.com/.

References

Bartenieff, Irmgard, and Dori Lewis. 1980. *Body Movement: Coping with the Environment.* New York: Gordon and Breach.

Davies, Eden. 2001. *Beyond Dance: Laban's Legacy of Movement Analysis.* London: Brechin Books.

Fernandes, Ciane. 2015. *The Moving Researcher: Laban/Bartenieff Movement Analysis in Performing Arts Education and Creative Arts Therapies.* London: Jessica Kingsley.

Halberstam, Judith. 1998. *Female Masculinity.* Durham, NC: Duke University Press.

Kestenberg Amighi, Janet, Susan Loman, and K. Mark Sossin. 2018. *The Meaning of Movement: Embodied Developmental, Clinical, and Cultural Perspectives of the Kestenberg Movement Profile.* New York: Routledge.

Mulvey, Laura. 1975. "Visual Pleasure and Narrative Cinema." *Screen* 16 (4): 6–18.

Newlove, Jean, and John Dalby. 2004. *Laban for All.* London: Nick Hern.

Code Word, "I Love You": Sisterhood, Friendship, and Trauma

Tracey Thomas

When viewers are first introduced to Jessica Jones, the titular character in Netflix's original series *Marvel's Jessica Jones* (2015), she speaks of a young girl, Hope, who has run away from home to be with a man: "She's either an idiot in love, or she's being conned. Which amount to pretty much the same thing" (ep. 1.01 "AKA Ladies' Night"). To Jessica, any kind of love—here, the romantic kind—is something to be scoffed at and pitied. This is not limited to romantic love, however; Jessica, seems to have little interest or care for any kind of definition of "love": romantic, platonic, familial. Her romantic entanglements are often recreational, her platonic friends are few, and her family is absent. However, Jessica makes an exception for one person: her best friend, Patricia "Patsy" Walker, or "Trish," as she comes to be known in the show. Jessica and Trish are opposites in many ways, but in others, very similar. This chapter explores both Jessica's and Trish's journeys from victims to empowered females throughout the first season of *Jessica Jones*. Importantly, this Netflix series demonstrates that a relationship between two women can exist to support and empower both parties without reducing their relationship to merely being about men and the men in their lives. While these men are catalysts for the women's abuse, it is also the men and their actions that galvanize Jessica and Trish into a stronger platonic relationship that becomes central to their characters and a foundation to *Marvel's Jessica Jones* as a whole.

This chapter is broken into three parts, with each part exploring concepts of sisterhood, friendship, and trauma, as well as how these connect the two women. Taken chronologically, the first part establishes how Jessica and Trish met as young teens, and how their respective traumas in their youth shaped their budding friendship and sowed the seeds of the sisterhood that would continue up to the events described in the next part of this chapter: the immediate backstory of Jessica and Kilgrave,[1] as well as Jessica's trauma. This part establishes Jessica and Trish as the characters we see on the television show, demonstrating how trauma tests their friendship and bonds. The final part demonstrates how Jessica's and Trish's previous traumas create a strong sisterly bond that perseveres beyond Jessica's trauma with Kilgrave and Trish's trauma with Will Simpson. This chapter explores their journey of self-discovery and their efforts to overcome their traumas to become stronger women and better friends, not to mention "heroes." This culminates in the final episode when Jessica says those all-important words, "I love you," to the most important person in her life: Trish Walker.

AKA: The Early Years

Debuting in 2015, *Jessica Jones* was part of a wave of successful television shows featuring Marvel characters that included *Daredevil* (2014), *Luke Cage* (2016), *Iron Fist* (2017), and *The Defenders* (2017). The show is based on the comic series *Alias*, written by Brian Bendis in 2001—a four-chapter volume that explores a meta-human with super strength and the ability to fly. The protagonist, Jessica Jones, is a conflicted character who bounces between presenting herself as Jewel, a superhero replete with costume and secret identity, and then later as Jessica Jones, a private investigator who does not consider herself a "superhero." The Netflix adaptation kept the character's super strength but not her flying abilities; the result roots the television show in a somewhat fantastical version of New York City without abandoning a sense of realism altogether. According to showrunner Melissa Rosenberg and Marvel coordinator Jeph Loeb, a core concept for translating *Alias* to television was this choice to root the narrative "in [the] world that [they] created of Hell's Kitchen and New York City" (Radish 2015). This ensures that, for viewers, Jessica is "a real woman with real problems," and the show "is about paying [her] rent and getting the next client" (Radish 2015). Furthermore, Rosenberg felt it was important that Jessica be someone who she "wanted to be friends with. It was important that there be somebody in [her] life who made it all look easy, but [who did] not necessarily [feel] that way" (Radish 2015). In this case, Rosenberg succeeded, as others have noted that "[Jessica], as a person, becomes more relatable due to the practical nature of the title character and her relatable 'real world' problems" (Kreuze 2016, 36).

Yet, female protagonists in television, especially as main characters, often suffer from being treated as sexualized objects or props for male characters, and therefore, their relatability toward the female sex can significantly drop as there is a lack of connection between audience and character. In a study conducted by the Center for the Study of Women in Television and Film, Dr. Martha Lauzen (2016) noted some interesting facts regarding women and their onscreen presence. While mostly limiting her analysis to cinema rather than television, Lauzen did note that gender stereotypes were prevalent in the top-grossing films of 2015, and that moviegoers were more likely to know the occupation of male characters than female characters. This is mirrored in *Jessica Jones* with the immediately recognizable careers of Will Simpson, Luke Cage, and Detective Clemons. However, *Jessica Jones* equalizes this dynamic by including characters such as Trish, Jeri Hogarth, and Claire Temple, who have very recognizable careers and whose work is directly alluded to throughout the show. The choice of casting ensures that Jessica is understood to be the protagonist, but the ensemble narrative that plays out over the thirteen episodes of season 1 is not just her own, as Trish, Jeri, and even Luke are given overarching plots that connect with Jessica's. Therefore, while "females comprised 22% of all clearly identifiable *protagonists*" in Lauzen's study (2016, 2; emphasis in original), this number does not accurately reflect *Jessica Jones*, whose protagonists (with the exception of Luke Cage) are all female. Furthermore, according to Loeb, *Jessica Jones* was one of the first properties Netflix developed for the Marvel Cinematic Universe (Radish 2015). The fact that Netflix planned the Marvel television shows around Jessica first, combined with the popularity of this female-driven cast, hopefully means that Lauzen's 22 per cent figure will soon grow.

When *Jessica Jones* was still in development with ABC and not Netflix, Rosenberg contemplated using Carol Danvers, who is one of Jessica's best friends in her *Alias* graphic, in the series. However, the shift from ABC to Netflix also meant a shift in narrative, which in turn resulted in greater exploration of the definition of heroism and of Jessica's journey of discovery. Furthermore, with Carol Danvers receiving a film of her own in the Marvel Cinematic Universe, the addition of Trish Walker "was better [than using Carol]," noted Rosenberg (Watts 2015). She continued in an interview with IGN: "this was because [Jessica's] best friend was not someone with powers. . . . [Rather, she was] a great mirror for her" (Watts 2015). Some of Carol Danvers's origin story made its way into the Netflix adaptation of Trish

Walker, however obliquely. In the comics, Carol was an alcoholic after experiencing a traumatic pregnancy while being psychically manipulated and raped by a man who pretended to be her partner (Kaveney 2008, 81). In conjunction with Trish, as a young child actress she participated in arson as a way to gain attention, and through the emotional manipulation of her mother, he engaged in substance abuse. As such, incorporating parts of Carol Danvers's origin into the character of Trish Walker helps to equalize the relationship between the two by bringing attention to the childhood traumas that both Jessica and Trish experienced. By beginning their stories and trauma together in childhood, Jessica and Trish are able to share an interesting connection that forms the basis of their friendship.

Perhaps their traumas and Jessica's and Trish's coping methods relate back to Jessica being "relatable," in contrast to most comic book characters. Laura Figueroa (2015) has found that female characters in television typically fall into two archetypes: in the first they can only be successful, independent, frigid, and strong, and in the second they are emotional, loving, and passive. There is no room for women characters to be all-encompassing, dynamic characters, as they must fall into just one of the two categories Figueroa explores. Jessica appears as strong and independent while maintaining a certain emotionally frigidity and enjoying a (marginally) successful career.[2] Never is she loving or passive! These all-encompassing identities, and Jessica's status as a multifaceted woman, however, are something that the show explores through its "AKA" episode titles, a nod to Bendis's original graphic run. When we first meet Jessica, we know that it is after her trauma and that she is in a vulnerable state of trying to rediscover herself. She is not sure who she is, as the woman she was previously is not someone she can go back to—that woman is gone. However, watching her as she struggles through her daily life and works to establish her identity yet again, we note that at her core, she wants to do something good, to contribute to the world. But in attempting to do so, she must overcome a host of personality issues (Radish 2015). While many "superhero" stories focus on self-discovery (and *Jessica Jones* is of course one such story), the Netflix show is more than just a "psychological thriller first and a superhero show second" (Radish 2015). It is also about sisterhood, friendship, and female support in the face of trauma.

These multi-faceted explorations into who Jessica Jones is play a central role in the Netflix narrative, and they are key to showing the growth that Jessica's character experiences over the course of the television show. Loeb explained in an interview that the choice to add "AKA" to the title of each episode was an attempt to imply that every single person (whether viewer or character) has an "also known as" in their life (Radish 2015). In other words, people often have a hidden, secret life that others are not always privileged to see and experience. Yet, we as the audience get to experience Jessica's "AKA" while watching the show, particularly through her relatability. Even more importantly, Jessica's storyline in season 1 focuses on who she is, showing that she always has been a hero, regardless of whether or not she puts on a costume to fight crime (Kaveney 2008, 72–3). Of course, it does take her some time to get there, stuck as she is in the idea that she is an either-or woman—either a superhero or not. However, as "[she] cannot forgive herself for the simple fact that she is a normal human being at the same time as being someone who can fight and fly . . . she sees contradictions where none exist" (Kaveney 2008, 78). The audience is in the same limbo as Jessica, attempting to discover who she is and what she is meant to be. Eventually, the audience—and Jessica—will discover a female superhero who is comfortably strong in her body and sexuality *and* is also vulnerable in love, who uses humour *and* fights injustice, who is inclusive and compassionate *and* decisive and deadly (Cocca 2014, 219).

"I Really Want to Be Your Friend"

Viewers of Netflix's *Jessica Jones* eventually learn how Jessica and Trish became friends, as well as the details of their initial traumas, through a series of non-chronological flashbacks. In episode 1.08, we learn how Jessica's family died: a car collision. Her trauma is framed by the argument between Jessica, her parents, and her younger brother Phil that occurred as the car collided with the back of the truck, and it is compounded by the typical family relationship leading up to the collision.[3] In the lead-up to the collision, Jessica argues with her brother, calling him various names in annoyance for breaking their shared Game Boy. These everyday familial images are juxtaposed against the horrific nature of Jessica's trauma. Jessica loses everything in a moment of her (assumed) making, becoming an orphan and carrying the guilt that her teenage angst was the cause of her family's death.

In comparison, the audience's first impressions of teenage Trish are that of a young Disney-style starlet who, as heard in a whispered conversation between her and her mother, Dorothy, passed out and set fire to a tablecloth in a nightclub. The only connection between Trish and Jessica at this point is that they are in the same class in school; they have not spoken, and they are certainly not friends—in fact, they do not yet know each other. Foreshadowing the girls' future as best friends is the *It's Patsy!* theme song. Running in the background in the hospital room, the song announces, "I really want to be your friend, I hope this day will never end, it's Patsy! It's Patsy! I really want to be a friend with you!"[4] Although the first true meeting between the two girls is engineered by Dorothy Walker as a photo op for the *It's Patsy!* show, Trish and Jessica's initial impressions are not necessarily fully negative or awkward, as it is Trish who notices Jessica is awake after she makes a callous remark about Jessica's family. This suggests that Trish, who is already unhappy being a teen star, has pushed aside her own unhappiness to empathize with someone else.

It is not until later in their linear timeline, in episode 1.11, that the audience learns of Trish's trauma, which extends beyond substance abuse and (accidental) arson. Shortly after moving in with the Walker family, Jessica overhears an argument between Trish and her mother regarding Trish's status as Patsy and Trish's hatred of playing someone she is not. The argument escalates to Dorothy assaulting Trish with a People's Choice Award, leaving her bleeding. Not only is Trish's trauma a result of physical violence, but there is also the implication of her mother mismanaging her as a child star and abusing her image to make "Patsy" a brand. After constantly reiterating in the argument, "I'm sick of all this Patsy shit. . . . I'm not Patsy!" (ep. 1.11, "AKA I've Got the Blues"), Trish experiences an identity crisis. Her trauma now stems, in addition to physical abuse, from a loss of identity and self, just as Jessica's very identity undergoes a similar metamorphosis. Furthermore, it is this scene in episode 1.11 that shows Jessica first using her super strength inadvertently. Yet, neither girl is ready to accept her new lot in life; Jessica refuses to let Dorothy know about her increased strength to avoid the same exploitation that Trish experiences, and Trish does not want her personal identity and imperfect image to be made public. At this point in their lives, Jessica is physically and mentally stronger than Trish and superior in her place (despite being an orphan), gloating, "If you tell anybody [about my powers], I'm gonna tell everybody that you're a pathetic victim of child abuse. They'll make a Lifetime movie about it: *Stolen Childhood: The Patsy Walker Story*. I'd be saving you" (ep. 1.11). Horrified at the potential loss of her carefully constructed identity, Trish succumbs to Jessica's blackmail, but with a caveat: "You don't tell anyone and you don't try to save me" (ep. 1.11).

However, it is not until Jessica *actually* saves Trish that the two girls begin to solidify their friendship into something deeper. When Trish's mother manhandles her, and then body-shames her by saying, "the camera adds ten pounds. . . . You want them to call you *Fatsy*?" (ep. 1.11), it is Jessica who barges in and tells Dorothy to stop, despite Trish's reservations:

Trish: You promised not to save me.

Jessica: I can't help it. [*Throws Dorothy into a wall, demonstrating her strength.*]

Trish: Now she knows.

Jessica: Good. (ep. 1.11)

Jessica sacrifices the safety of her anonymity, something she felt strongly about in the light of Dorothy's exploitation, to save Trish from something she was being forced into—in this case, becoming Patsy. By giving up something precious to her, Jessica begins to reassemble her identity, just as Trish re-evaluates hers.

Ladies' Men: Kilgrave and Simpson

Although Jessica's choice to save Trish from her mother established a bond between the two girls, it resulted in an act of violence. When Bendis created Jessica Jones, he made sure that the audience knew that something bad had happened to her in the past. This is a reflection of the story's complexity, because it shows that Jessica does not think of herself as a hero (Kaveney 2008). The violent actions taken against Jessica, including those aimed specifically at women and resulting in trauma, become facilitators of Jessica's narrative and identity, thereby creating conflict. This is problematic, as it requires a traumatic event *in addition to* the earlier one that established Jessica as a "superhero."

Kaveney notes that the original *Alias* run was about who Jessica came to be, but this first depended on her becoming crime-fighting Jewel, someone who is "always pretty and always bright and cheerful," with her "costume of virginal white, sky blue and pastel pink" representing an innocent age or way of looking at things (2008, 71). Jewel is someone who desperately wants to save people, and this is reflected in her name, costume, and ideology. This also happens in the television series between Jessica and Trish. In episode

1.05, Jessica is selling hoagies on a New York street corner when a little girl walks by her, ignoring the fact that her father has stopped at the crosswalk to look at his cell phone. The girl continues into the street, where a taxi blares its horn and attempts to brake. Jessica, witnessing this, gasps and steps in front of the girl with her hands outstretched and placed on the hood of the vehicle, stopping it completely. Jessica feels appreciated when the little girl says, "the sandwich saved me. Thank you." This pivotal moment in Jessica's life brings her to Trish, who in a nod to the *Alias* comics holds up Jessica's superhero costume, only for Jessica to respond, "The only place anyone is wearing that is trick-or-treating or as part of some kinky role-playing scenario" (ep. 1.05, "AKA The Sandwich Saved Me"). Although not fully committed to the idea of assuming her role as a superhero, she knows that it is something that Trish wishes she could do. So when Trish asks, "So you're really gonna do it? You're gonna be a hero?" Jessica replies only with, "We'll see" (ep. 1.05). The television show often alludes to Jessica assuming the worst of humanity— especially when referring to being "saved" and through her dubious belief in heroism. Much of this revolves around the idea that Jessica thinks people only "save" others when there is something in it for them (particularly seen in episodes 1.04, 1.05, and 1.10, where she complains about the state of people, heroes, heroism, and her own understanding of it; but most notably in episode 1.11, when Jessica says, "Humanity sucks and they don't deserve saving"). The television show therefore contrasts Bendis's Jessica/Jewel, who happily went about becoming a superhero pre-Killgrave, to Rosenberg's Jessica, who is only interested in saving people on *her* terms and without hiding her identity or having her alter ego.

Of course, Jessica only considers becoming a superhero because Trish so clearly wants to be one herself, as the establishment of their teenage friendship had constantly revolved around the concept of "saving" Trish. At the beginning of episode 1.05, the audience learns of Jessica's past, just before she met Kilgrave. After quitting her day job, where she uses her fledgling detective skills to blackmail her fraudulent boss, Jessica meets Trish at a bar for drinks. She humiliates a man hitting on Trish at a punching arcade game, resulting in Trish lamenting the misuse of Jessica's abilities:

> Trish: You could use your abilities for something more useful. I mean, you can fly . . . well, jump.

Jessica: It's more like guided falling. [*Pauses.*] Hey, I have an idea. Why don't you put on a cape and go run around New York?

Trish: You know I would if I could.

Jessica: I don't get you. You have money, looks, a radio show, creepy if not adoring fans, and you're a freaking household name. What more do you want?

Trish: To save the world, of course.

Jessica: You wanna be a hero? I'll show you how to be a hero. [*To everybody in the bar*] Shots on Trish Walker, everybody! (ep. 1.05, "AKA The Sandwich Saved Me")

Jessica's response is about diminishing the idea that superheroes are selfless or altruistic, as she claims that people do not want a superhero with a cape and costume to rescue them; they want to have a good time. Where Trish sees the glass half full, Jessica sees it only dirty and smudged. Perhaps the worst part, for the audience, is knowing that the only time Jessica truly saves someone, the only time she truly acts like a superhero on her own—her good deed of saving Malcolm—calls Kilgrave's attention to her and begins six months of further trauma, all because Jessica helped someone, or as she says, "I made a difference" (ep. 1.05).

Roz Kaveney criticizes Bendis's female characters, suggesting that there is always a problematic relationship with their status as "heroes" (2008, 74). In the graphic novel, Kaveney notes, "Jessica becomes Kilgrave's whipping girl for every defeat he had ever had at the hands and fists of male superheroes" (93). The relationship between the two becomes a power struggle between hero and villain, whereas in the Netflix version, Kilgrave is a misogynist and a critic of the whole superhero ethic instead of someone who feels like he must tear down superheroes to make himself feel better. The television version is more about gender power and superheroes versus power and humiliation. This is because in *Alias*, Kaveney states, Bendis avoids the obvious—Killgrave did not rape Jessica. He constantly humiliates her in every other sexual way possible, as "rape would have been the cliché . . . leaving [Bendis] open to the charge of being a man who did not understand the issue" (93–4). Yet in the television show, he *does* rape Jessica. Rape becomes a trauma that is contextualized within a more justifiable framework of domestic violence, betrayal, and self-defence in a way that humiliation is not (Quintero Johnson and Miller 2016).

Often, when women are shown committing acts of violence on television, there are gender-based explanations, writes Jessie Quintero Johnson and Bonnie Miller in their article, "When Women 'Snap': The Use of Mental Illness to Contextualize Women's Acts of Violence in Contemporary Popular Media" (2016). They note that these situational circumstances are linked to mood disorders, intense anxiety and frustration, or trauma—all of which ultimately can be used to explain why a woman might "snap" and become violent. Jessica's response to the trauma inflicted upon her is to withdraw socially, becoming moody, tense, and aggressive toward others. Quintero Johnson and Miller state that this sympathetic violence is due to social and personal circumstances beyond the perpetrator's control. This also occurs with Trish in her dealings with Will Simpson.

Before becoming a member of the New York City Police, Will Simpson was in the United States military. He uses his military contacts and equipment to aid Trish and Jessica, as well as his knowledge and understanding of how to trap Kilgrave. However, his military past is also shrouded in secrecy and the usual comic villainy, as the audience quickly learns that while he was in the military, Simpson was part of a project that gave soldiers performance-enhancing drugs (called "Combat Enhancers" in the show), which gives him super strength and excessive aggression. These qualities make him particularly enticing to Kilgrave, who places him under his mental control; it is only after Jessica frees him, and once his guilt in attacking Trish manifests itself, that he decides to try and stop Kilgrave. Therefore, Trish falls victim to the troubling "knight in shining armour" narrative whereby women who have been hurt and treated poorly by men (and who previously decided that they did not want to date such men) allow grand gestures to eclipse their partner's earlier questionable actions. Trish begins to date Simpson, and while the two get along, with Simpson even helping the two women plot against Kilgrave, he quickly begins to disagree with Jessica's plan. In episode 1.10, while Simpson is drugged, he physically attacks Trish, who in response locks him outside the room she is in. This becomes her first indication that Simpson is not fully in control of his faculties, and his mental state continues to deteriorate. In episode 1.03, the audience learns that Trish, who already converted Jessica's bedroom in her apartment into a gym, needed a place "to train. . . .

No one touches me unless I want them to," she says in response to her mother's abuse as she learns to take control of her body. Reacting to Simpson's abuse, Trish then takes control of the situation in ways she previously could not. In the fight between Jessica and Simpson, Trish becomes the hero, saving Jessica instead of the other way around. It is now the one with superpowers who needs to be saved, while the "normal" human does the saving. This scene highlights the importance of the concept of heroism for the two women's identities. Furthermore, it explores the notion of Trish's heroism, something that comes from within—from conviction and a desire to help, rather than from superhero abilities. It is Trish's storyline in the series that teaches Jessica that her powers do not control her (in the sense of how Kilgrave took control of *her*, using his power to abuse *her* powers). Jessica instead learns that inner strength is the necessary ingredient in becoming a hero, and that no matter what she does, Trish would be there for her.

Girl Power

Exploring the multiple traumas that Jessica and Trish have experienced in their lives, and which created the basis of their friendship, as portrayed in season 1 of *Marvel's Jessica Jones*, provides interesting avenues of discussion and analysis vis-à-vis the role of women in comic adaptations and women on television, and particularly the bonds between them. However, while there are parallels between the two women and their traumas, it is the relationship between them that is particularly important, because beyond their traumas, the two can constantly support each other, thereby facilitating their journeys of self-discovery. They become stronger women, better friends, and overcome their traumas in positive ways. Referring to the graphic novel *Alias* and the show's original script, Kaveney describes Carol Danvers's friendship with Jessica Jones as the reason why these two damaged women represent such powerful support mechanisms for each other. This bond, of course, goes far beyond their casual banter about men (Kaveney 2008)—as female superheroes are often included in storylines that revolve around men in some fashion or another. The characters of Carol and Jessica are both reflected in storylines that revolve around the traumas done to them *by* men, and both overcame male villains. For the Netflix version, Trish is no alcoholic, but she certainly shares a traumatic backstory that turns on her sense of self as it closely relates to her childhood alter ego, Patsy. Although Kaveney questions how someone can be a superhero and self-conscious of their strengths and weakness at the same time, Rosenberg had a plan for that, as reported by Loeb:

> What's most important is the relationship between [Trish] and Jessica, and how these two women who are, in some ways, sisters, in terms of their friendship, could be that different, and yet believe in the same kinds of things. That question of, what is it to be a hero and the responsibilities that you have when you have abilities, is something that brings them together, but also continually pushes them apart. (Radish 2015)

The relationship between Jessica and Trish constantly affirms the role of the hero, the act of "saving" someone, and how this ties into the two women's identities. Both come from different angles and ideologies, but both offer valid points while demonstrating respect for each other. Where Jessica uses her powers to save Hope, Trish uses her powers of emotional support to save Jessica. The push-pull relationship between Jessica and Trish reflects Figueroa's earlier description of the either-or scenario; to achieve an encompassing existence, they must first move beyond the limits of their preconceived identities and their pasts and do so with each other. This observation echoes that of Carolyn Cocca, who notes that female heroes are "strong, community-minded 'woman warriors' who consult, protect, and rely on friends, [who] present an alternative to a hierarchical, individualistic, patriarchal society" (2014, 215).

These two women have a friendship that is unique to television—one in which they can be both competitive and friendly, can love each other and hate each other, and in which they can draw on a shared history while still saving each other when it is most necessary (Radish 2015). Ranging from Trish (slightly) invading Jessica's private life ("You've been keeping tabs on me?" in episode 1.01) to sticking with each other when things are rough ("I'm life-threatening, Trish. Steer clear of me" in episode 1.02), the two constantly reaffirm the importance they play in each other's lives. Whether it is "saving" the other, or just being there, Jessica and Trish embody strong female protagonists who do not let their lives revolve around their pasts and/or male-driven traumas. Instead, they overcome each trauma, each hurdle together, discovering something new about themselves each time as they figure out their identities, but also how they can be "heroes." As shown in the final episode of season 1, Jessica and Trish plan to stop Kilgrave, but they need a special code word to show that he is not controlling them:

> Trish: We should have a code word. If you say it, you're still you. Something you would never say. Like "pickle juice" or "sardines."

> Jessica: Or "I love you."

> Trish: [*Pause*.] Yeah. That'll work. (ep. 1.13, "AKA Smile")

While Jessica might be a superhero due to her abilities and her choice to save others, it is Trish who is Jessica's hero: her beautiful, strong best friend who means more to her than anything.

NOTES

1   Readers should note that in the original *Alias* graphic novel, this name is spelled with two *l*s ("Killgrave"), whereas in the Netflix television show, it is spelled "Kilgrave." I will use these two spellings to denote which character version—graphic novel or television—I am referring to.

2   Interestingly, Trish can appear as the opposite: she is loving, emotional, and passionate, embodying a softness that contrasts with Jessica's hardness. However, Trish has progressed further than Jessica in her work to encompass all these traits in her identity, as she is successful and independent. She lacks the same frigidity and strength that Jessica embodies, but she attempts to make up for this fact with her martial arts training.

3   For example, Jessica snaps at her brother with comments like "I'm going to kill you if you don't leave me alone," and "twelve hours in a car with you? Fine, leave without me" (ep. 1.08, "AKA WWJD?").

4   The star of the television show *It's Patsy!*, Trish absolutely hates her alter ego, and indeed any reminder of her position as a teen starlet. The audience learns of this when she awkwardly blurts out, "This is torture" (ep. 1.11, "AKA I've Got the Blues").

References

Cocca, Carolyn. 2014. " 'It's About Power and It's About Women': Gender and Political Economy of Superheroes in *Wonder Woman* and *Buffy the Vampire Slayer*." In *Heroines of Film and Television: Portrayals in Popular Culture*, edited by Norma Jones, Maja Bajac-Carter, and Bob Batchelor, 215–35. Lanham, MD: Rowman and Littlefield.

Figueroa, Laura M. 2015. "A Good Girl, a Graduate, a Gynecologist, and a Gladiator: A Qualitative Analysis of Representations of Women in Four Television Shows." Honour's thesis, Trinity College, Hartford, CT. Trinity College Digital Repository, http://digitalrepository.trincoll.edu/theses/524.

Kaveney, Roz. 2008. "The Heroism of Jessica Jones: Brian Bendis' Alias as Thick Text." In *Superheroes! Capes and Crusaders in Comics and Films*, 63–99. London: I. B. Tauris.

Kreuze, Alette. 2016. "The Female Hero: Finding Her Place in the Male Dominated World of Film." Master's thesis, University of Leiden.

Lauzen, Martha M. 2016. *It's a Man's (Celluloid) World: Portrayals of Female Characters in the Top 100 Films of 2015*. San Diego, CA: Center for the Study of Women in Television Film.

Quintero Johnson, Jessie M., and Bonnie Miller. 2016. "When Women 'Snap': The Use of Mental Illness to Contextualize Women's Acts of Violence in Contemporary Popular Media." *Women's Studies in Communication* 39 (2): 211–27.

Radish, Christina. 2015. "*Jessica Jones*: Melissa Rosenberg and Jeph Loeb Talk Characters, Tone, Action and More." *Collider*, July 29, 2015. http://collider.com/jessica-jones-tone-action-melissa-rosenberg-jeph-loeb-interview/.

Watts, Steve. 2015. "Captain Marvel's Carol Danvers Was Originally on Jessica Jones." *IGN*, November 19, 2015. https://www.ign.com/articles/2015/11/20/captain-marvels-carol-danvers-was-originally-on-jessica-jones.

"I Can't Leave": The Iconography of Hysteria and the Anti-superhero

Sorouja Moll

"I watched Jessica Jones *and it reminded me of you," somebody said to me in a public message on Facebook.*

—Mo Daviau 2016.

Mo Daviau is not a superhero. She is a survivor. She is also a writer who reflects on the day-to-day implications of living through the haunting torment of an abusive relationship, and on how, even though she is now departed from its physical space, she is never really able to escape. Daviau suffers from the effects of post-traumatic stress disorder (PTSD), and the suggestion that she watch *Marvel's Jessica Jones* perhaps arrived as a salve prescribed to soothe a friend's pain and to express that she is not alone; there is someone else out there who survived gender-based violence. Yet, Daviau recalls that while sitting on her bed, laptop open streaming the cleverly packaged reanimation of her experienced violence, she related less to Jessica Jones than to the figure of Hope. The two characters (Jessica and Hope) are cut from the same cloth—rape culture. Jennifer Keishin Armstrong (2016) argues that the series's representation of the female anti-superhero serves "a purpose"; she points out that "they [female anti-heroes] might hold up a mirror to our society's own worst traits," or "they might offer a story of redemption . . . and some of the best of our anti-heroines also trace their fatal flaws back to their struggles with, specifically, womanhood." In this chapter, I explore the "purpose" of the anti-superhero exemplar in *Marvel's Jessica Jones*. I argue that the gendered, sexualized, and popularized representations of transgression are pooled to reinforce patriarchal hierarchies and hysteria stereotypes with ideological strategies that make the former and latter inescapable. To do this work, I undertake a comparative discourse analysis in order to show that the show's narratives and visual tropes representing transgression are not a recent phenomenon, but in fact have a long history. They were reanimated, documented, and archived in a nineteenth-century Paris asylum, La Salpêtrière. Jean-Martin Charcot (1825–93), a French neurologist and professor of anatomical pathology, was a researcher and teacher at the hospital. Known as the "daring Caesar of hysteria" (Showalter 1997, 31), Charcot directed, recorded, and disseminated images of hysteria as choreographed tableaux produced for the public during his *leçons due mardi*, or Tuesday lectures. Charcot devised, in a way not unlike the Netflix series, performances in which transgression and hysteria are bound as twinned representations of the struggles with womanhood specifically, drawn from examples from antiquity and also the work of William Shakespeare. Comparing these contextual histories with *Marvel's Jessica Jones*, I evaluate the repeated objectification and gendered renderings of hysteria amplified by Jones's fight against, and Hope's fall within, the apparatus of patriarchy symbolized in the misogynistic arch-enemy Kilgrave.

I begin by examining the underlying contexts and methods used in the popularized examples of hysteria and their applications appearing in iconic and pedagogical representations of such figures as Hillary Clinton during the 2016 US presidential race. I then carry out a comparative analysis of Jessica Jones, Hope Shlottman, and Charcot's use of Shakespearean characters with his patient Louise Augustine Gleizes (known as Augustine or "A") to exemplify hysteria for his audiences. The legacy of this representation reappears in Jessica and Hope. Further, I examine how Charcot evokes the playwright's figures as an ideological teaching method as they impart the gendered discourses of hysteria in order to demonstrate and sustain inequitable power relations, social hierarchies, and sexual violence. Finally, I argue that the series's characters are rooted in forms of gender-based violence. The show's normalization of abuse continues to popularize stereotypical qualities of hysteria as transgressive agency, and thus reinforces rather than transforms a patriarchal apparatus.

Context and Constructions

Unlike Clea (1964), Ms. Marvel (1968), and Elektra Natchios (1981), Jessica Jones's character is a recent incarnation of a female superhero. Brian Michael Bendis and illustrator Michael Gaydos debuted Jones's character in 2001 for the *Marvel Max Alias* monthly series. The creators are credited with breaking Marvel's gendered catalogue, which up to that point was typified by overly competent heroines donning shiny, size-zero latex outfits and who use their superhero powers to fight crime (Riesman 2017). Jones, in contrast, lives in a messy, Jim Beam–strewn Hell's Kitchen apartment. She dresses in androgynous casual wear: tank top, leather jacket, and jeans. She is a loner. Volatile. A short-fused mess. She is a no-nonsense, alcoholic private dick, and makes no bones about being a sexual free agent with a penchant for expletives and a keen sense for one-liners delivered with the flair of a badass film noir anti-hero. David Betancourt (2015) describes the series as part of a "meaner, edgier and more seductive *Marvel* universe . . . this is an adult show based on adult comic." The choice to develop the female *anti*-superhero was considered a break from the established Marvel lineup. For the series's narrative, Jones's rogue persona is haunted. She embodies her PTSD as a survivor of aggravated rape perpetrated by the show's villain, Kilgrave. The manifestation of hallucinations, anxiety, addiction, and anti-social behaviours are integral to Jones's character development and her divergence from the Marvel norm. The culmination of these elements gives her a *purpose*: to save Hope. The sexual violence at the series's core gravitationally coalesces the two characters under Kilgrave's command; this gender-based violence resonates with viewers because of the prevalence of violence in various social, economic, and political milieus. It affects Mo Daviau. It affects us all. The character Hope Shlottman is an undergraduate student from Omaha, Nebraska, who lives and studies in New York City. She came under the influence of Kilgrave, who used his powers of mind control to kidnap her, rape her, and force her to murder her own parents. Hope is made to serve two life sentences for this crime. Jessica Jones, for her part, is determined to prove Hope's innocence by forcing Kilgrave to either confess or expose his powers. The "hope" Jones embodies in the act of emancipating Shlottman from her patriarchal prison concomitantly dispatches Jones as a metaphoric and vicarious agent of hope that might save us (faithful series audience) from the intersectional violence encountered in our own lives. Yet how do the unconventional attributes of an "anti-hero" still contain Jessica Jones within the patriarchal lexicon of hysteria?

The language of "hysteria" appears within ancient medical discourse as an abstract Greek noun: *hystera*, or womb. It reappears in the nineteenth century as a neurosis ubiquitously represented in the female body as a nervous condition or one that appears as an unhealthy emotion or as excessive excitement. When the subject disobeys laws set in stone by the patriarchal order, they are held in contempt, and placed outside of the normalized and opposing state of the feminized obedient body that is deemed civilized, well-behaved, and not nasty. Patriarchy determines the rules of transgression (housed by language); therefore, resistance remains bound within the established structure, even and most especially when excluded from it. The question is: Are demonstrations of disobedience *purposeful* in order to make intelligible the complexities and contradictions of gendered obedience and thus to sustain it?

During the third and final debate for the 2016 American presidential election, for instance, Donald Trump called Hillary Clinton "a nasty woman." As soon as Trump delivered his remarks, tweets stormed the Internet with the hashtag #strongwomenarenastywomen. Trump's misogyny-fuelled rhetoric publicly disparaging a strong, intelligent, and non-compliant woman received blowback in the form of a counter-discourse from individuals who decided to "own it": "Yes, as a matter of fact, I am nasty." This form of resistance is not new. How, then, is Jessica Jones's character held within a parallel framework? She, too, "owns" a character type that is "transgressive" because she is categorized as non-compliant within Marvel comic book norms and its constructed narrative. Are these assertions of agency that kick back against patriarchal bombast actually transformative, or are they reiterations of flagrant enunciations that stabilize dominant codes of power—even in their resistance?

Jessica Jones's character is "nasty" and damaged and scarred. Her hysteria manifests not only in her character's PTSD but is also projected materially and symbolically in the figure of Hope; both experience the consequences of being captured in Kilgrave's mind-controlling power and thus centre questions of agency, free will, and concepts of autonomy and resistance. As Maureen Ryan (2015) explains in a review of the show, "these elements allow Rosenberg [the show's creator] to construct intelligent, well-crafted mediations on the ways in which women are manipulated by social pressures to conform and sacrifice part of themselves to avoid being labeled troublemakers." The upshot of Ryan's circular observation is that the stereotype of "troublemakers" is unavoidable because of the "social pressures" from patriarchal constraints. Kilgrave's insistence that Jones's character "smile," as an example, conforms to gendered coding that demands acquiescence and the sacrifice of agency (ep. 1.05, "AKA The Sandwich Saved Me"). Resistance does make the structure visible—I agree—but is the structure transformed over the course of the series or does it adhere to a hegemonic model of gendered obedience—again, even in acts of resistance? "Transgression" is an act that goes beyond a law, rule, or command; it is an offence, a violation, a sin. Thus, transgression is hysteria's handmaiden in that to be cast as hysterical is to break gendered codes of conduct, laws, and rules. Judith Butler (2006) locates "gender in the repeated stylization of the body, a set of repeated acts within a highly rigid regulatory frame that congeal over time to produce the appearance of substance, of a natural sort of being" (45). Butler further explains that "a political genealogy of gender ontologies, if it is successful, will deconstruct the substantive appearance of gender into its constitutive acts and locate and account for those acts within the compulsory frames set by the various forces that police the social appearance of gender" (45). What, then, are the *repeated acts* being played out in the ontological representation of Jones and her trauma? How does it continue to conform to patriarchal structures even against the *intelligent mediations* of the show's director? How has sexual violence imbued and policed ontological states of being to the point that it not only defines subjectivity but also controls act of resistance?

Michel Foucault (1978) famously described what he called "the law of transgression and punishment, with its interplay of licit and illicit. Whether one attributes to it the form of the prince who formulates rights, of the father who forbids, of the censor who enforces silence, or of the master who states the law, in any case one schematizes power in a juridical form, and one defines its effects as obedience" (84). In the Netflix series, transgression as a gendered act is paradoxically treated as a form of structural obedience that is marked as and combined with sexuality and violence, which is continually governed, dictated, fetishized, and popularized because it is predictable, reliable, and familiar behaviour. "Hysteria," as Elaine Showalter (1997) describes it, "has come to imply behaviour that produces the *appearance* of disease," and there remains an unfixed diagnosis (14). Yet, throughout medical history, Showalter shows, hysteria has been associated with women (15). How, then, do we make meaning, how do these meanings sustain themselves, and why are they necessary? Stuart Hall (1997) contends that "meaning is *not* in the object or person or thing, nor is it *in* the word. It is we who fix the meaning so firmly that, after a while, it comes to seem natural and inevitable" (21; italics in original).

Acquiring obedience takes time, and so, too, does the nailing of meaning to dependable outcomes. Foucault (1977) examines the implementation of docile bodies and the art of distribution as the technique of disciplining, with the result that "what was then being formed was a policy of coercions that act upon the body, a calculated manipulation of its elements, its gestures, its behaviour" (138). After murdering her parents, and at the apex of her hypnotic state under Kilgrave's control, Hope tells Jessica to "smile"; the action distributes, by proxy, the disciplining of gendered protocols and the transference of power that runs parallel in Trump's and Clinton's respective campaigns. During the 2016 race, Hillary Clinton was publicly criticized for her unapproachable manner and her inability to "connect" with the electorate. The feminized and interpersonal sentiments were articulated in the suggestion, so often directed at to Clinton, that she "Smile. You just had a big night" (Zarya 2016).

The longer history of gendered and socialized coercion is found in the *Malleus Maleficarum* (1487; see Mackay 2009). This lengthy treatise, written by Catholic clergymen Heinrich Kramer and Jacob Sprenger, was used as a reliable method to profile, accuse, and persecute individuals suspected of witchcraft. It established the rules of evidence and the canonical measures by which alleged witches were subsequently tortured and executed. Similarly, in his quest to conceptualize madness, Charcot employed techniques used during the witch hunts, such as identifying hysterical stigmata on bodies and "pricking or writing on the sensitive skin of patients" (Showalter 1997, 32). The pedagogical foundation for communicating what constitutes a "witch," "deviant," "transgressor," "whore," "hysteric," or "nasty woman" operates through what Giorgio Agamben (2009) describes as the apparatus. Agamben contends that living beings are captured by the apparatus (which comprises education, prisons, governments, laws, language, religion, military, etc.), and that within this "capture" there is a continual struggle. It is through this struggle that the living being is processed as a subject (Agamben 2009, 13–17). In other words, it is the subjectification of us. Objects are used to create a continuum of desires to keep living beings captured and serviced through capitalism, and these include everything from the Internet, microwaves, mortgages, porn, cars, *The Real Housewives*, love, phones, protests, music, pens, Facebook, bathroom tiles, cars, soy milk, Ritalin, comic books, hope, Netflix, etc. These objects of desire are the power of the apparatus. The subjectified subject then uses their acquired objects and never-ending desires to masquerade as an assumed "identity" and environment—or to declare this is "I." The subjectification of a living being is within the apparatus's blueprint, and over time gendered etymologies and ontologies are infused with codes to enforce power relations such as morality and its counterpoint, transgression. Foucault (1978) reminds us that "there is no binary and all-encompassing opposition between rulers and ruled at the root of power relations and serving as a general matrix. . . . One must suppose rather that the manifold relationships of force that take shape and come into play in the machinery of production, in families, limited groups, and institutions, are the basis for wide-ranging effects of cleavage that run through the social body as a whole" (94). Thus, while Foucault argues that there is no binary, those with a stake in existing power relations use such artificial constructions to reduce and polarize in order to create zones of intelligibility—otherwise known as common ground. Consequently, power relations use established binaries to determine who we are based on assessments of the other, the excluded, and the disobedient. Moral indignation, for instance, is oriented as an ethical compass in the directional process of subjectifying living beings in an effort to locate meaning and self-concept in the apparatus—who I am and who I am not—all guided by capitalism, patriarchy, and gender-based violence. When Jones attempts to explain to lawyer Jeri Hogarth the constraints she confronts when battling against Kilgrave, she identifies aspects of the apparatus: "Hope Shlottman is getting crucified in the media. . . . My story will put me in the same position as Hope." "Incarcerated," Hogarth replies. Jones continues, "Kilgrave leaves a trail of broken people behind him. . . . I am busy trying to bring Kilgrave in, change public perception, and victims will come forward" (ep. 1.03, "AKA It's Called Whiskey"). Jones perceives the apparatus's interlocking points as a carceral network through which beings flow and bio-power moves. Within the schematic of the apparatus, "this bio-power was without question an indispensable element in the development of capitalism; the latter would not have been possible without the controlled insertion of bodies into the machinery of production and the adjustment of the phenomena of population to economic processes" (Foucault 1978, 140–1).

An institution that deployed, and indeed constituted, discourses of transgression and hysteria with the insertion of bodies into the machinery was at La Salpêtrière. George Didi-Huberman (2003) calls it "the fair of monstrosities" (235), "a kind of feminine inferno . . . confining four thousand incurable or mad women" (xi). When producing his iconography of hysteria, Charcot reinforced a gendered template with his *attitudes passionnelles*, using titles such as "summons," "amorous supplication," "mockery," "menace," "eroticism," and "ecstasy," as well as the "resolution" that culminated in the performance of the subject's redemption (Showalter 1997, 33). The objective was to cure transgression, which necessitated the subject's obedience toward redemption by being sexually and intellectually exploited. The asylum was famous. Writers saw it as a "museum," but "Salpêtrière was the capital of smoke screens" (Didi-Huberman 2003, 235). In 2017, and still in 2024, the preoccupation with established gendered stereotypes continues and this preoccupation's association with the body through varying forms of medical and pop-culture performances. Melissa Rosenberg explains the process by which she adapted Jessica Jones's *Alias* comic book to television as follows: "What we did throughout the first 13 hours, you would take a nugget from the comic book and expand upon it . . . so you're constantly filling in" (Hill 2015). Yet, from which part of the apparatus does Rosenberg draw in order to "fill in" these gaps?

Augustine and Hope and Jessica Jones

Charcot's lectures at La Salpêtrière were held on Tuesdays. The asylum's "mastery over repetition was already highly instrumentalized—and in the sense that it was almost ideally accepted—on these hysteric bodies that had become nearly transparent representative agencies, deprived as they were of resistance" (Didi-Huberman 2003, 232–3). Sigmund Freud called a body deprived of resistance "ideal" (Didi-Huberman 2003, 233).

When Freud's paradigm is compared to the series, Kilgrave's instrument of mind control to manipulate individuals as empty vessels follows a routinized patriarchal model. Jones's refusal to be governed by Kilgrave was not a Freudian "ideal"; nevertheless, she is still within the apparatus. Jones's investigation into Hope's disappearance, for instance, doubles as a spiralling excursion into her own present trauma; she is ushered in by the hotel's concierge as she enters: "Ms. Jones. I thought that was you. Welcome back." (ep. 1.01, "AKA Ladies' Night"). The hotel bedroom scene in episode 1.01 is the performative locus that fuses together Jones and Hope. Daviau describes the scene as follows: "I am alone in my bed with the first episode of *Jessica Jones* on my laptop. I felt fine until we meet the character Hope lying in a puddle of her own piss in a hotel bed, refusing to get up and leave under orders of the villain who has mind-controlled her to stay put" (Daviau 2016). Daviau contemplates the loss of agency as she makes visible the disciplining mechanics of the apparatus. Jones must pry Hope from the bed. The symbolic struggle of wills between the two characters materializes the conflicts against the embodied and externally forced gendered limitations that keep each woman imprisoned. Hope's repeated declaration, "I can't leave" (ep. 1.01, "AKA Ladies' Night"), is emblematic of the perpetual violence that underscores not only her present condition but also her (and Jones's) historical chains. Hope's "phase of tonic immobility" (Didi-Huberman 2003, 123) while screaming "I can't leave!" from Kilgrave's bed is a repeated act from Charcot's catalogue of hysteria that resonates for Daviau in the twenty-first century. It is an echo of Charcot's patient Augustine: "The 'image' of hysteria in the nineteenth century—and certainly something of it remains with us today—the vulgarized image of hysteria was the one produced and proposed by Charcot" (Didi-Huberman 2003, 235).

"Augustine" is the name Charcot used to identify her. She was the most photographed of all of the asylum's "hysterics" (Showalter 1997, 35). In 1875, Augustine was fifteen years old when her mother left her at La Salpêtrière. Throughout her young life, she endured sexual abuse. Augustine's so-called hysterical attacks emerged at the age of thirteen after her employer, a man who was also her mother's lover, raped her (De Marneffe 1991, 88). For five years, Charcot exploited Augustine as he directed her, along with other women and girls, to perform during his Tuesday lectures, where they would pose for the patriarch and his international, multidisciplinary audience (see figure 13.1 below). These actions repeat with Hope when she tells Jones, "he made me jump for hours as high as I could" (ep. 1.02, "AKA Crush Syndrome"). Augustine performed the phases of hysteria from a bed not unlike the bed in Kilgrave's hotel room that imprisoned Hope. Charcot used photography as the medium with which to repeat his ideological choreography; likewise, in the series Jones discovers Kilgrave's room plastered with her photographed images (ep. 1.03, "AKA It's Called Whiskey"). Jones is subsequently compelled to photograph herself in order to maintain Kilgrave's archive and as a

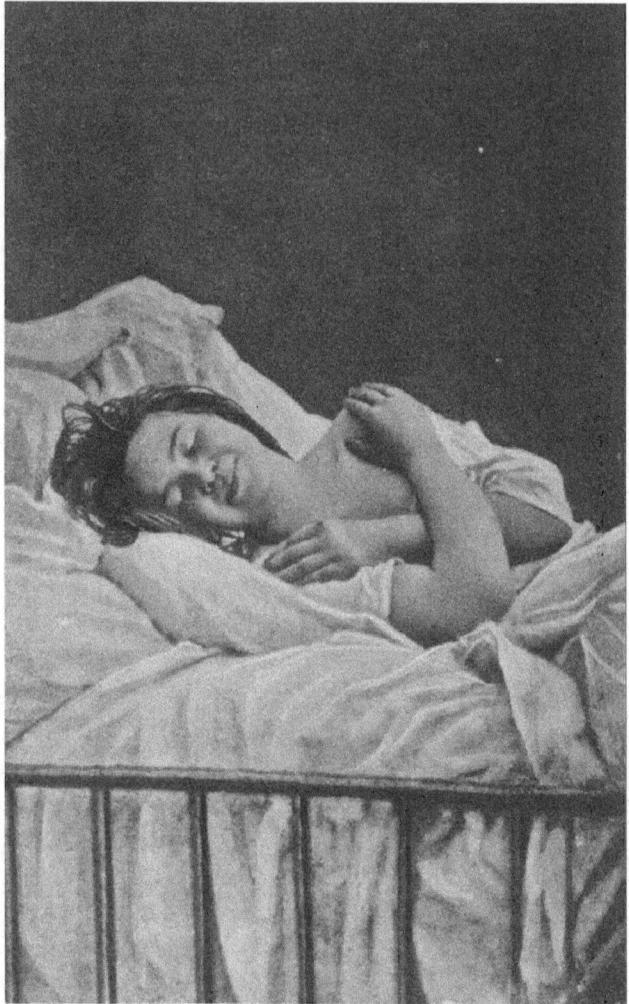

Fig. 13.1. *Attitudes Passionnelles Erotisme*, 1878, Paul-Marie-Léon Regnard (French, 1850–27). J. Paul Getty Museum, Los Angeles. Digital image courtesy of Getty's Open Content Program.

way of policing her behaviour (ep. 1.04, "AKA 99 Friends"; ep. 1.05, "AKA The Sandwich Saved Me").

While Jones's defiance, disobedience, and brazen sexuality conform to a gendered "disciplinary partitioning" (Foucault 1995, 199), her rebellious character reinforces the apparatus of patriarchy based on a gendered hierarchy and desire. An excerpt from Augustine's 1878 patient transcript reveals her resistance against Charcot and the containment of institutionalized sexual violence: "I won't uncross my legs! . . . Oh! You really did hurt me. . . . No, you won't manage! . . . Help! . . . Camel! Lout! Good-for-nothing! . . . Pardon me! Pardon me, Monsieur! Leave me alone. . . . It's impossible!" (quoted in Didi-Huberman 2003, 83). Her voice resonates in Jones's delivery when confronting Kilgrave, from which point she is no longer represented as being under his control:

Jessica: I told you not to touch me

Kilgrave: God's sake. Come on, Jessie.

Jessica: Do not call me that.

Kilgrave: We used to do a lot more than just touch hands.

Jessica: Ya, it's called rape.

Kilgrave: What? Which part of staying in five-star hotels, eating in all the best places, doing whatever the hell you wanted is rape?

Jessica: The part where I didn't wanna do any of it. Not only did you physically rape me, but you violated every cell in my body and every thought in my god damn head.

Kilgrave: That's not what I was trying to do.

Jessica: It doesn't matter what you were trying to do. You raped me again, and again, and again. (ep. 1.08, "AKA WWJD")

While Jones's character makes visible the power dynamics of subjugated bodies in the apparatus, her persona replicates the "disciplinary mechanism" (Foucault 1977, 197) that constrains her character as a transgressive woman who is abject, outcast, hysterical, and indifferent; and in this way, the narrative reproduces the familiar exclusion of a strong woman gone awry. The scene identifies the boundary lines as well as the temporal and spatial (exclusion-inclusion) dynamics of being captive in an apparatus that repeats and sustains sexual violence as it perpetually constrains women and girls by guilt and/or shame. The cycle is represented when Jones pleads to the police to institutionalize her because she feels it is her only recourse: "Now I'm confessing. Open and shut. . . . I am sick. I am dangerous and I belong in supermax" (ep. 1.07, "AKA Top Shelf Perverts"). The supermax prison represents the most secure level of custody for those deemed the highest security risk because they pose a threat to both national and global security. Jones's inability to control her fate is shown in a paralysis that figuratively manifests in the patriarchal "master" Kilgrave, who ultimately controls the system and Jones's agency.

Showalter examines the role of hysteria in the media and notes that interest in the discourse as a form of resistance surfaced in feminist scholars' writing on women's history: "nineteenth-century hysterical women suffered from the lack of public voice to articulate their economic and sexual oppression, and the symptoms—mutism, paralysis, self-starvation, spasmodic seizures—seemed like bodily metaphors for the silence, immobility, denial of appetite, and hyper-femininity imposed on them by their societies" (1997, 54–5). Diane Price-Herndl (1988) suggests that "hysteria can be understood as a woman's response to a system in which she is expected to remain silent, a system in which her subjectivity is denied, kept invisible" (53). Yet, Jessica and Hope's articulations of resistance ultimately are captured, iconized, and commodified so as to service popular culture. As a parallel, the patients' experiences in the nineteenth-century asylum were transcribed to service not only popular culture but also science. As Jones's friend Trish explains to her when usurping Jones's plan to respond to systemic violence by volunteering to be incarcerated, "You've lost it, Jess, and I get it, I really do, but you are not thinking clearly. . . . You have guilt and shame and it's clouding your judgment. . . . You can't do anything in prison. You can't save Hope. You can't protect anyone, or yourself" (ep. 1.07, "AKA Top Shelf Perverts"). At the institutional level, her lawyer reinforces the diagnosis of Jones's hysteria as she removes her public voice: "You have gone off the deep end. I want to have a psych eval. We will be pleading incompetence. . . . Your judgment is severely impaired" (ep. 1.07, "AKA Top Shelf Perverts").

While Augustine was imprisoned in the asylum, she performed hysteria as directed for Charcot and his audiences; her body, gestures, and refusals were reduced to a sign within a structural hierarchy entrenched in sexual violence. "The sign," as Jacques Derrida (1982) asserts, "represents the present in its absence. It takes the place of the present. When we cannot grasp of or show the thing, state the present, the being-present, when the present cannot be presented, we signify, we go through the detour of the sign. We take or give signs. We signal. The sign, in this sense, is deferred presence" (9). In a parallel example, when attributing a "sign" to a living being, Antonin Artaud (1958) speaks about the struggle of language when deciphering life: "When we speak the word 'life,' it must be understood we are not referring to life as we know it from its surface of fact, but to that fragile, fluctuating center which forms never reach" (13). Augustine, Hope, and Jessica are "deferred" beings in search of their "fluctuating center." In each of their respective transgressions they materialize the ambiguous space in which the iconic image of hysteria floats, lands, and floats again in the pursuit of meaning. Augustine's representation of hysteria landed in medical, social, and commodity discourses, in such fields as theatre, medicine, mass media, photography, popular fiction, and in adaptations of literary works such as those of William Shakespeare, all of which fed the consumptive desires as "signs" that divert us from that which can never be reached—the being of hysteria, transgression, resistance, and our fluctuating living selves. For instance, "the Tuesday Lectures . . . are written, or rather rewritten, just like plays, with lines, soliloquies, strange directions, asides by the hero" (Didi-Huberman 2003, 243). The lectures were "a site of catharsis (for the actresses even more than the spectators), in the sense in which tradition speaks of the catharsis of *humeurs peccantes*, which comes from the verb *peccare*: to sin, to fail, to commit evil and trick others" (244). It was necessary for hysteria as a transgression to be cured, to be put in its place, and to reinforce the power relations that engage gendered hierarchies. To do this work, the *sign* of hysteria had to be disseminated.

The "Tricks i' th' World": Augustine, Hope, Jessica Jones, and Shakespeare

Charcot's international audiences comprised approximately five hundred people, including physicians, writers, artists, scientists, and scholars, and he "delighted his largely nonmedical public" (Didi-Huberman 2003, 235). In Charcot's archived transcriptions, images, and his "theatre of medicine," Augustine is represented as Ophelia-like. Didi-Huberman describes her transcribed and explicit resistance to Charcot's science and to the institutionalized court as "an irruption of the past act 'in person,' the raw, gesticulated hallucination of the act out of a simple suggestion to remember. A theatre of the return of memory . . . then, like flames rekindled . . . as one reads in Shakespeare" (232). In his description, Didi-Huberman isolates moving parts within the apparatus:

> And indeed the doctor is a full partner in this abrupt rekindling of memory in "his subject." He is the partner and actor of

transference, and the figure of the Master. This is why he needs more than the signifying deposition of the event. . . . He needs, in addition, mastery over the reproducibility of this deposition (its theatre reproduced and repeated in photographic procedures). (232)

Charcot and Kilgrave assume the role of "master" as they circumscribe agency in the practice of sexual violence by subjugating girls and women into the role of the hysteric. Showalter explains that during the late nineteenth century, Dr. Charles Bucknill, president of the Medico-Psychological Association in London, England, observed Ophelia to be among a "class of cases by no means uncommon. Every mental physician of moderately extensive experience must have seen many Ophelias. It is a copy from nature, after the fashion of Pre-Raphaelite School" (quoted in Showalter 1994, 86). Ophelia's body is reduced to an object of desire in the apparatus for cultural, social, and economic profit, or to be what Jacques Lacan calls "the object Ophelia," enabling control and furthering patriarchal agendas (Showalter 1994, 77). In a sense, Hope is the series's Ophelia. Her madness, grounded in sexual violence and patriarchal desire, dramatizes the psychological and material warfare that consumes all characters within the series. Consider how Ophelia is watched as she sings her "mad songs" before the court:

Says she hears

There's tricks i' th' world, and hems, and beats her heart,

Spurns enviously at straws, speaks things in doubt

That carry but half sense. Her speech is nothing,

Yet the unshaped use of it doth move

The hearers to collection. (*Hamlet* act 4, scene 5, lines 4–9)

The word "nothing" appears thirty-one times in Shakespeare's *Hamlet*. "Nothing" comes from the Old English *nān thing*, or "no" and "thing." Shakespeare teased out the irony of the word endlessly in his plays; for example, Laertes responds to Ophelia's mad songs with "This nothing's more than matter," and as "A document in madness" (act 4, scene 5, lines 172–5).

Ophelia, in an earlier instance, verbally spars with Hamlet in a sexualized exchange, which also becomes an arena in which Hamlet can project his misogyny (Greenblatt 2008, 329–30):

Hamlet: Do you think I meant country matters?

Ophelia: I think nothing, my lord.

Hamlet: That's a fair thought to lie between maids' legs. (act 3, scene 2, lines 105–7)

"Country" is also a pun on the word "cunt," and the wordplay continues in the scene when the word "nothing" suggests female genitals, which is often linked to the shape of a zero (a ubiquitous Shakespearean trope), or "no thing." The "thing" here represents male genitals, and to have "No thing" (act 3, scene 2, line 109), as Hamlet implies, foreshadowing Laertes's remark that "This nothing's more than matter," is to have a vagina. The female body's synonymous engagement with madness has a long history. Ancient Egyptians offer early descriptions dating to 1900 BCE in the Kahun Papyrus, which "identifies the cause of hysterical disorders in spontaneous uterus movement within the female body" (Tasca et al. 2012, 110). Cecilia Tasca et al. (2012) explain that in the Greek world, argonaut and physician Malampus deemed the revolt of the virgins as madness "derived from their uterus being poisoned by venomous humours" and "uterine melancholy" (110); furthermore, the authors locate the first use of the term "hysteria" in the fifth century BCE in the works of Hippocrates, who believed "that the cause of this disease lies in the movement of the uterus ('hysteron')" (111). The meaning continues to float and land across a historical trajectory leading to Salem, Massachusetts, in 1692, where several outbreaks of hysteria are recorded during the witch trials (115). Hope's "delusion" as diagnosed by her lawyer in episode 1.03 (AKA "It's Called Whiskey") "as fully formed" runs in parallel with the trials of witches and the judgment of Ophelia, who engages in a counter-discourse, her mad songs, among the institutional powers (police, doctors, lawyers, media, prison officials, the court) and communicates the crimes, tricks, and transgressions that the agents of patriarchy have committed (*Hamlet*, act 4, scene 5, lines 152–95). While still incarcerated, Hope confesses her "sanity was touch and go for a while there" (ep. 1.10, "AKA 1,000 Cuts"). Kilgrave holds the key. In episode 1.10, "AKA 1,000 Cuts," Jones engages Kilgrave in a Faustian bargain to locate Hope. As Kilgrave states, "You want what I have. . . . I have Hope. . . . She's a living embodiment of your guilt, isn't she?" The concept of guilt is predicated on transgression. Consequently, guilt and its gendered connection to hysteria are aptly located in Charcot's use of patients to demonstrate the range of madness when staging, for instance, the guilt-ridden figure of Lady Macbeth. Charcot's electric director, Duchenne de Boulogne, would apply electric shocks to his patients to evoke "expressions of cruelty" (Didi-Huberman 2003, 227) on the faces of women and girls, which were then photographed and displayed as evidence for the public and archive: " 'Yet, there's a spot. . . . ' While the same Lady Macbeth notoriously reiterates her crime and her guilt, a little doctor, in the shadows at her side, says: 'Hark! She speaks. I will set down what comes from her, to satisfy my remembrance the more strongly' " (Didi-Huberman 2003, 232).

Another figure Charcot draws from the apparatus's deep narrative well is Saint Joan of Arc (see figure 13.2 below). He describes her as a "transgressive hysteric" (quoted in Showalter 1997, 32). Slavoj Žižek (2004) argues that "the charge against Joan at her trial can be summed up as follows. In order to regain mercy and be readmitted into the Catholic community, she was to (1) disavow the authenticity of her voices, (2) renounce her male dress, and (3) fully submit herself to the authority of the church (as the actual terrestrial institution)" (57).

Joan of Arc appears in Shakespeare's Henry VI,[1] where her depiction could be perceived at either end of the conventional gendered binary: virgin or whore. Joan of Arc's military intelligence and might played a major role in England losing its war against the French. Unsurprisingly, then, Shakespeare depicts the French warrior as a witch and hysteric, a "fallen woman," as described by the character Richard, Duke of York: "Strumpet, the words condemn thy brat and thee / Use no entreaty, for it is in vain" (act 5, scene 6, lines 84–5). The duke seals her fate: "Break thou in pieces, and consume to ashes" (act 5, scene 6, lines 91–2). Joan of Arc is burned at the stake. As Jean E. Howard (2008) explains, "The English respond to this powerful but disarmingly down-to-earth peasant girl by calling her a witch and a whore" (293). Joan of Arc is a figure not unlike Jessica Jones. In battle, Young Talbot attributes Joan's skills to witchcraft, rather than acknowledging her agency and expertise as a leader. Joan of Arc, like Jones, "is an unmarried woman who has turned soldier and assumed the garments of a man." An unwed woman was perceived as being susceptible to Satan's will (Howard 2008, 293–4).

Fig. 13.2. Artist unknown, ca. 1485. Only surviving representation (a verified image has not been found) of Saint Joan of Arc, in the collection of Centre Historique des Archives Nationales, Paris, AE II 2490.

Shakespeare and Charcot effectively alter the historical narrative of Joan of Arc, transforming her from a powerful French warrior into an abject and unnatural monster of war whose downfall on stage bolsters English pride as military propaganda: "this structure is one of neither drama nor knowledge; it is the point where history is immobilized in the tragic category which both establishes and impugns it" (Foucault 1988, xii). Howard (2008) describes the representation of powerful women as anomalies, and thus potentially iconic, as signifying and satisfying what is desired and what is not: "they could be read as criminals or fiends rather than as miraculous exceptions to their cultures' expectations concerning virtuous women" (293).

After years of being held against her will by Charcot, and after her many attempts to escape the institution, one morning Augustine dressed like a man and walked out of the asylum's front doors. Augustine disappeared into the streets of Paris. Her self-emancipation ironically reflected the nineteenth-century trope of the so-called New Woman (who wears masculine attire such as pants), and it points to Jessica's fantasy of using her agency (power) to escape Kilgrave by leaping from his rooftop and riding away (bareback—another gendered Victorian transgression) on an awaiting white stallion (Rosenberg 2015). Jessica remains. Augustine, on the other hand, was never seen again.

What, then, happens to Jessica Jones? The series concludes with Jones returning to her role as a private investigator for two more seasons. In the comic book series, Jessica Jones marries Luke Cage, and in 2015, Marvel released *Secret Wars: Secret Love* no. 1. Writer Jeremy Whitley created a storyline that included Jones and Cage as a married couple helping friends to solve their domestic woes (Fay 2015). When reflecting on Jones, Rosenberg has remarked, "What I love about this character is she's so unapologetically who she is" (quoted in Hill 2015). But is she? I argue that she is a reconstruction of a transgressive subject who maintains gendered hierarchies and hegemonic valuing based on sexual violence. Perhaps this *is* what we want her to be. Jones telling Kilgrave to "smile" (ep. 1.13, "AKA Smile") before she kills him is cathartic relief indeed, but the act is merely a reversal of gendered codes of violence and as such is predicated on and governed by the patriarchal expectations and desires of the apparatus. As Foucault explains, "it [madness] is also the most rigorously necessary form of the quid pro quo in the dramatic economy, for it needs no external element to reach a true resolution. . . . It has merely to carry its illusion to the point of truth" (1988, 34). But what truth is being sought in the gendered representation of the transgressive body?

Conclusion

Kilgrave is dead. Hope is sacrificed. Jessica Jones is domesticated. Patriarchy lives on. As Jones explains, "knowing it's real means you gotta make a decision: (1) keep denying it, or (2) do something about it" (ep. 1.01, "AKA Ladies' Night"). The meta-discourse germane to Jones's dilemma necessitates the questioning of what is *real*. In this chapter, I examined how popular culture constructs the "real" within patriarchal plot lines of the apparatus that depict strong female characters operating through sexual violence rather than transforming the gendered hierarchies and familiar tropes that, not unlike Charcot and Kilgrave, continue to control and dominate them. While Jones attempts to leave the apparatus by "taking myself out of the equation," we are left to wonder if this is at all possible (ep. 1.07, "AKA Top Shelf Perverts"). Jones's trauma, hysteria, and resistance repeat a narrative in which viewers like Daviau and myself, not unlike the members of the Kilgrave Victim Support Group, find a kinship as well as perhaps a salve (ep. 1.09, "AKA Sin Bin"). Misogyny and violence are experienced daily within the apparatus: "I couldn't stop smiling. He wouldn't let me," as a Kilgrave survivor recounts (ep. 1.04, "AKA 99 Friends"). Is the elusive masquerade of an assumed self so manufactured and normalized that our living beings and our *fluctuating centres* are lost to us? Maybe Augustine took herself out of the equation. Maybe I watch *Jessica Jones* to feel my rage vicariously played out by fulfilling a cathartic desire to escape what is otherwise inescapable. "They say everyone is born a hero, but if you let it, life will push you over the line until you are the villain. Problem is you don't always know that you crossed that line. Maybe it's enough if the world thinks I'm a hero; maybe if I work long and hard, maybe I can fool myself" (ep. 1.13, "AKA Smile"). Still, if there is any hope of transforming the apparatus that determines and controls desires with the purpose to incarcerate us, we need to stop fooling ourselves about the roles played, sustained, as well as silenced within the patriarchal system. We need to somehow *remove ourselves from the equation* and pursue our *fluctuating centre*. As Jessica explains, "I can't save you. The whole time he had me, there was some part of me that fought. There was some tiny corner of my brain that tried to get out. But I'm still fighting. I won't *stop* fighting. But if you give up, I lose" (ep. 1.05, "AKA The Sandwich Saved Me").

NOTE

1   See also "Henry VI, Part 1, Appendix: Joan la Pucelle, or Joan of Arc," Folger Shakespeare Library, accessed March 22, 2024, https://www.folger.edu/explore/shakespeares-works/henry-vi-part-1/appendix-joan-la-pucelle-or-joan-of-arc/.

References

Agamben, Giorgio. 2009. *What Is an Apparatus? And Other Essays.* Translated by David Kishik and Stefan Pedatella. Stanford, CA: Stanford University Press.

Artaud, Antonin. 1958. *The Theatre and Its Double.* Translated by Mary Caroline Richards. New York: Grove Press.

Betancourt, David. 2015. "Marvel/Netflix's Game-Changing 'Jessica Jones': A Fanboy's Five-Point Review." *Washington Post*, November 20. https://www.washingtonpost.com/news/comic-riffs/wp/2015/11/20/marvelnetflixs-game-changing-jessica-jones-a-fanboys-five-point-review/?utm_term=.dfe5bd445e35.

Butler, Judith. 2006. *Gender Trouble: Feminism and the subversion of identity.* New York: Routledge.

Daviau, Mo. 2017. "This Is Not Another Jessica Jones Think Piece Written by an Abuse Survivor by Mo Daviau." *Nailed*, February 21, 2017. http://www.nailedmagazine.com/editors-choice/not-another-jessica-jones-think-piece-written-abuse-survivor-mo-daviau/.

De Marneffe, Daphne. 1991. "Looking and Listening: The Construction of Clinical Knowledge in Charcot and Freud." *Signs* 17 (1): 71–111.

Derrida, Jacques. 1982. "Différance." In *Margins of Philosophy*, 3–27. Translated by Alan Bass. Chicago: University of Chicago Press.

Didi-Huberman, Georges. 2003. *Invention of Hysteria: Charcot and the Photographic Iconography of the Salpêtrière.* Translated by Alisa Hartz. Cambridge, MA: MIT Press.

Edmunds, Joan M. 2008. *The Mission of Joan of Arc.* London: Temple Lodge Press.

Fay, Matthew. 2015. "Love Is a Battleworld in 'Secret Wars': Secret Love #1." *PopMatters*, September 2, 2015. https://www.popmatters.com/196919-secret-wars-secret-love-1-2495490873.html.

Foucault, Michel. 1977. *Discipline and Punish: The Birth of the Prison.* Translated by Alan Sheridan. New York: Pantheon Books.

———. 1978. *History of Sexuality.* Vol. 1, *An Introduction.* Translated by Robert Hurley. New York: Vintage Books.

———. 1988. *Madness and Civilization: A History of Insanity in the Age of Reason.* Translated by Richard Howard. New York: Vintage Books.

Greenblatt, Stephen. 2008. "The Tragedy of Hamlet, Prince of Denmark." In *The Norton Shakespeare: Tragedies*, edited by Stephen Greenblatt, Walter Cohen, Jean E. Howard, and Katharine Eisaman Maus, 2nd ed., 323–35. New York: W. W. Norton and Company.

Hall, Stuart. 1997. "The Work of Representation." In *Representation: Cultural Representations and Signifying Practices*, edited by Stuart Hall, 15–74. London: Sage/Open University.

Hill, Libby. 2015. " 'Jessica Jones' Showrunner Melissa Rosenberg Talks Rape, Adaptation, and Female Sexuality." *Los Angeles Times*, November 22, 2015. http://www.latimes. com/entertainment/herocomplex/la-et-hc-st-jessica-jones-melissa-rosenberg-rape-female-sexuality-20151120-story.html.

Howard, Jean E. 2008. "The First Part of Henry the Sixth." In *The Norton Shakespeare: Tragedies*, edited by Stephen Greenblatt, Walter Cohen, Jean E. Howard, and Katharine Eisaman Maus, 2nd ed., 287–96. New York: W. W. Norton and Company.

Keishin Armstrong, Jennifer. 2016. "These Are the Anti-heroines We've Been Waiting For." *BBC*, July 16, 2016. http://www.bbc.com/culture/story/20160707-from-unreal-and-veep-to-jessica-jones-when-women-go-bad.

Mackay, Christopher S. 2009. *The Hammer of Witches: A Complete Translation of the Malleus Maleficarum*. Cambridge: Cambridge University Press.

Price-Herndl, Diane. 1988. "The Writing Cure." *NWSA Journal* 1 (1): 52–74.

Riesman, Abraham. 2015. "Who Is Jessica Jones? And Should I Watch Her TV Show." *Vulture*, November 19, 2015. http://www.vulture.com/2015/11/jessica-jones-alias-explainer.html.

Ryan, Maureen. 2015. "TV Review: 'Marvel's Jessica Jones.' " *Variety*, November 17, 2015. http://variety.com/2015/tv/reviews/jessica-jones-review-krysten-ritter-netflix-1201636528/.

Showalter, Elaine. 1994. *Representing Ophelia: Women, Madness, and the Responsibilities of Feminist Criticism*. London: Macmillan.

———. 1997. *Hystories: Hysterical Epidemics and Modern Media*. New York: Columbia University Press.

Tasca, Cecilia, Mariangela Rapetti, Mauro Giovanni Carta, and Bianca Fadda. 2012. "Women and Hysteria in the History of Mental Health." *Clinical Practice & Epidemiology in Mental Health* 8:110–19.

Zarya, Valentina. 2016. "There Is Literally No Facial Expression Hillary Clinton Can Make to Please Male Pundits." *Fortune*, September 27, 2016. http://fortune. com/2016/09/27/hillary-clinton-smiling-debate/.

Žižek, Slavoj. 2004. "From Antigone to Joan of Arc." *Helios* 31:51–62.

Representations of Rape and Race

Pree Rehal and Caitlynn Fairbarns

In 2016, CBS rejected the pilot for a series called *Drew*, which would have been the first series to depict the character Nancy Drew as a person of colour, despite it having tested well with audiences. This was because *Drew* allegedly "skewed too female" (Ahsan 2016). However, the success of contemporary shows like *Orange Is the New Black* (2013–19) and *Transparent* (2014–19), and films like *Star Wars: A Force Awakens* (2015) and *Mad Max: Fury Road* (2015), continue to prove that femme-centred narratives are capable of being relevant, interesting, and commercially successful. While Netflix conceals specific viewership analytics, third-party research from Symphony Technology Group (STG) provided an estimate of *Jessica Jones*'s viewership based on a sample size of fifteen thousand people (McFarland 2016). Between September and December 2015, STG's automatic content recognition technology counted 4.8 million viewers of *Jessica Jones* over a thirty-five-day cycle, suggesting that shows with women in lead roles are relatable, and evidently lucrative. Although Netflix contested these figures, it nonetheless confirmed that it viewed *Jessica Jones* as a sort of gateway for its users to the wider lineup of Netflix Marvel television series. Vice-President Todd Yellin has stated that although *Daredevil* was the first Netflix Marvel show, the service's data shows that most viewers began with *Jessica Jones* (Dumaraog 2017). Therefore, among these particular series, *Jessica Jones* might in fact be considered the most remunerative.

This chapter will analyze the ways in which *Jessica Jones* demonstrates feminist media progress, while problematizing the ways it creates the illusion of progress as a white feminist show. Dreama G. Moon and Michelle A. Holling argue that, "As a progressive intervention into patriarchy, feminism has traditionally centered (white) women's experience, yet when sex and gender are combined with race, feminism tends to lose its progressive edge" (2020, abstract). In this way, the centring of women's experience becomes a double-edged sword to the extent that it endeavours to advocate for all women while operating from a singular identity or positionality that consequently jeopardizes the feminist project. We'll begin by contextualizing *Jessica Jones* in its genre, positioning ourselves as the authors, defining our terms, and further delving into the nuances of feminism in relation to the show. We do this by analyzing Jessica in the big picture before zooming in on Jessica and her relationships with racialized characters on the show.

Media Representation, Feminist Theory, and *Jessica Jones*

To further understand the important progress that *Jessica Jones* has made for superhero narratives, we must look at the work of influential comic book author Gail Simone, including but not limited to *Deadpool* (1997–2017), *Birds of Prey* (1999–2011), and *Wonder Woman* (2011–17). Simone compiled a selection of comic book superheroines who have been severely brutalized, raped, and murdered.[1] Her work contributes to the discussion of how women have been constructed within comic books to further the story of men. The catalogue of names shows how violence against women is commonly written to drive the plot and character development of masculine superheroes. Gendered and sexualized violence is depicted in popular culture—specifically the comics industry—as a plot point that does not engage with or further the discussion of rape culture. Simone's website shows that within the world of comics, violent acts are shown through the gaze of the perpetrator (and of the superhero who deals with the aftermath of the violence), rather than from the perspective of the victim. The constructed gaze of an assumed cisgender man has a large impact on the ways in which victims are depicted for media consumption.

Despite fan campaigns for more diverse and femme-driven comic content, *Jessica Jones* was the first Marvel television show with a woman lead. For the purposes of this chapter, "women" refers to trans women, cisgender women, and anyone who identifies as a woman (including queer, non-binary, and gender non-conforming folks who claim this label). Fans have been working and fighting hard for more nuanced representation. #WeWantWidow, an online campaign that took place in 2015, is an example of a community joining to fight for Black Widow to get her own television show or movie. It took years of protest for studio heads to do more than merely acknowledge such requests. The *Black Widow* film, starring Scarlett Johansson, was eventually released in 2020. *Captain Marvel* was the first Marvel movie to be released with a woman lead. Creators have stated that Captain Marvel is the strongest superhero in the entire Marvel Cinematic Universe (MCU) (Buchanan 2016). While the movie earned $1 billion at the box office, it was met with sexist trolling, fake reviews, and bad Rotten Tomatoes ratings (Abad-Santos 2019). There was a lot of pushback against its success. This is because the future of women superhero stories was reliant on the financial and critical accomplishments of Captain Marvel in Marvel and Wonder Woman in DC Comics. Since Captain Marvel was the first woman-led Marvel movie ever, there was a lot of pressure for it to be successful. Due to *Captain Marvel*'s financial success, we can hope for a Kamala Khan/Ms. Marvel story.[2] Kamala's story starts after Carol's and is heavily reliant on the Captain Marvel origin story. While studio heads have not given us an exact date for when we will be introduced to Kamala, we need the story of a young woman of colour in the MCU. Especially in the current political climate, we need Kamala on the screen, to also tell the story of a Muslim woman superhero.

Looking at gender and media depictions of rape and sexual assault, this chapter uses *Jessica Jones* as a reference point in its discussion of rape myths. We use the term "rape myths" to define attitudes and beliefs about rape and sexualized violence that perpetuate rape culture. Rape myths are widely shared attitudes that perpetuate victim blaming and slut shaming while excusing or erasing the actions of the perpetrator. We explore how rape myths are commonly represented in media and how they inaccurately portray the reality of survivors and negatively affect consent culture. By engaging critically with *Jessica Jones*, we will investigate how her narrative dismantles rape myths that are commonly depicted within film and television.

In order to analyze this text critically, we find that it is important to begin by establishing our tone and voice. This chapter has been put together in a collaborative manner and the perspective used here is one of "we" and "our." But although this chapter is written collaboratively, the use of "we" and "our" is not meant to imply any equivalence between our respective identities and privileges. As sexual assault survivors, we are approaching the Marvel series *Jessica Jones* with our own histories, experiences, and privileges.

As a descendent of settlers on Turtle Island, and as a brown-skinned, queer, non-binary person who is a survivor of sexual assault, I (Pree) acknowledge that I still benefit from many privileges. I acknowledge these privileges as a cis-passing, caste-privileged, visibly able-bodied person, without an accent that alarms xenophobes, in possession of a graduate education, and as a beneficiary of anti-Black and anti-Indigenous racism as a non-Black person of colour (and settler). As a multiplicitous survivor, I contribute to this chapter so as to validate survivors and to hold space for nuanced conversations within fan studies and cultural studies.

As a cisgender, visibly able-bodied, white queer woman who is a sexual assault survivor, I (Caitlynn) acknowledge that my voice comes from a place of privilege. I am not subjected to the violence and oppression that trans, Black, Indigenous, and racialized folks experience, especially within the larger conversation on sexualized violence and whose story of violence gets to be told. Engaging with *Marvel's Jessica Jones*, I am looking through a critically canonical feminist lens and am using sources that support queer experiences as such voices are often left out of conversations around sexualized violence.

Our chapter is written in solidarity with and in relation to intersectional feminists, and more specifically Black feminist and queer writers. We engage with Kimberlé Crenshaw's (1991) theory of intersectionality to validate the multiple oppressions that Black women and other marginalized people face at the intersection of factors including race and gender. Crenshaw (1991) writes, "Although racism and sexism readily intersect in the lives of real people, they seldom do in feminist and antiracist practices" (1242). We recognize that these oppressions happen as a synthesized experience and are not suffered individually. As we discuss trauma, sexual assault, and rape, we write from our own histories and experience while still addressing stories that are not ours to include multiple voices in the discussion.

To analyze consumption, we will be invoking the concept of "the gaze" throughout this chapter. We will examine how the gaze affects stories of sexualized violence and how the gaze differs in *Jessica Jones* compared to other depictions of rape. Laura Mulvey's work on the "male gaze" within cinema is used as a starting point for our exploration of the Marvel show. Mulvey explores the gaze in two different modes, the passive (feminine) and the active (masculine). Her work looks at how women in media are "looked at" by men, and how women are constructed for masculine pleasure and how this creates the idea of "looked-at-ness" (Mulvey 1999, 833–44). Although Mulvey's ideas work within a gender binary, her theories are relevant to our research on how survivors of sexual assault are depicted for the "male gaze" within movies and television. To expand on "looked-at-ness," we explore how viewers and consumers of media bear witness to sexualized violence. In consuming media of a violent nature without creating action, are we passive witnesses to the events? While watching Jessica's story, are we active or passive viewers?

Throughout its first season, *Jessica Jones* engaged with rape unlike any other Marvel property that we have seen so far. Marvel comic books have portrayed sexualized violence in horrific ways—for example, in *The Avengers* no. 200 (1980) when Ms. Marvel is raped. The comic addresses sexual assault by illustrating incest, abduction, and abuse without addressing the consequences of violence upon the victim. Gender-based violence and assault was shown in Marvel's movie or television properties until *Jessica Jones*. Very clearly and without hesitation, Jessica tells Kilgrave that he raped her (ep. 1.08, "AKA WWJD"). This is a critical moment of the show as we witness a Marvel superheroine define consent culture. In this scene, Kilgrave is confused as to how his actions could be classified as rape, and Jessica responds concisely by saying that she did not want "to do any of it." Activist and popular culture researcher Roz Kaveney (2008) argues that,

> Like pornography, superhero comics always teased, they always offered more than they could ever deliver, on splash covers where grinning villains played with our heroes and heroines as figures on a giant chessboard, or spun them on a wheel of death. Part of the thrill was always that, no matter how powerful superheroes were, they always managed to find themselves in a jeopardy commensurate with their strength. (2)

Jessica Jones stands out against other television shows because we do not often see victims given the opportunity to express their emotions or tell their own stories. Stories about gender-based violence are repeatedly portrayed in the perspective of the attacker or of the manly saviour while eschewing a greater dialogue about trauma and consent. Laura Hudson elaborates on this lack of victims' perspectives in her article *Rape Scenes Aren't Just Awful. They're Lazy Writing*:

> The same is true of rape scenes, which so often end up being stories about how men feel about women getting raped, rather than how those women feel about their own assaults. As one woman noted after creating a statistical breakdown of rape in *Game of Thrones*, although the rapes of 117 women have been described

thus far in the novels, "only two rape victims in books tell their own story rather than having a man tell it for them—and they're both villains." Too often, women and their abuse are treated as a tool for inspiring feelings, reactions, and character development in men; the story of their rape is not about them, or how it affects them: It's about a man, and how it affects him. (Hudson 2015)

When the media does not provide nuanced stories of sexualized violence and portrayals of survivors of violence, it perpetuates rape myths that reinforce ideas of hegemonic masculinity.

Entertainment Weekly and Variety have criticized shows like Game of Thrones (2011–19), Downton Abbey (2010–15), and House of Cards (2013–18) for their unnecessary portrayal of rape and for catering to common tropes of sexualized violence (Valby 2014). In her book Watching Rape: Film and Television in Postfeminist Culture, Sarah Projansky (2001) examines more thoroughly how tropes of sexual violence in the media normalize abuse and obscure the stories of victims:

Sexual violence is a normalized phenomenon, in which male-dominant environments . . . encourage and sometimes depend on violence against women, in which the male gaze and women as objects-to-be-looked-at contribute to a culture that accepts rape, and in which rape is one experience along a continuum of sexual violence that women confront on a daily basis. (9)

Projansky further highlights how the media socially constructs narratives around rape that do not reflect the reality of many victims and survivors. By creating women as objects to be looked at, it perpetuates rape myths that objectify women and reinforce victim blaming and slut shaming. Having women within media cater to ideas of the "male gaze" further enforces rape culture, which says that men are entitled to women's bodies. We can see how the Jessica Jones narrative pushes against the normalization of violence by not showing acts from Kilgrave's perspective. Within the show, there is no representation of how Kilgrave abused Jessica; rather, we only see how she deals with the repercussions of the abuse. The show follows her perspective and how she copes with trauma on a daily basis. Jessica's behaviour illustrates how women suffer from and survive violence, rather than how men abuse women. We consume Jessica's rape through her trauma and observe it as an ongoing violent process involving traumatic tremors and aftershocks—and this is shown from her own perspective, rather than through the male gaze.

One way to examine how we enter the gaze in this series is the quality of Jessica's character development, and that of those with whom she interacts—most of whom happen to be women. The show attempts to resist the sexual objectification that we have come to expect with the likes of Scarlet Johansson in skin-tight pleather. However, one criticism we came across was Daniel Murphy's piece for *Pop Matters*, where he identifies the following issues: "Jessica sleeps while wearing a full face of makeup, is conventionally attractive, and has a propensity to lounge around her apartment suggestively in revealing tank-tops while partially (and sometimes, very) intoxicated" (PopMatters Staff 2016). While we agree that Jessica still sports makeup and is attractive (read: thin and white), we argue that her brooding expression, hunched shoulders, and searing gaze subvert our ideas of what an MCU hero (and heroine) looks like. Generally, characters who are woman are visualized as busty but thin, well-dressed, with erect postures and brushed hair, and often with their posteriors in the eyeline of the camera, rather than as stylized badasses. From our point of view, Jessica's at-home apparel doesn't read as "suggestively revealing." Instead, analyses like Murphy's contribute to rape culture, and while he may be well-intentioned, suggesting that a woman is depicted as anti-feminist or as a sex object for wearing a thick-strapped tank top in her domain is bizarre.

From our perspective, Jessica looks like a real human rather than a sexy superheroine, but does the show grant other characters a feminist release from the white cis-hetero patriarchy as well? Spoiler alert: no. Nancy Fraser writes that "the feminist perspective is elitist, white, upper class" (1997, 117).

Disturbing Nuances of Rape, Trauma, and Their Media Representation

As television, film, and advertising continue to tell the same narrative around gendered violence, thereby perpetuating rape culture, specific imagery becomes associated with victims and perpetrators. A common rape myth is the idea of "stranger danger," which implies that violent attacks on women are random or isolated incidents. According to Tina Mahony (2017), 82 per cent of sexual assaults happen with the victim knowing the perpetrator. Like most survivors, we already, unfortunately, know this to be true, and the point is that rape culture has already established an environment in which victims of violence don't feel safe or comfortable coming forward with their experiences. By showing stories that fail to reflect 82 per cent of the population, mainstream media further isolates these victims.

Kwame Opam identifies why *Jessica Jones*'s depiction of rape, rapists, and their survivors are so revolutionary:

> It's easy to identify the monstrous, predatory rapists, and to depict them on TV. But when schools are creating consent classes because the topic is so poorly understood, the problem becomes all the more horrifying, not in spite of but because of its mundanity. Men needn't be evil or superhuman in order to use their power to take advantage of women. They just have to live in a society that allows for it. (2015)

The fictionalized superhero story *Jessica Jones* reflects the type of experience that many others have gone through. From the moment he met her, Kilgrave controlled Jessica's mind, forced her into being his "girlfriend," and made her cater to his needs. Jessica represents a large number of victims who have felt manipulated and controlled in "relationships" where sexual acts lacked consent. The abuse Jessica experiences speaks to how rape is not only a violation of a person's body, but also of their agency.

In season 2, we learn that when Trish was fifteen she was raped by Max Tatum, a forty-year-old film and television producer. It is revealed that Max has assaulted other young actors. Trish makes it very clear that there can't be consent between a child and an adult. Discussions of coercion and abuse of power within the MCU are relevant, and while we initially wrote this chapter in 2017, we're editing it in 2024, in a post-Weinstein and post-Cosby era, when we continue to learn that assaults within the industry are being committed by people that were once trusted and admired. That being said, "yet another example of (white) feminism's penchant for marginalizing women of color is the whitening of #MeToo and #TimesUp, evident in their popularization and visibility extended to white women's victimage. Only later was the founder of Me Too, Tarana Burke, a Black woman acknowledged, while testimonies of Black and Latina actresses were ignored" (Moon and Holling 2020, 255). And so, while watching Jessica's post-traumatic stress, triggered memories, and alcoholism is difficult—it's a struggle for many people to watch while wanting her to be better, be different—watching her prey on the Black husband of the

Black woman she murdered is also disturbing. The show shows us an unsettling example of how *hurt people hurt people*. White women's experience of sexual violence are allowed to be nuanced and complex, while the experiences of Black survivorhood is invisible in the show.

Luke Cage calls Jessica a "hard drinking short-fused mess of a woman," but the audience struggles to watch our hero(ine)'s mess. Popular notions of the "right way" for a victim of sexualized violence to behave makes it hard to bear witness to Jessica's life as it spirals out of control. A rape myth that needs to be criticized more is the idea that there is one perfect way for a victim to deal with rape and sexual assault. We are continuously shown that if a woman has made it out of violence and abuse alive, she has handled it well. If she reported the incident, she has handled it well. If she can move on quickly from the assault, she has handled it well. The myth plays into the idea that victims need to handle their trauma in a way that is convenient for others. Sadie Gennis (2014) further elaborates on this in relation to the shows *Downton Abbey* and *Scandal* (2012–18):

> Anna's rape and her attempt to hide it for the sake of her husband is reminiscent of Mellie's recent sexual assault on *Scandal*, in which Fitz's father rapes—and possibly impregnates—the first lady, but Mellie doesn't speak up in order to protect her husband's political career. Both shows frame Anna's and Mellie's decisions to stay quiet as noble, portraying them as martyrs for their husbands' livelihoods. Because in the end, their assaults aren't about providing commentary on rape culture or empowering these female characters as they find ways to overcome and heal. Their rapes are about their husbands and the honorable selflessness of women who do anything to protect the men in their lives.

In showing a "perfect victim" in the media, it's illustrating that there is only one way to handle trauma, and it must be in a way that serves someone else. These constructs and ideas lack individual experience and are rape myths that unify all acts of sexual violence. There is no perfect way to behave, there is only one person's reality and their way of coping. The process of healing is non-linear and individual. We should not be made to cope in a manner that serves someone else. *Jessica Jones* is about an individual's way of coping and dealing with trauma, even if it's hard to watch.

Victims are frequently presented as docile and passive, to be easily consumed for patriarchal ideas of sexualized violence. The passive woman after her abuse is more manageable for an audience to watch, specifically for viewers that are assumed to be heterosexual cisgendered men. Lindy West (2015) recently discussed the nuances of victimhood in the following terms: "Victimhood is passive. It is neutral. It is not shameful. It is not something you can choose to accept or reject, because it is imposed upon you by other people and outside cultural forces."

The choice to create passive victims is not necessarily a bad thing, but when it becomes the dominant portrayal of survivors, it proliferates the idea that they have to be easily consumable for audiences. Media products that are created to share stories of abuse and to put the victim's experience in the forefront place less stereotypical societal expectations on survivors to behave a certain way. Exploring post-traumatic stress that leads to alcoholism does require more complex examination and engagement, making it more difficult to mindlessly consume or binge-watch. When depicted, sexualized violence should be represented in a way that allows viewers to engage with the media and to create a larger dialogue around rape and sexual assault, as opposed to encouraging viewers to blindly accept the tropes that have been presented to them. A more complicated story that explores the psychological consequences of violence takes more time to make and more time to understand. *Jessica Jones* disrupts the current media representations of consent culture and amplifies the voices of victims.

Some showrunners have chosen to not have any sexual assault or rape in their shows because of the politics surrounding the issue (Valby 2014); this was the choice made by Bryan Fuller, for example, in the shows *Hannibal* (2013–15) and *American Gods* (2017–21). No matter what genre of media, one can frequently find narratives of trauma that are handled without the necessary care. Creating nuanced stories that reflect reality is a challenge, and a lot of showrunners have created victims that lack depth because it is believed that they will be easier for viewers to understand. Instead of engaging in the lifetime effects of trauma, storytellers cater to tropes that show victims as either passive or as "damaged goods." Rape is complicated and includes various stories and perspectives that some creators are not ready to explore. Our observation as survivors is that rape is generally portrayed as an isolated event, in the same way a car accident would be, with little to no mention of its consequences once some time has passed.

As a series, *Jessica Jones* engages in discourses around rape culture in a productive and potentially less triggering way. Rather than employing on-screen sexual assault, the show uses emotional abuse, post-traumatic stress syndrome, and the politics of consent as vehicles for framing rape as an ongoing challenge in the lives of survivors. As a cancer survivor and a sexual assault survivor, I (Pree) can attest to the fact that these kinds of traumas become daily navigational issues. These can and often do lead to the kinds of addictive behaviour that we see in Jones. In an interview with the *Hollywood Reporter*, executive producer Melissa Rosenberg commented on the way the show narrates rape in comparison to dominant representations:

> It's becoming ubiquitous, it's become lazy storytelling and it's always about the impact it has on the men around them. It's like, "Oh his wife was raped and murdered so he's going to go out and destroy the world." That's so often what it's about, just this kind of de rigueur storytelling to spice up often male characters. It's damaging. It's just hideous messaging, and so coming into this, the events have already happened and this is really about the impact of rape on a person and about healing, survival, trauma and facing demons. To me it's much richer territory. If you turn on any television show or, for that matter, film these days, nine out of 10 of them seem to open with a naked, tied-up, dead woman with her undies around her ankles. I think I've been calling them the NTSDs, which stands for naked, tied-up, dead, I can't remember. They've just become so ubiquitous, it's like numbing the audience to what is a horrific violation. (Fienberg 2015)

While Jones is not "NTSD," she's also not unscarred. Her trauma could (and potentially should) be held responsible for her alcoholism, toxic relationships, avoidant personality, trust issues, difficulty being truthful, and guarded personality. The one thing the different items in this limited list share is that these are valid and unpleasant—real human experiences and popular media doesn't hold space for unpleasant women, especially as superheroes. Is Jessica subversive in being a superhero that is a shitty friend/person? Is she a generally unstable yet strong person while still being a badass? Well, yes, mostly, because why not? Batman is distant and traumatized, but he is also cool and sexy. No one questions the desirability of Batman (or Bruce Wayne), nor that of Ironman, nor, occasionally, Joker. Mainstream popular culture and its participants are generally harsh critics of women, and the culture itself can be a breeding ground for misogyny and the reduction of underdeveloped women characters to narrative tropes, sex objects, or accessories.

Outside of her own show, Jessica has been the victim of a narrative trope, specifically in the Marvel Netflix show *The Defenders*. The series represented Jessica along the lines of the "Smurfette" trope according to which the men on the team experience most of the action and adventure while the women are there for emotional support. Although Jessica was merely in an emotional support position, her role in the group was to focus more on support than leadership. Qualitatively and quantitatively speaking, Jessica and her backstory are assigned less screen time than her masculine pals. And while *The Defenders* did feature more women than initially anticipated, including Misty Knight (*Luke Cage*), Claire Temple (*Daredevil*, *Luke Cage*, and *Iron Fist*), Karen Page (*Daredevil*), and Colleen Wing (*Iron Fist*), these characters tended to provide support for their masculine counterparts and were not themselves the main focus.

Race, Representation, and (White) Feminism

Jessica's interactions with Luke continue in the direction of the historical hyper-sexualization of Black men. The white gaze trained on Black folks reinforces hegemonic white colonial views of sexuality and Black masculinity. Although the narrative suggests the characters' feelings for one another are reciprocated, the ways in which the camera shows them in relation to each other is historically violent. The framing of the dark-skinned Black character with this large, muscular body, in contrast to her small, white body, presents an intentionally racialized contrast. For example, when Jessica tears off Luke's shirt (ep. 1.03, "AKA It's Called Whiskey"), the lighting emphasizes the muscular contours of his body, while the camera traces the contrast of his dark skin against her whiteness. And things then get messy (read: violent), because Jessica continues to pursue a relationship with Luke, even though she previously murdered his late wife, Reva, a light-skinned Black woman. While our heroine was under Kilgrave's spell when she killed Reva, murdering a Black woman who happens to be his wife and choosing to withhold all of this information from him deeply traumatizes and dehumanizes Luke. This is especially unethical and dehumanizing while Jessica continues to be intimate with and consume him. Withholding information like "I actually killed your wife" robs Luke of his ability to provide informed consent, and of the right to decide whether or not he wants to be intimate with his wife's murderer. Within the limited confines of what rape is and can be, it would be easy to simply write this off and to say that Jessica did not in fact rape Luke. However, rape is about power and robbing the victim of consent and their own agency, and in this context, we argue, Luke is forced into a web of sexual violence, fetishism, and necropolitics—all harms that Jessica is materializing, and which were catalyzed by Kilgrave.

Jessica and Luke's dynamic continues to flatten his experience of Blackness, masculinity, and survivorhood, and it subjects him to a colonial gaze that positions the viewer as a consumer of an anti-Black stereotype known as the "Magical Black Person" (MBP) trope. Similarly, Black queer scholar Kwame Anthony Appiah proposes the "Saint" trope. The Saint is "the noble good-hearted black man or woman, friendly to whites, working class but better educated than most class Americans, and oh so decent" (1993, 80). Appiah's content analysis links this to roles played by Danny Glover in films like *Lethal Weapon*, as "the Saint's macho incarnation." And in reference to the *Lethal Weapon* movies, he writes that "in each of them [1987, 1989, 1992, 1998] it's the white cop who's crazy." Sound familiar? In *Jessica Jones* we see this familiar duo replicated in the unhinged private investigator, Jessica, and our friendly boy next door, Cage, who invites shifty Jessica into the bar even though he just caught her creeping into the window yet again (ep. 1.01, "AKA Ladies' Night").

Appiah also highlights Morgan Freeman's transformation from his role as a pimp in *Street Smart* (1986) to that of the Saint in *Driving Miss Daisy* (1989), *Robin Hood* (1991), and *The Power of One* (1992). Ten years later, Matthew W. Hughey defined "Magical Negro films" as "cinema highlighting lower-class, uneducated, and magical Black characters who transform disheveled, uncultured, or broken white characters into competent people" (2017, 543). In Hollywood, the MBP stereotype tends to be applied to same-gender relationships, with an overly committed Black man helping a broken white man. Freeman provides yet another example when he literally plays the role of God in *Bruce Almighty* (2003). And while he does indeed play the character of God, he commits to the side gig of being a personal as well as spiritual guide to Bruce (played by Jim Carrey). And so, in *Jessica Jones*, the crazy white man and Black Saint tropes are replaced with a crazy white woman, which is emblematic of white feminism at large, to say nothing of the *two steps forward, one step back* nature of *Jessica Jones*. The dynamic between Jessica (a white woman) and Luke (a Black man), in combination with their respective Marvel series (which carry very different tones), amplify the use of this trope. In reference to MBP films, Hughey writes,

> These films all possess a mutual resemblance regarding how the positive and progressive attributes of strong, magic-wielding [B]lack characters [in this case, our bulletproof Luke Cage] are circumvented by their placement as servants to broken and down-on-their-luck white characters [Jessica Jones]. This on-screen relationship reinforces a normative climate of white supremacy within the context of the American myth of redemption and salvation whereby whiteness is always worthy of being saved, and strong depictions of blackness are acceptable in so long as they serve white identities. (2017, 548)

Luke is constantly shown as being saint-like, self-martyring in his inability to see past what Jessica presents herself to him as, whether as a love interest or a down-on-her-luck white character. Cerise L. Glenn and Landra J. Cunningham interpret Appiah's use of the Saint trope as a category that "serves to offset the racial stereotypes that White audiences generally aim at the Black characters as well as draw upon the superior moral nature associated with the oppressed" (2009, 138).

Jessica Jones is praised for its feminism and representation of (white) women in various roles, but it is inherently a white feminist show that puts the agency and liberation of its Black characters on hold. One might play devil's advocate and assume that the MBP still shows Black folks in a "positive" light. But Hughey explains that

> The interracial cooperation between broken whites and MNs[3] with exceptionally safe and happy attributes may appear progressive to some. If they are, then they concurrently represent a desire for audiences to solve interracial tensions via individual acts of black servitude, rather than through a rearrangement of racialized social structures or the contestation of dominant racial narratives. (2017, 557)

While the MBP trope may engender warm feelings among some viewers, it does nothing to challenge misogynoir, anti-Blackness, or the status quo more broadly. This chapter focuses on *Jessica Jones*; however, a dedicated content analysis contrasting depictions of race (and racism) in *Jessica Jones* and the *Luke Cage* series would be jarring. While this comparison is beyond the scope of this chapter, it's safe to say the former is demonstrating "the underlying fetishistic . . . [desire to] transform Black-white friendship into a use-value commodity for white characters' salvation" (Hughey 2017, 561). The choice to continue using and showing these racist tropes is harmful considering how Black folks continue to be treated. bell hooks argued that

> Otherness has been so successful because it is offered as a new delight, more intense, more satisfying than normal ways of doing and feeling. Within commodity culture, ethnicity becomes spice, seasoning that can liven up the dull dish that is mainstream white culture . . . fantasies about the Other can be continually exploited, and that such exploitation will occur in a manner that reinscribes and maintains the status quo . . . frank expression of longing, the open declaration of desire, the need to be intimate with dark Others. The point is to be changed by this convergence of pleasure and Otherness. (1992, 21–2).

The show disturbingly pushes Reva's murder to the periphery, while Luke and Jessica's relationship takes centre stage. Their dynamic is an extension of historical and contemporary violence rooted in colonialism and slavery, whereby white women sexually exploited Black men, and the romanticization of this violence in *Jessica Jones*, while not surprising, is nonetheless harrowing. In 1944, a fourteen-year-old Black boy, George Stinney, was wrongfully convicted of the murder of two white women (Garcia-Vargas 2014). Stinney was the youngest person to be executed in the United States, and his execution, like that of Emmet Till's (who was also a child at the time of his state-sanctioned murder), is an example of the ways in which Black masculinity is viewed, even for teenaged boys.

There are many occurrences throughout history of white women falsely accusing Black men of raping them. In the antebellum South, the hyper-sexualization of Black men and boys reinforced white supremacy through sexual violence. Although these dynamics are rooted in colonialism and slavery, we continue to see them playing out in public today. As this chapter was being written, Lena Dunham had only recently apologized to Odell Beckham Jr. for her racially charged comment accusing him of not wanting to sleep with her at the Met Gala (Williams 2016). Dunham seemed to be assuming that Black men owe white women sex and that they should desire white women automatically. Lara Witt speaks further to this issue by commenting on how white women responded to the cast of the film *Moonlight* (2016) modelling for a Calvin Klein underwear campaign:

> The objectification of black men by white women leaves such a lingering stench. I certainly can't ignore it and find it appalling to hear white women dehumanize and lust after black dick and black bodies without ever seeing the irony of their justified demands for their own right to agency and lack of objectification by all men, but especially white men. (Witt 2017)

The sexualization of Black men by white women (and non-Black people more broadly) underwrites anti-Black racism. So, while *Jessica Jones* is transgressive in its white feminism and slightly subverts the problematic MBP stereotype (which generally involves a Black man being depicted as a token aid to a white man), it is responsible for further perpetuating racist stereotypes about Black masculinity. This includes Luke and Jessica's one (yes, *one*) other Black friend, Malcolm. *Jessica Jones* is responsible for empowering the white survivor while framing Black survivors like Luke as impermeable and treating Black characters like Malcolm and Reva as disposable. We argue that these contrasts relegate both Luke and Malcolm to the status of beautiful, inspiring sidekicks who serve ultimately to empower their white pal.

This chapter has sought to show how the *Jessica Jones* series portrays sexual violence and consent while also problematizing its feminism by contrasting Jessica's empowerment and Luke's oppression and fetishization. What *Jessica Jones* does well is accurately portray the flawed realities of human beings who struggle with alcohol, PTSD, unresolved issues, and abuse through the lens of a white woman. That being said, the show is a white feminist (wet) dream and employs misogynoir and the MBP trope alongside technical choices that exploit Luke's agency, and this reflects its anti-Black racism and understanding of sexual violence. What feminist audiences tend to overlook in their response to the show is how some of the survivors it portrays (namely, white women characters) are entitled to healing from their trauma while also engaging in further cycles of harm and abuse.

NOTES

1   See the website Women in Refrigerators at https://lby3.com/wir/.

2   In the time since this chapter was first drafted, the MCU has grown to include the *Ms. Marvel* series on Disney+ (released in 2022). The series was met with particularly positive reviews of Iman Vellani's performance of Kamala Khan/Ms. Marvel.

3   As non-Black authors, we prefer to use the "MBP" shorthand introduced above, but we should note that Hughey's text refers to this as the "Magical Negro" trope.

References

Abad-Santos, Alex. 2019. "Captain Marvel Is Officially a $1 Billion Box Office Hit." *Vox*, April 3, 2019. https://www.vox.com/culture/2019/4/3/18287032/captain-marvel-box-office-one-billion.

Ahsan, Sadaf. 2016. "CBS's Nancy Drew Television Series Remake, Starring Sarah Shahi, Cancelled for Being 'Too Female.'" *National Post*, May 17, 2016. https://nationalpost.com/entertainment/television/cbs-nancy-drew-television-series-remake-starring-sarah-shahi-cancelled-for-being-too-female.

Appiah, Kwame Anthony. 1993. " 'No Bad N[——]': Black as the Ethical Principle in the Movies." In *Media Spectacles*, edited by Marjorie Garber, Jann Matlock, and Rebecca L. Walkowitz, 77–90. New York: Routledge.

Buchanan, Kyle. 2016. "Kevin Feige Says Brie Larson's Captain Marvel Will Be the Strongest Superhero Yet." *Vulture*. 21 October 21. http://www.vulture.com/2016/10/captain-marvel-movie-director-kevin-feige.html

Dumaraog, Ana. 2017. "Most Popular Viewing Order of Marvel/Netflix." *Screen Rant*, August 27, 2017. http://screenrant.com/marvel-netflix-defenders-viewing-order-most-popular/.

Fienberg, Daniel. 2015. " 'Jessica Jones' Boss on Losing Carol Danvers, Exploring Rape Responsibly and Season 2." *Hollywood Reporter*, November 22, 2015. https://www.hollywoodreporter.com/live-feed/jessica-jones-rape-season-two-842318.

Fraser, Nancy. 1997. *Justice Interruptus: Critical Reflections on the "Postsocialist" Condition*. New York: Routledge.

Garcia-Vargas, Andrea. 2017. "In 1944, We Executed a 14-Year-Old Boy. Why Did It Take 70 Years for Us to Exonerate Him?" *Upworthy*, December 17, 2017. http://www.upworthy.com/in-1944-we-executed-a-14-year-old-boy-why-did-it-take-70-years-for-us-to-exonerate-him.

Gennis, Sadie. 2014. "Downton Abbey and the Insensitive Portrayal of Rape on TV." *TV Guide*. February 20, 2014. http://www.tvguide.com/news/downton-abbey-rape-plot-device-tv-1078013/.

Glenn, Cerise L., and Landra J. Cunningham. 2009. "The Power of Black Magic: The Magical Negro and White Salvation in Film." *Journal of Black Studies* 40 (2): 135–52.

hooks, bell. 1992. *Black Looks: Race and Representation*. Boston: South End Press.

Hudson, Laura. 2015. "Rape Scenes Aren't Just Awful. They're Lazy Writing." *Wired*, June 30, 2015. https://www.wired.com/2015/06/rape-scenes/.

Hughey, Matthew W. 2009. "Cinethetic Racism: White Redemption and Black Stereotypes in 'Magical Negro' Films." *Social Problems* 56, no. 3 (2009): 543–77. doi:10.1525/sp.2009.56.3.543.

Mahony, Tina. 2017. "Women in Canada: A Gender-Based Statistical Report." Statistics Canada, June 6, 2017. https://www.statcan.gc.ca/pub/89-503-x/2015001/article/14785-eng.htm

McFarland, Kevin. 2016. "Meet Symphony, the Company Calculating Netflix TV Ratings." *Wired*, January 15, 2016. https://www.wired.com/2016/01/meet-symphony-the-company-that-tracks-netflixs-elusive-ratings/.

Moon, Dreama G., and Michelle A. Holling. 2020. " 'White Supremacy in Heels': (White) Feminism, White Supremacy, and Discursive Violence." *Communication and Critical/Cultural Studies* 17 (2): 253–60.

Mulvey, Laura. 1999. "Visual Pleasure and Narrative Cinema." In *Film Theory and Criticism: Introductory Readings*, edited by Leo Braudy and Marshall Cohen, 833–44. New York: Oxford UP.

Opam, Kwame. 2015. "On Jessica Jones, Rape Doesn't Have to Be Seen to Be Devastating." *The Verge*, November 23, 2015. https://www.theverge.com/2015/11/23/9786180/jessica-jones-game-of-thrones-rape-consent-television-2015.

PopMatters Staff. 2016. " 'Jessica Jones' and Gendered Forms of Seeing." *PopMatters*, March 9, 2016. https://www.popmatters.com/jessica-jones-and-gendered-forms-of-seeing-2495451026.html.

Projansky, Sarah. 2001. *Watching Rape: Film and Television in Postfeminist Culture*. New York: New York University Press, 2001.

Valby, Karen. 2014. "Hey TV: Stop Raping Women." *Entertainment Weekly*, February 27, 2014. http://ew.com/article/2014/02/27/tv-rape-scenes-downton-abbey-house-of-cards-scandal/.

West, Lindy. 2015. "Hi! I'm Lindy West, and I'm a victim." *Bitch Planet*, no. 5 (September). Berkeley, CA: Image Comics.

Williams, Alex. 2016. "Odell Beckham Jr. Responds to the Lena Dunham Dust-Up: 'I Have to Learn More about the Situation.' " *New York Times*, September 7, 2016. https://www.nytimes.com/2016/09/08/fashion/odell-beckham-jr-lena-dunham-met-gala-response.html.

Witt, Lara. 2017. "You Love Black Men's Bodies but Do You Care about Their Lives?" *Wear Your Voice*, February 28, 2017. https://wyvarchive.com/love-black-mens-bodies-care-lives/.

"AKA WWJD?" Interrogating Gendered Ideologies and Urban Revanchism

Arun Jacob and Elizabeth DiEmanuele

As the saying goes, we do not know what happens behind closed doors. There are always stories, histories, and experiences that we simply cannot know, especially when it comes to our relationships with one another and ourselves. The broken door to Jessica's apartment—which, after breaking early in the first episode, has cardboard in place of the window that reads, "Fragile. Handle with care."—is a recurring motif in *Jessica Jones*, positioning viewers as witnesses to Jessica Jones's life as a survivor of sexual trauma and a reluctant hero who is determined to save people from the dangers of Kilgrave and the city with her exceptional abilities (ep. 1.01, "AKA Ladies' Night").

A broken door represents more than a rupture of silence; its gendered histories reveal much about our protagonist and the city in which she lives. Doors offer privacy and they are essential in keeping unwanted people out. They also hold a history of gendered politics; in this context, doors operate as the divide between the public and private spheres, ensuring that women stay in their place away from all the dangers of the outer world. In *Jessica Jones*, the broken door—complemented by the "Fragile. Handle with care." sign—tugs at the vulnerabilities we might associate with a woman living alone in a dangerous part of the city. Jessica's client Mr. Shlottman aptly echoes these concerns for safety early on in the season. After his wife tells him to forget about it, he responds, "Leave a woman living alone in this city? With no lock, no door? It's not safe," vocalizing the belief that women are fragile (and perhaps require protection from a masculine system) (ep. 1.01, "AKA Ladies' Night").

In addition to demonstrating the ways in which fear, privacy, safety, and gender inform one another throughout the series, Mr. Shlottman's questions open up a broader conversation about how urban politics interpolate with men's fears and threats to middle-class, white masculinity. Urban geographer Hille Koskela (1999) emphasizes the centrality of space to women's fear, noting that "space and social characteristics are mutually modifying, interacting dimensions that deeply affect the nature and shape of women's fear. Fear of crime is constantly modifying women's spatial realities. . . . [However] space is not just a medium for interaction but is also produced by this interaction" (112). Sexual objectification of women in public space through harassment and sexist imagery not only produces fear but is also part of the social production of patriarchal urban space. While Jessica may not always show her fear openly, the broken door and its sign remind us of why: Jessica's past with Kilgrave and all of his abuses is far more terrifying than anything that may barge through that door. She has already lived the nightmare.

We believe it is productive to explore these relationships in *Jessica Jones* through the economies of revanchism. The neoliberal society of the United States and Canada suffer from a vicious "revanchism" that Neil Smith (1998) describes as a "blend of revenge with reaction," a mean-spirited movement that denies the social responsibilities of government while exacting distress upon the most vulnerable in society (2). Revanchism circulates the belief that society is dangerous and threatening, that, in the words of Leslie Kern (2010), "fear of the other justifies displacement and redevelopment, and the need for redevelopment (highest and best use) legitimizes the violence of displacement and marginalization" (210). What makes Leslie Kern's work especially fascinating is her gendered approach. If revanchist urbanism reinforces masculine power relations, wherein the privileged and the ruling class respond to the threat of losing power and status through gentrification, its survival also depends upon the idea that the safety of women (their offspring, the city's futurity, and so on) are under threat if action is not taken. Notably, gentrification operates as an important tool of revanchism in the series, often used as a means to "protect" the ideal citizens and keep undesirable citizens out; in many cases, gentrification operates as a means to confine women to private spheres, so as to keep them safe from "undesirable" living conditions and people. For the purposes of this discussion, *gentrification* will refer to the process of renovating and upgrading dwellings and cityscape so that they conform to middle- and upper-class standards of living.

Phil Hubbard (2004) opines that "it is possible to re-read spaces of neoliberal gentrification as landscapes that revalue (and *capitalise*) Masculinity through distinctive commodity forms and aesthetics" (679); keeping women "in check" through fear and social narratives is one way in which neoliberalism upholds this masculinity. In the revanchist cityscape, these narratives are often bolstered by presenting social problems (such as crime) as the preserve of individuals. As a case in point, consider the notion of slut shaming, which is the action of stigmatizing a woman for engaging in behaviour judged to be promiscuous or sexually provocative; people (the hegemon is/are usually men, but sometimes white women) often criticize women for appearing too sexual (according to their standards of acceptable sexuality) in order to control them. They also often blame women for being victims/survivors of rape by using similar appearance-based criticisms. The non-compliance (or un-adaptability) of the subject to a neoliberal consumer society is viewed as not only immoral but, inevitably, as unlawful. This use of shame to dominate and control women is an example of how these narratives can operate in the revanchist city under the guise of the individual's problem, and it is certainly mirrored in the narratives that unfold in *Jessica Jones*. For instance, Hope's arrest for murdering her parents under Kilgrave's command turns her into a criminal and public object of scrutiny (ep. 1.01, "AKA Ladies' Night"). We witness her arrest and questioning, as well as public reporting of her guilt throughout the series. The social terror that arises out of the experience is so bleak that even Jessica Jones, with all of her physically exceptional strength, refuses to come forward with her own story (ep. 1.03, "AKA It's Called Whiskey").

And yet, despite these obstacles, the series presents women as powerful survivors in a city that demands their silence. The revanchist city expresses "terror felt by middle- and ruling-class whites who are suddenly stuck in place by a ravaged property market, the threat and reality of unemployment, . . . and the emergence of minority and immigrant groups, *as well as women, as powerful urban actors*" (Smith 1996, 207; emphasis added)—an idea rooted in the fear of losing power and control. Who is more threatening to such an ideal than Jessica Jones, a woman who can lift cars, hold her own in a bar fight against a group of rugby players, and sleep in an apartment with a broken door, despite living in a densely populated, threatening city? Who is more threatening than a woman who can survive on freelance work and who forgoes stringent ties to any organization or person? While the Marvel franchise certainly presents us with other characters who threaten the revanchist city narrative, we are fascinated by the way Jessica's very real narrative of survival (of violence, assault, trauma, and so on) also acts as a motif for survival in a gentrified society, whose very existence and sense of safety depends upon women's silence and complacency. Jessica's decision to confront Kilgrave's violence in conjunction with the trauma she experienced and continues to endure is not just a personal triumph, but also a decision to reject the revanchist city's goal to silence and contain the uncontrollable. In Jessica's own words, "[The people in this city] want to feel safe. They'd rather call you crazy than admit I can lift this car or that I can melt your insides with my laser eyes" (ep. 1.01, "AKA Ladies' Night"). Even knowing that society desires her to maintain a certain degree of predictability and "safety," Jessica knowingly pushes forward, vocalizing her message for survivors of Kilgrave's violence and using her abilities to do the right thing, even when it makes others uncomfortable.

Facing the Hell of Hell's Kitchen

The first line of *Jessica Jones*, "New York may be the city that never sleeps, but it sure does sleep around," immediately presents the city through the lens of a scorned lover (ep. 1.01, "AKA Ladies' Night"). Combined with the visual of Jessica working with her camera as a private investigator who takes photos of people—often men—cheating on their spouses, we learn right away through Jessica's eyes that other people are morally damaged and cannot be trusted. "A big part of the job is looking for the worst in people," she says. "Turns out, I excel at that. Clients hire me to find dirt, and I find it. Which shouldn't surprise them—but it does."

We cannot simply dismiss the role "dirt" plays in the gritty landscape that is Hell's Kitchen, nor can we ignore the gendered history it holds in the labour that Jessica performs. Morag Shiach's (2004) work in women's labour helpfully unpacks the role technology once played in distancing women from "intimate forms of dirt" (73). The professions Shiach examines were once hidden from the public sphere due to their "shameful" status and closeness to spaces that would otherwise be reserved for women, such as caretaker and housekeeper roles. Technology, like the washer, operated as a way of helping women maintain their social dignity in professions that were already precarious due to their proximity to men. Jessica's camera represents an evolution of these technologies, as it becomes her professional tool to collect and distribute "dirt" for payment from a distance. When she says, "cheaters are good for business," she echoes fear-driven narratives related to women's labour the "dirt" with which it was associated; however, she does so with a twist: she is not ashamed or fearful, and in fact, she operates her camera by choice. Right away, she challenges the revanchist desire for her to be vulnerable to the city and its people, as she exposes the "dirt" of those who "deserve it."

Dirt seeps into many aspects of Jessica's life and comes to signify how neoliberalism births new forms of urban inequality, cleaving society and space along visible fault lines. Take Jessica's dwelling. She lives in a run-down apartment building; her clothes are strewn across the floor and cockroaches crawl from her sink. The occupants of the building are poor, visible minorities, homeless teenagers, drug-addled vagrants, and other socially undesirable types, people whose very presence in the central city is deemed untenable. The series makes a bold statement about gentrification in the city by placing its protagonist-hero and the majority of its minorities in this undesirable space: by placing our protagonist-hero in a setting that is (from a gentrified lens) undesirable and unsafe, the series in some ways suggests that these circumstances are unjust, perhaps even unwarranted. We know right away with the open door that Jessica feels more at home in Hell's Kitchen than she ever did living with Kilgrave or even elsewhere. At the same time, the cockroaches, broken doors, and dirt of Jessica's apartment complex operate as determinants of social worth and imply early on that those living with her in Hell's Kitchen are difficult, problematic, or unworthy within the revanchist city.

Luke Cage acts as the one exception, and once again, concepts of cleanliness and worth come into play. The first time Jessica enters Luke's bar, she says, "I've never seen a dive bar this clean. Because you care about it." To Jessica—and by extension, to us viewers—everything about Luke is moral and good. As his strength, however, the cleanliness of Luke's bar is not typical. We cannot dismiss the fact that visible minorities do not hold a significant place in the city. As viewers, what are we to make of the fact that the other residents in Jessica's building possess similarly undesirable living arrangements? What are we to make of Luke's clean bar by contrast? Just as the series creates distinct lines between cleanliness and dirt within the heart of Hell's Kitchen, these social cues also operate to satisfy the impressions and expectations of a potential middle- and upper-class viewership and/or anyone with access to Netflix culture. Those who binge-watch Netflix have access to media technologies and social infrastructures, which could range from high-speed Internet to 4K televisions and securitized condominiums. The Netflix subscriber cleaves to the more clichéd regimens of daily life: the hermetic capsule of the daily commute, the constant effort to avoid contact with strangers, and the welcome redoubt of the home. More simply, in many cases, the Netflix subscriber has the privilege of separating themselves from the circumstances of the characters on the screen.

Jones's friend Trish Walker, a media personality, resides in a fortified luxury condominium tower, one that satisfies the ideals of the gentrification process with its cleanliness, upgraded technology, and location in the downtown core. We believe the contrasting living arrangements of Jessica and Trish are emblematic of how urban pro-growth agendas intensify social and territorial inequalities within cities. Where Trish resides in the scenic, aestheticized, and revitalized downtown enclave, Jessica schleps around Hell's Kitchen, a name synonymous with onscreen urban blight, fear, and violence. These onscreen depictions further our understanding of how the characters are meant to be primarily understood as participants in the neoliberal consumer society. It should come as no surprise that Trish's apartment is described as "the fortress," a place protected from unwanted bodies and people. Not one person has a spare key (ep. 1.01, "AKA Ladies' Night"). While Mr. Shlottman may not have provided a definition of the perfect space for "a woman living alone in the city," we imagine that Trish's fortress would be the ideal: clean, private, silent, surveilled, and unbreakable.

If Jessica's broken door reveals her invulnerability to the city's dangers, Trish's surveilled fortress is everything else: it exemplifies the fear, vulnerability, and helplessness the city seeks to ignite in women. Trish's containment places her in the city's hold, stripping away her power and agency as a working woman and public figure in the process (ep. 1.04, "AKA 99 Friends"). While she later fights alongside Jessica, the belief that Trish should stay protected in her fortress remains a running concern throughout the series. Such a relationship reminds us of Koskela's (2000) work on video surveillance, where the principle of surveillance is considered to be "much the same as the principle of the 'ideal prison': to be seen but never to know when or by whom" (243). The threats revanchism places on self-sufficient women like Trish fits within this line of thinking. The more contained the city's citizens and agents can be, the better, especially if those citizens are considered to be unpredictable, uncontainable, or threatening to the status quo. Following this analogy of the prison, consider the living arrangements of Hope and Trish. While polar opposites in terms of luxury, Hope's prison cell and Trish's fortress are both informed by urban threat. The unpredictability of Hope's perceived crime creates enough public fear that she must remain in prison without bail.

On the other end of the spectrum, Trish's privileged lifestyle enables her to mobilize a high-quality surveillance system to remain safe from Kilgrave. In both instances, gentrification operates as the system that ensures their containment as well as their invisibility to the public.

It's Not Your Fault: Surviving the Revanchist City

Abusive relationships are, at their core, about control. Abusers will assert control over their partners any way they can, often employing sophisticated tactics: manipulating their victims with mental and verbal abuse, scaring them into submission, isolating them from their communities, and ultimately convincing them that their pain and suffering is completely their own fault (Healicon 2016, 65). Kilgrave does all of this but through the metaphor of a superpower. His power mirrors the ways in which abusers break down and control their victims, subduing their will, regardless of their personal strength or integrity. Kilgrave's psychological abuse of his victims, his absolute and total control, his manipulation, and his dominance over their agency are all part of what makes him utterly terrifying: his powers are subtle exaggerations of very real human abilities.

Jessica's self-annihilation is a direct response to the horrifying revelation that she remembers everything Kilgrave did to her and how she felt while it was happening. Her memories remind us that Kilgrave's victims are not automatons or zombies; they are instead forced to witness what they have done, and they experience it as something they did themselves. They cannot escape the resulting guilt and they never stop wondering what part of themselves made their obedience to Kilgrave possible. It is not often that popular audiences encounter a rape survivor confronting her rapist and refusing the gaslighting he uses to avoid the word "rape."[1] Jessica's relationship with Kilgrave is the primary focus of this behaviour because he is a master of strategy. Kilgrave distorts the truth of Jessica's experiences in an effort to make her question her own version of reality.

The relationship between Kilgrave's power to distort reality, his manipulation, and his agency within the revanchist city is crystallized in his choice to purchase Jessica's childhood home (ep. 1.08, "WWJD"; ep. 1.09, "AKA Sin Bin"; ep. 1.10, "AKA 1,000 Cuts"). Kilgrave's wealth enables him to reconfigure a space that holds Jessica's innocent memories, as he negotiates terms for her to stay with him. Part of these terms are that he will not use his powers to make her stay. She stays in the home of her own "free will," though every action is met with some form of blackmail, wherein he threatens to hurt others if she does not follow through on her promise. Flashbacks play a prominent role in these episodes. Each time Jessica remembers some aspect of her family, she is pulled back into the present by something that happens with Kilgrave.

Though these flashbacks are powerful, we are especially fascinated by one that involves her living arrangements with Kilgrave, back when they lived in his condominium (ep. 1.10, "AKA 1,000 Cuts"). In this flashback, Kilgrave wears an expensive-looking suit and Jessica wears a yellow sundress, which is significant, as we learn earlier that Jessica does not like wearing dresses, preferring instead the jeans and tank tops she displays throughout the series. They are on the condominium's patio and have the most picturesque view of the Brooklyn Bridge. From the dress to the view to the way he brushes Jessica's hair aside for a kiss, the "gentrified picture" tells us right away that Kilgrave owns everything about this scene, from the clothes Jessica wears to the condo they live in. We then cut to the present, when Kilgrave says, "I timed it. I didn't ask you to do anything. For eighteen seconds, I wasn't controlling you. And you stayed with me because you wanted to" (ep. 1.10, "AKA 1,000 Cuts"). Not letting Kilgrave get away with his gaslighting, Jessica responds with, "I remember vividly. I had waited so long for that moment; for one single oppor-tunity to get away from you." The flashback plays again, only this time, it is Jessica's memories, and the scene is less clear. She backs out of the kiss and says she will meet him inside. When Kilgrave leaves, she walks to the edge of the building and looks down, fantasizing about her own escape from the situation on a white horse. In this fantasy, she saves herself and escapes the city; however, before she can jump off the rooftop, Kilgrave calls her inside and forces her to return. Jessica and Kilgrave then fight about what happened and whose memory is accurate. The interplay of memory, control, and the cityscape offers viewers a glimpse of what Jessica endured and survived, disrupting Kilgrave's idealized version of their relationship and, in some ways, the gentrified picture. Jessica's vocalization of her suffering reminds viewers that even during what Kilgrave views as the highs of their relationship, Jessica has experienced layers of suffering and trauma.

Just as Jessica's physical strength enables her to resist the city's threats, her vulnerability and resilience as a survivor are what make her an even greater threat—to Kilgrave and to the city that seeks to silence her voice and abilities. Our use of the word "survivor" here is quite purposeful. Jessica survives the crash that killed her parents. She survives Kilgrave's abuses. She survives Hell's Kitchen. She survives Kilgrave chasing her down. Jessica's experiences and strength as a survivor are integral because they give her something of which Kilgrave is incapable: a capacity to empathize and care about the well-being of others. While Jessica may be passive-aggressive in almost all of her interactions, her understanding of the confusion, pain, and guilt that Kilgrave's survivors experience is what gives her the motivation to keep fighting; it is also what affords us a new glimpse of the "untenables" in her building. As previously mentioned, Jessica's current living arrangements place her alongside minorities, drug addicts, and other "undesirable" types in the gentrified cityscape; yet these are the people who survive in spite of a city that seeks their silence. They are the ones who fight alongside Jessica, not the police or officials who are there to "keep the city safe" (ep. 1.10, "AKA 1,000 Cuts"). They, too, survive and protect one another in the process.

NOTE

1   To clarify what we mean by "gaslighting," this term refers to a form of emotional abuse whereby information is twisted, spun, or selectively omitted to favour the abuser. The ultimate goal is to make victims doubt their own memory, perception, and sanity. It is a devastatingly effective tactic, allowing an abuser to more easily manipulate their victim (Abramson 2014).

References

Abramson, Kate. 2014. "Turning Up the Lights on Gaslighting." *Philosophical Perspectives* 28 (1): 1–30. https://doi.org/10.1111/phpe.12046.

Healicon, Alison. 2016. *The Politics of Sexual Violence: Rape, Identity and Feminism.* Basingstoke, UK: Palgrave Pivot.

Hubbard, Phil. 2004. "Revenge and Injustice in the Neoliberal City: Uncovering Masculinist Agendas." *Antipode* 36 (4): 665–86.

Kern, Leslie. 2010. "Gendering Reurbanisation: Women and New-Build Gentrification in Toronto." *Population, Space and Place* 16 (5): 363–79.

Koskela, Hille. 1999. " 'Gendered Exclusions': Women's Fear of Violence and Changing Relations to Space." *Geografiska Annaler, Series B: Human Geography* 81 (2): 111–24. https://doi.org/10.1111/j.0435-3684.1999.00052.x.

———. 2000. " 'The Gaze without Eyes': Video-Surveillance and the Changing Nature of Urban Space." *Progress in Human Geography* 24 (2): 243–65.

Shiach, Morag. 2004. "Technologies of Labour: Washing and Typing." In *Modernism, Labour and Selfhood in British Literature and Culture, 1890–1930*, 57–99. Cambridge: Cambridge University Press, 2004. 57-99.

Smith, Neil. 1998. "Giuliani Time: The Revanchist 1990s." *Social Text*, no. 57 (Winter): 1–20. https://doi.org/10.2307/466878.

Considering *Jessica Jones* as a Moment in Time

Jessica Bay

As a Netflix original series, *Jessica Jones* combines the popularity of super-hero stories (and those of the Marvel Cinematic Universe in particular) with the grit of a film noir–esque detective series in a single product that appeals to a mass audience. Rather than draw viewers into a strict version of appoint-ment viewing by releasing one episode per week, Netflix chose to release the series as one complete season to be binge-watched by those viewers with the time and then rewatched immediately and at their leisure by fans. Common to most Netflix original series, this decision influences the type of content Netflix chooses to produce as well as the ways in which audiences under-stand serial narrative. This popular impact also offered the show's creators an opportunity for immediate and helpful feedback that directly influenced the show's storyline, similar to how Netflix's use of data gleaned from its users helps it to determine what content to create. The result was a show that is representative of its time in terms of both content and production.

Through analysis of the viewing habits of its audience and minute classi-fication of its content, Netflix is better able to recognize the products that will appeal most to its audience than traditional television studios. Combining this direct knowledge with daring business practices, Netflix is displaying a confi-dence in the content that comes from a new and more accurate kind of mar-ket research. Netflix usually releases its original content in complete seasons. This has been extremely successful for the company as people make plans to stay home and binge-watch the entire season of their preferred show—creat-ing a new form of event television. In fact, Netflix uses this strategy because it has determined how to retain viewers for a new series. That is, it knows which episode tends to make a skeptical viewer decide to stay up for three days to binge-watch an entire season of a particular show (O'Reilly 2016). This hook episode is never, according to the company's research, the pilot of any show, which is why Netflix regularly buys a show based on its concept rather than ordering a pilot and then deciding to green-light the rest of the series—the practice used by traditional networks to keep viewers committed and loyal, to render them returning customers (Baldwin 2012; O'Reilly 2016). Knowing that this is how viewers engage with these series gives creators a new way to provide narrative content. Rather than structuring their stories in a way that ensures viewers recall content and maintain a continued interest in the show over an extended period, series created specifically for Netflix distribution can play with the structure since many viewers treat the season of a Netflix show almost as an extended film—that is, they may watch thirteen episodes in one weekend. Media critic Djoymi Baker suggests that these series be considered "epics" and our binge or marathon viewing of seasons a type of "epic-viewing" (2017, 40–1). In fact, as Baker writes, "Netflix encourages customers to think of its products as best experienced in the overall *epic* duration" (40).

We see some of this in the first season of *Jessica Jones* when the storytelling slows down at the moment Jessica and Kilgrave come together in one house (1.08, "AKA WWJD?"). Instead of continuously rushing forward toward the goal of capturing Kilgrave to secure Hope's release, the show allows the audience to consider the possibility of Kilgrave's rehabilitation and Jessica's role and feelings of responsibility in that rehabilitation. This ability to slow down a little rather than moving from action to action is extremely important in a show that comments so obviously on rape, PTSD, trauma, and their after-effects. Ultimately, Jessica decides that it is not her job to save her abuser, and that saving Hope is more important, but the time it takes to consider this possibility helps to flesh out Jessica's motivations while also giving the audience a closer look at Kilgrave's character. Obviously, this is not something that Netflix invented, and the company owes a lot to HBO, AMC, and other producers that position themselves as "more than TV" for popularizing the "narratively complex" long arc in storytelling (Mittell 2006).

In addition to the element of narrative structure, Netflix offers showrunners some flexibility in terms of the maturity of their shows. *Jessica Jones*, for example, was in development at ABC as early as 2010 before finally being passed over by the network in 2012 (Acuna 2015). Kirsten Acuna of *Business Insider* suggests that *Jessica Jones* is "basically an R-rated Marvel adaptation made for the small screen" (2015), and it is unlikely that ABC would ever have been the right place for this woman who drinks, is promiscuous, and only begrudgingly helps her neighbours when they're in need. We can see that Netflix produces something different from traditional television—something that can be enjoyable while opening up the opportunity for greater conversations—and *Jessica Jones* is one such site of discursive pleasure.

In the preceding chapters, we were introduced to the character of Jessica as presented in this first season. The season as a whole focuses on what it means to be a hero, the different ways to be a supportive friend, the aftermath of trauma, the normalization of gaslighting, and the effects of toxic masculinity. In these episodes we are given some insight into the lives of survivors who have left their abusers but without ever fully escaping their past torments, including in the characters of Robin, Kilgrave's parents, Jessica, Trish and her mother, Simpson and his colleagues in the military, the entire survivor's group, Malcolm, etc. But it is also a story about people working through their demons—as in the cases of Malcolm and drugs, Jessica and misandry/alcoholism/guilt/feelings of inadequacy, Trish feeling weak, Luke and his experience of loss and feelings of weakness. Moreover, it is a story of strength, too, as we saw in part 2 of this collection, where we encountered many different types of masculinity: Simpson and his need to exert control despite the fact the he is never quite the strongest or smartest and is never in charge; Luke Cage and his emotional softness despite his "unbreakable" physicality; Malcolm and his overwhelming need to help those around him even when he can't help himself. We also witness a multitude of femininities: Jessica's typical "strong" female stereotype; Hogarth as the woman who has had to imitate men to get where she is; Trish, who has been weak and refuses to be seen as such, and so fights back with her words while she learns to push back physically, even as she barricades herself in her home; Pam, who seems to be subservient and weak, but who defends Jeri physically and stands up for what she believes in, both in her relationship and ultimately in her life; Wendy, whose whole world is falling apart around her, but who still has an ace up her sleeve; and finally Claire, who sees more "powered" people and a larger situation opening before her and who trusts them to solve her problems while offering whatever aid she can, both in terms of her medical knowledge and her experience with superpowers. Moreover, the show still manages to give us glimpses of wonderful relationships amid the many forms of turmoil charted here (e.g., between Jessica and Malcolm, and especially between Jessica and Trish).

Are there problems with this series? Absolutely. The focus on strong women who all seem to be fighting against each other is a glaring concern in a show so strongly focused on the aftermath of abuse. Season 2 of the series, while not discussed in the preceding chapters, was made available on Netflix on March 8, 2018, and fans and critics alike were excited to see what the show would tackle next. This season followed the introduction of all four Defenders characters (Daredevil, Jessica Jones, Luke Cage, and Iron Fist) in their own individual series, as well as the combined *The Defenders* series, so quite a bit had happened in New York within the story world of *Jessica Jones*, and Jessica herself would presumably have some new demons to overcome.

After the second season was released, reviewers continued to find the show enjoyable, but they voiced a greater degree of criticism compared to the first season. Many viewers, and particularly racialized fans and critics, were disappointed with the show's continued focus on white women saviours and its lack of people of colour (Caroll 2018; Collins 2018; Flint 2018; Glover 2018; Jasper 2018; Sperling 2018). While the show continues to focus on women's stories, it does so at the expense of people of colour, and women of colour in particular. There is a discernable shift in season 2, with Jessica in recovery and her appearing to move on in terms of her romantic relationships and her interactions with others in general. This season spends more time focusing on substance abuse and the devastation that it can cause to relationships, as well as illness and the accompanying loss of hope; it also lingers on Jessica's struggle with her sense of self and her family relations. For a show that has been so groundbreaking in terms of its realistic portrayals of women survivors of abuse, *Jessica Jones* let its audience down by continuing to focus on—and seemingly forgive—the white survivors despite their increasingly monstrous actions. At the same time, as critics have shown, the show didn't just ignore women of colour, it used those characters recklessly to further the stories of the main characters (Flint 2018; Glover 2018; Jasper 2018).

When we consider the show alongside the other Netflix-Marvel collaborations, we can see how Jessica came to have such a huge responsibility placed on her shoulders. *Luke Cage* is very obviously a show with racial themes, as some of our contributors have briefly shown in their chapters (Fairbarns and Rehal; Stang; Seymour). *Iron Fist* has been openly and repeatedly criticized for appropriating Asian tropes (Bramesco 2017), but it has also been a space for conversation around the role of women in Asian American action films as well as highlighting the place of the white saviour (if not within the show, then definitely in the discourse surrounding it). And *Daredevil* offers audiences a character who represents a version of disability. If Jessica represents women in this quartet, then her show *should* work to represent all women, rather than just white women. Is it really so much to ask that a superhero show set in one of the most diverse cities in America reflect the community in which it is set? Luckily the discourse surrounding the show has led to some real change. After the first season, *Jessica Jones*'s showrunner, Melissa Rosenberg, ensured that every episode in season 2 was directed by a woman, which further secured the show's feminine voice. After the criticism levelled at season 2 and the show's creators, Rosenberg acknowledged her own blind spot by stating that "it just didn't occur to [her]" (Sperling 2018) that the main characters were white and that she was killing off all of the women of colour. While this response is ultimately quite harsh and tone-deaf, it did lead to some changes.

Season 3 of *Jessica Jones* was released on June 14, 2019, and it took a hard look at the show's own history. The story follows Trish's journey from sidekick to hero to villain as the character of Hellcat, while also introducing a typical, generic, white guy stalker as the season's main villain. Essentially, the villains of the season are, as Patricia Grisafi at the *Mary Sue* suggests (2019), "white entitlement personified." So, while there are also a few new women of colour added to the show, the creators decided to turn Jessica's ever-present camera lens around and point it at themselves with this third and final season to consider the problems caused by white feminism. At the same time, it is undoubtedly true that all three seasons of *Jessica Jones* centre trauma, masculinity and femininity, and the role of the hero in the modern world.

It is clear that Jessica and *Jessica Jones*, both the character and the show, continue to start conversations. While it is unfair to expect her to be the representative for all women superheroes on screen, viewers and critics are right to demand that the show better represent the world its titular character inhabits, particularly given its insistence on placing her in the real world. When *Jessica Jones* was first released in 2015, she was in good company with other women superheroes such as Agent Peggy Carter and Melinda May. By the time the final season was released in 2019, however, Marvel had actually dropped *Agent Carter* (2015–16), *Agents of S.H.I.E.L.D.* (2012–20), though with many more women superheroes, was only a year away from ending its run, and the promised release of the stand-alone *Black Widow* movie was pushed back (it was finally released in 2021). The future of Marvel's women superheroes at the time seemed to lie with *Captain Marvel* (2019; 2022), the character of the Scarlet Witch (*WandaVision* [2021]), and Kate Bishop in the Disney+ series *Hawkeye* (2021). Despite the progress made by *Jessica Jones* in its final season, it seems Marvel is looking forward to a very white future. It is therefore all the more important that we consider the initial release of *Jessica Jones* and consider the show's continued influence and impact on the industry as Marvel works to integrate its catalogue into the new Disney+ streaming service. Sonia Saraiya at *Variety* points out just how relevant to the cultural moment Jessica has been:

> Jessica Jones is not just Marvel's only female frontwoman, but the franchise's personification of female rage—a force that has become so potent, in the years since her first appearance, that half a million people marched on Washington, Oprah flirted with running for president, and rapists, abusers, and harassers have been dragged out of the highest halls of power and privilege, practically kicking and screaming as they go. Creator Melissa Rosenberg's interpretation of Brian Michael Bendis' comic-book heroine could not have been more prescient. (Saraiya 2018)

This is the character that Marvel and Disney need to consider bringing back to the screen to encourage more adult viewership on the latter's new streaming service: a character and show capable of representing the current moment while also taking criticism and growing because of it. Considering the legacy *Jessica Jones* has created, fans and viewers alike should push Marvel to continuously grow and adapt to the present social and political moment in their other adult Marvel Cinematic Universe content on Disney+ to ensure better women heroes who truly represent their world and allow for public conversations about relevant, if difficult, topics.

References

Baldwin, Roberto. 2012. "Netflix Gambles on Big Data to Become the HBO of Streaming." *Wired*, November 29, 2012. https://www.wired.com/2012/11/netflix-data-gamble/.

Baker, Djoymi. 2017. "Binge-Viewing as Epic-Viewing in the Netflix Era." In *The Age of Netflix: Critical Essays on Streaming Media, Digital Delivery and Instant Access*, ed. Cory Barker and Myc Wiatrowski, 31–54. Jefferson, NC: McFarland & Company.

Bramesco, Charles. 2017. "What Is the 'Iron Fist' Controversy? (Also, What Is 'Iron Fist'?)." *New York Times*, March 17, 2017. https://www.nytimes.com/2017/03/17/watching/iron-fist-review-roundup-controversy.html.

Carroll, Michelle. 2018. "Netflix's 'Jessica Jones' Has a Race Problem, But It's Fixable." *Wear Your Voice*, April 5, 2018. https://wearyourvoicemag.com/netflixs-jessica-jones-race-problem-fixable/.

Collins, Hannah. 2018. "Ultimately, Jessica Jones' Feminism Fails Women of Color." *CBR*, March 25, 2018. https://www.cbr.com/jessica-jones-feminism-no-women-of-color/.

Flint, Hanna. 2018. "Problematic Faves: Marvel's Jessica Jones." *SyFy Wire*, October 23, 2018. Available via the Internet Archive: https://web.archive.org/web/20181024014219/https://www.syfy.com/syfywire/problematic-faves-marvels-jessica-jones.

Glover, Cameron. 2018. "White Feminist Heroes: 'Jessica Jones' Continues Leaving People of Color Behind." *Bitch Media*, March 22, 2018. Available via the Internet Archive: https://web.archive.org/web/20180322195505/https://www.bitchmedia.org/article/reviews/jessica-jones-leaves-black-women-behind.

Grisafi, Patricia. 2019. "The Villains of *Jessica Jones* Season 3 Are White Entitlement Personified." *Mary Sue*, June 21, 2019. https://www.themarysue.com/marvel-netflix-jessica-jones-season-3-villains-white-entitlement/.

Jasper, Marykate. 2018. "Jessica Jones Is Great at Examining Trauma—Unless It Happens to Women of Color." *Mary Sue*, March 14, 2018. https://www.themarysue.com/jessica-jones-women-of-color/.

O'Reilly, Lara. 2016. "Netflix Lifted the Lid on How the Algorithm That Recommends You Titles to Watch Actually Works." *Business Insider*, February 26, 2016. https://www.businessinsider.in/Netflix-lifted-the-lid-on-how-the-algorithm-that-recommends-you-titles-to-watch-actually-works/articleshow/51158848.cms.

Saraiya, Sonia. 2018. "TV Review: 'Marvel's Jessica Jones' Season Two." *Variety*, February 28, 2018. https://variety.com/2018/tv/reviews/jessica-jones-season-2-review-krysten-ritter-marvel-netflix-1202711405/.

Sperling, Nicole. 2018. "*Jessica Jones* Creator Melissa Rosenberg on Power and Pitfalls of Female Rage." *Vanity Fair*, March 21, 2018. https://www.vanityfair.com/hollywood/2018/03/jessica-jones-season-2-netflix-marvel-melissa-rosenberg-krysten ritter.

List of Contributors

Jessica Bay (she/her) is a PhD candidate in the Joint Graduate Program in Communication and Culture at York and Toronto Metropolitan Universities. She previously completed an MA thesis in popular culture at Brock University titled "The New Blockbuster Film Sequel: Changing Cultural and Economic Conditions within the Film Industry" (2011) and an MA thesis in English at the University of Lethbridge titled "Re-writing Publishing: Fanfiction and Self-Publication in Urban Fantasy" (2014). Her current research examines the marketing strategies of Hollywood franchises in relation to teen fangirls and their practices. Luckily, this research has involved reading a lot of YA fiction and attending a lot of fan conventions—some of Jessica's favourite pastimes.

Dr. Bridget Blodgett (she/her) is an associate professor and chair of the Division of Science, Information Arts, and Technology at the University of Baltimore. Her research analyzes Internet culture and its social impacts on offline life. Her current research takes a critical eye to online game communities regarding gender, inclusiveness, and identity. *Toxic Geek Masculinity in Media* (co-authored with Anastasia Salter) was released in 2017 by Palgrave Macmillan and is the summation of this work to date.

Natalja Chestopalova (she/her) is a senior researcher, writer, and multimedia producer at the Wapatah Centre for Indigenous Visual Knowledge, OCAD University. Her work is informed by popular culture aesthetics and psychoanalysis and focuses on transformative sensory experiences and multimodality in film, the graphic novel medium, site-responsive performances, and virtual or AI-generated spaces. At Wapatah, Natalja is providing research project oversight for a range of initiatives, including the Indigenizing the (Art) Museum virtual series, *Arctic/Amazon: Networks of Global Indigeneity,* an exhibition and major publication produced in partnership with Toronto Metropolitan University and the Power Plant Contemporary Art Gallery, and the Virtual Platform for Indigenous Art, a custom digital tool that uses a wiki-style approach and 3D photogrammetry for mobilizing artwork and facilitating Indigenous access and contributions to Indigenous art in museum and gallery collections around the world. Natalja's publications have been featured in *Collections: A Journal for Museum and Archives Professionals*, the *Canadian Journal of Communication*, and Dialogue, and her latest book chapters can be found in the collections *The Comics of Alison Bechdel: From the Outside In*, *Who's Laughing Now? Feminist Perspectives on Humour and Laughter*, and *Television Series as Literature*.

Elizabeth DiEmanuele (she/her) is a digital communications professional in higher education and student affairs. She currently works at McMaster University and serves on the board of directors at Rainbow's End Community Development Corporation. In 2020, she was part of the McMaster University team that received a silver Prix d'Excellence for Best Use of Social Media ("Encouraging students to think global") from the Canadian Council for the Advancement of Education. She completed her MA in English at McMaster University. For the last eight years, Elizabeth's work has focused on Gen Z research and social media, websites, and storytelling. She currently works at McMaster University's Student Success Centre and co-chairs the university's IT Student Advisory Committee. Elizabeth holds a bachelor's degree in English language and literature (Western University, 2014), and a master of arts in English (McMaster University, 2015).

Caitlynn Fairbarns (she/her) is an artist and arts community organizer in Toronto. Under the name Fake Geek Girls Like Us, she produces art that explores gender, sexuality, mental health, and pop culture. When she isn't working on her own art practice, she is coordinating events, murals, and zines.

Ian Fitzgerald (he/him) is an independent researcher specializing in genre cinema. He has been published in the *Canadian Journal of Film Studies* and the textbook *The Spaces and Place of Canadian Popular Culture*, where he wrote about mall multiplexes. Ian completed his master's at York University, where he wrote about the contemporary romantic comedy, and currently works for the Government of Alberta.

Arun Jacob (he/him) is a doctoral candidate at the Faculty of Information, University of Toronto. He completed his master of arts in cultural studies and critical theory and master of arts in work and society at McMaster University in Hamilton, Ontario, and his master of professional communication from Toronto Metropolitan University. Arun's doctoral work unites media genealogy, intersectional feminist media studies, and critical university studies to explore how contemporary university data-management techniques and information-management systems shape our socio-cultural relations, experiences, and knowledge. Arun's publications have appeared in *Debates in Digital Humanities 2023, Interdisciplinary Digital Engagement in Arts & Humanities, Digital Studies/Le Champ Numérique*, the *College Quarterly, Digital Humanities Workshops: Lessons Learned, Alternative Historiographies of the Digital Humanities*, and *Real Life in Real Time: Live Streaming Culture*.

Dr. Catherine Jenkins (she/her) holds a PhD from the Joint Graduate Program in Communication and Culture at Toronto Metropolitan and York Universities in Toronto, Canada. Her dissertation, "Older Patient-Physician Communication: An Examination of the Tensions of the Patient-Centred Model within a Biotechnological Context," was nominated for the Governor General's Academic Gold Medal. She is an award-winning lecturer in the School of Professional Communication at Toronto Metropolitan University, where she teaches a Communicating with Comics course. In addition to her literary publications, her current research interests include the medicalization of comic book superheroes.

Dr. Michelle Johnson (she/her) holds an MA in dance (culture and performance studies) from the University of Hawai'i at Mānoa and a PhD in dance studies from York University. She is a certified movement analyst and somatic practitioner, and her research applies Laban movement analysis to popular media, focusing on the female body in live-action and animated film and television.

Mary Grace Lao (she/her) is a PhD candidate in the Joint Graduate Program in Communication and Culture at York and Toronto Metropolitan Universities and an instructor in the Faculty of Arts and Sciences at Humber Polytechnic. Her doctoral research looks at media(ted) discourses of gender-based violence and rape culture. She is part of a SSHRC-funded project, "The

Embodied Tween: Living Girlhood in Digital Spaces," that examines media constructions of girlhood and its intersections with race and class. Her favourite superhero is Superman.

Dr. Sorouja Moll (she/her) has a PhD in humanities (Concordia) specializing in the fields of communication, English, and art history. She also holds a BA and an MA in English from the University of Guelph. As an interdisciplinary communication scholar, her research-creation practice undertakes a multimodal critical discourse analysis of all forms of media, including adaptations of Shakespeare in Canada, and an intersectional approach to nineteenth-century archival and narrative-based communication structures and applications and their present-day manifestations in, among other areas, nation, memory, and identity. Moll's areas of research include the oral histories of mixed-race identity; Indigenous and non-Indigenous relationship rebuilding practices and education as meaningful and sustainable; and creating spaces in which transgression, enunciation, ambiguity, and emancipation can be explored through performance, creative writing, and research practices. Sorouja teaches communication, theatre, and performance studies at the University of Waterloo in the Department of Communication Arts.

Kiera Obbard (she/her) is a PhD candidate in literary studies in the School of English and Theatre Studies at the University of Guelph in Ontario, Canada. Her SSHRC-funded project "The Instagram Effect: Contemporary Canadian Poetry Online" examines the complex social, cultural, technological, and economic conditions that have enabled the success of social media poetry in Canada. She completed an MA in cultural studies and critical theory at McMaster University and an honours BA with a joint major in English and communication at the University of Ottawa. She is currently a graduate resident at the Humanities Interdisciplinary Collaboration Lab and an editorial board member of the Centre for Media and Celebrity Studies and WaterHill Publishing,

Dr. Brett Pardy (he/them) is an instructor in the School of Culture, Media, and Society at the University of the Fraser Valley. His research focuses on the emotional impact of media on learning and unlearning conceptions about racism, masculinity, community, and mental health. He has previously published work on the militarization of *The Avengers*.

Pree Rehal (they/them) is an independent researcher with a master's from the Joint Graduate Program in Communication and Culture at York and Toronto Metropolitan Universities. Pree has taught at College Montmorency in Quebec, currently resides in Toronto, and often teaches workshops across the Greater Toronto Area. Their research interests include cosplaying, critical race studies, navigating non-monogamy for racialized trans and queer folks, and the Panjabi diaspora. You can generally find Pree playing Yoshi's Island, making zines, or buying more plants.

Eric Ross (he/him) is a doctoral candidate in cultural studies at George Mason University, where he currently teaches social justice courses for the School of Integrative Studies. His research and teaching interests include museum studies, memory studies, political subjectivity, and cultural policy.

Dr. Anastasia Salter (they/them) is a professor of English at the University of Central Florida, and the author most recently of *Playful Pedagogy in the Pandemic: Pivoting to Games-Based Learning* (with Emily Johnson; Routledge, 2022); *Twining: Critical and Creative Approaches to Hypertext Narratives* (with Stuart Moulthrop; Amherst College, 2021); *Adventure Games: Playing the Outsider* (with Aaron Reed and John Murray; Bloomsbury, 2019); and *Toxic Geek Masculinity in Media* (with Bridget Blodgett; Palgrave Macmillan, 2017).

Dr. Jessica Seymour (she/her) is an Australian researcher and lecturer at Fukuoka University, Japan. Her research interests include children's and young adult literature, Tolkien studies, popular culture, and literary adaptation. She has contributed chapters to several essay collections on a range of topics, from fan studies, to online/transmedia writing, to TV series like *Doctor Who* and *Supernatural*, to eco-criticism in the works of J. R. R. Tolkien.

Dr. Sarah Stang (she/her) is an assistant professor of game studies in Brock University's Department of Digital Humanities, where she teaches courses in the Game Design and Game Studies Graduate Programs. Sarah is part of the executive committee for the Canadian Game Studies Association as well as the secretary for the International Communication Association's Game Studies Division. She is on the board of reviewers for *Game Studies* and on the advisory board for *Eludamos*, and she is also the former editor-in-chief of

Press Start and the former essays editor for *First Person Scholar*. She received her PhD from the Communication and Culture Program at York University. Her research primarily focuses on gender representation in both digital and analog games. Her published work has analyzed topics such as female monstrosity, body horror, androgyny, parenthood, interactivity, and feminist game studies, and can be found in journals such as *Games and Culture*, *Game Studies*, *Critical Studies in Media Communication*, *Human Technology*, and *Loading*, as well as in several edited collections.

Tracey Thomas (she/her) is a PhD candidate in the Department of Humanities at York University in Toronto, Canada, and currently is a communications specialist for a credit union. Her dissertation research explores superheroes in the CW's Arrowverse through the adaptation of graphic novels to the television screen, particularly how superhero characteristics, traits, costumes, settings, and narratives are translated in various mediums. She questions why some elements from the graphic form are kept for adaptation while others are discarded to understand the evolving function of superheroes in our contemporary world. Her other research interests include pop culture adaptation (manga, anime, comics, books), cultural studies, and film studies.

Index

Superman, 25–26, 31, 52, 56, 64, 81; "The Myth of Superman," 23; *Superman* (series), 25
superpower, 1, 23, 25–26, 42, 50, 74, 84, 87–88, 115, 124, 143, 152, 178, 185, 199, 249, 255
support group, 57, 108, 132, 221
surveillance, 5, 67–72, 74–78, 113, 248–249, 251
synopticon, 70. *See also* panopticon

T

Tennant, David, 126, 128, 135, 138, 156
Thor, 26, 125; *Marvel's Thor* (film), 140
time effort, 175, 187. *See also* space effort; Laban Movement Analysis
tomboy, 177–178
Tony Stark (*See* Iron Man)
Trauma: Sexual trauma, 63. *See also* sexual assault; trauma theory, 8–9, 151
Trish Walker, 3, 6, 46, 77, 103, 109, 111, 156, 174, 177, 190–192, 197, 248. *See also* Patsy Walker
Trump, Donald 94, 206
Turner, Brock, 96–97, 132, 139–140, 147, 155

U

urban revanchism, 153, 243

V

vigilante, 25, 28–29, 74, 76, 80, 86, 95
villain, 8, 26, 28, 36, 49, 52, 57–58, 60–61, 67, 72–73, 83, 86, 96, 101, 119, 123–130, 132, 134, 137–141, 143–144, 156, 197–199, 205, 211, 221, 229–230, 257; supervillain, 25, 54, 56, 124, 137–138, 141, 143, 145, 202–205, 207, 209, 211–214, 216, 220–221, 226–234, 237, 239–240, 242, 244, 246, 248, 251
violence, 3, 5, 8, 29, 39, 41, 45–47, 51, 58, 60–62, 64–65, 79–80, 82–83, 88–89, 91, 93–95, 97, 100, 102–106, 112–117, 119–122, 138, 143, 145–146, 152–153, 157, 159–162, 167–170, 194–195, 198; domestic violence, 39, 45, 160–161, 198; gendered violence, 8, 162, 231; sexual violence, 226–230, 233–234; breaking the silence, 167–168

W

Watchmen, 28–30, 33, 49, 63–64, 85–86, 116. *See also* Moore, Alan
weight effort, 175, 182. *See also* direct space effort; indirect space effort
white supremacy, 93, 97, 152, 238–239. *See also* racism
Will Simpson, 7, 55, 72, 94–95, 100, 103–105, 108–109, 111, 113, 115–121, 182, 190–191, 195, 198–199, 255. *See also* Frank Simpson; Nuke
Wonder Woman, 26, 36, 56, 84–85, 202, 227; *Wonder Woman* (comic), 56; *Wonder Woman* (film), 226; *Wonder Woman* (series), 25

X

X-Men, 27, 81, 122; *X-men* (series), 141

Z

Zebediah Killgrave, 24, 27, 139. *See also* Kilgrave; Purple Man